"This is a bold book, destined to become [...] of worn-out science-and-religion debates, Paul Tyson reclaims theology as the first truth discourse that tells us what science is and how it should function. Rather than look through the lens of science to theology, *A Christian Theology of Science* turns the telescope around and asks us to consider the scientific implications of creedal Christianity. Tyson's book is both erudite and lucid. Rarely have the foundations of modern science been subjected to a more penetrating critique."

—**Hans Boersma**, Nashotah House Theological Seminary

"For decades, the disciplines of theology and science were in open conflict, banal agreement, or mutual isolation. In this work, Paul Tyson reimagines their engagement with great clarity and erudition to provide a theological analysis of science as the knowledge of nature. This is an excellent and timely book which significantly enhances our understanding of the natural sciences and their relation to theology, history, and metaphysics."

—**Simon Oliver**, Durham University

"Tyson argues that the City of God must operate on its own terms rather than on those of the City of Man. This demands that it find the courage to recover Christian theology as a first truth discourse with an associated Christian theology of science. This work offers a highly lucid account of how to begin the recovery operation. It is likely to become a classic text bridging several disciplines."

—**Tracey Rowland**, University of Notre Dame, Australia

"This book enters territory that has long been awaiting intelligent attention, not because it is a forgotten backwater but because it is a no-man's-land, caught between self-interest and fear. Tyson is a trusty guide, navigating a minefield with secure footing in metaphysics, showing how the assumptions behind nineteenth-century science and religion have cordoned off parts of our lives and corralled them into separate camps. He characterizes those camps and their various relationships and highlights flaws in the assumptions that led us into them. He suggests a way out, guided by light, Plato and Augustine, Aristotle and Aquinas, and Socrates. Tyson's overview is crystal clear. He wears his impressive learning lightly, and his footnotes and references are extensive. This book is highly original and deserves a wide readership."

—**Spike Bucklow**, University of Cambridge

"One of the basic tasks in the effort to help bring about a genuine paradigm shift in a culture's way of understanding some fundamental idea is to articulate the new approach in a succinct and compelling manner, accessible to any reasonable person with or without any special expertise. This is just what Tyson accomplishes with this new book, which represents a significant moment in the growing concern to rethink and indeed reorder the relationship between 'science' and 'religion.' In this powerful little text, Tyson clears away the myths that continue to rule the popular imagination and replaces them with lucid, theologically and metaphysically nuanced insights that resonate with undeniable truth."

—D. C. Schindler, the Pontifical John Paul II Institute

"Panoramic in its breadth and stunning in its depth, Tyson's genealogy exposes our often-hidden presumptions regarding our fraught discussions on faith and science. This book equips people of faith and people of science with the right infrastructure for each to come to a true and fruitful encounter with the other. This could very well become the standard text for courses on this crucial crosspoint."

—Matthew John Paul Tan, Vianney College

A CHRISTIAN THEOLOGY OF SCIENCE

A CHRISTIAN THEOLOGY OF SCIENCE

REIMAGINING A THEOLOGICAL VISION OF NATURAL KNOWLEDGE

PAUL TYSON

FOREWORD by DAVID BENTLEY HART

Baker Academic
a division of Baker Publishing Group
Grand Rapids, Michigan

© 2022 by Paul Tyson

Published by Baker Academic
a division of Baker Publishing Group
PO Box 6287, Grand Rapids, MI 49516-6287
www.bakeracademic.com

Printed in the United States of America

Library of Congress Cataloging-in-Publication Data
Names: Tyson, Paul G., author.
Title: A Christian theology of science : reimagining a theological vision of natural knowledge / Paul Tyson ; foreword by David Bentley Hart.
Description: Grand Rapids, Michigan : Baker Academic, a division of Baker Publishing Group, [2022] | Includes bibliographical references and index.
Identifiers: LCCN 2022004814 | ISBN 9781540965516 (paperback) | ISBN 9781540965790 (casebound) | ISBN 9781493437498 (ebook) | ISBN 9781493437504 (pdf)
Subjects: LCSH: Religion and science. | Theology.
Classification: LCC BL240.3 .T97 2022 | DDC 261.5/5—dc23/eng20220405
LC record available at https://lccn.loc.gov/2022004814

Baker Publishing Group publications use paper produced from sustainable forestry practices and post-consumer waste whenever possible.

22   23   24   25   26   27   28   7   6   5   4   3   2   1

Contents

Foreword

DAVID BENTLEY HART

An elegantly brief book should not be burdened by a ponderously long foreword, so I will confine myself to a few general remarks. This is not a text, in any event, that requires either apology or explanation; it is a model of expository lucidity, and it speaks for itself more than adequately. One would expect nothing less from Paul Tyson. He has distinguished himself in the past by the acuity with which he has addressed the intersections and ruptures and misunderstandings and reconciliations that constitute the relationship between science and theology in the modern world, and by the sophistication (though also by the charity) with which he dismantles many of the prevailing biases and self-delusions on both sides of the divide.

It was not very long ago, in relative terms, that academic polemicists could get away easily with simpleminded caricatures of "science" and "religion," each term being construed as indicating a single fixed and invariable essence, and each being understood as inimical to the other. In a great deal of popular discourse, moreover, these caricatures persist. "Science," so the story told by many of religion's cultured despisers goes, is a single, discrete, strictly empirical discipline, largely inductive and scrupulously purged of metaphysical assumptions, while "religion" is the sphere of "unreasoning faith" and consists in a collection of convictions based neither on logic nor on evidence but solely on authority, emotional dependency, and metaphysical prejudice. And, far too often, the apologetic riposte to this picture on the part of believers is either to accept its fundamental terms but then argue that faith is "compatible" with a scientific worldview or else to retreat into fundamentalist obscurantism.

Thus understood, however, both "science" and "religion" are essentially modern forms of ideology that do little more than reinforce one another's logical deficiencies. In fact, what is at stake in the encounter when it proceeds in this fashion is neither science nor religion in any genuine sense. "Science," in this context, becomes a name not for any particular regimen of method and theory, but rather for a metaphysics, one in which method has illegitimately assumed the status of a purely "physicalist" ontology of nature. By the same token, the word "religion" has come to mean not any actual tradition or traditions of thought and practice, but rather a fideistic adherence to this or that set of dogmas in abstraction from the systems of reasoning they express. More to the point, neither scientific nor theological culture can really be complete in itself when wholly divorced from the other, because there is no sane way of completely dividing their proper spheres of custody. So violent a division impoverishes both by forcing each to reject the probative relevance of the other in areas of shared concern. The sciences as they have been understood since the rise of the mechanical philosophy do not possess—*on principle*—the resources of internal critique that would allow them to distinguish properly between method and metaphysics, between aetiology and ontology, between mechanical causation and sufficient reason, and so on. Theology, as it has been understood since the early modern triumph of the obscene pieties of pure biblicism and dogmatic positivism, has lost the capacity to be qualified, fecundated, or illumined by discoveries in "natural philosophy" (to use the more venerable term).

The conversation must begin again, and on a far more intelligent, historically informed, and philosophically refined basis. This is where Tyson excels, and where this book makes a humble but signal contribution. Tyson is one of those scholars in the Anglophone world doing the most to create a new paradigm of engagement, and in the process to help free the modern cultures both of the sciences and of philosophical theology from the limitations that their unnatural schism has condemned them to. This really is a small gem of a book.

Acknowledgments

As is always the case in an acknowledgments section such as this, there are many more people to thank than the ones I will mention. But of particular importance as intellectual friends in the writing of this book, I wish to acknowledge John Milbank, William Desmond, David C. Schindler, Knut Alfsvåg, Sotiris Mitralexis, Isidoros Katsos, Spike Bucklow, José Garibaldi, Luke Costa, and Jonathan Horton.

As a metaphysical theologian interested in applied and sociological matters, I must confess I was not that interested in the "science and religion" space until relatively recently. I am thankful to Stewart Gill and David Brunckhorst, both of whom I worked for between 2016 and 2018, for drawing me into the theological exploration of modern science. Stewart took the starting punt on me, and then David was highly supportive at the crucial early stages in my pursuit of the hunches that have resulted in this book. Many thanks, Stewart and David!

Over the past few years, I have been at the Institute for Advanced Studies in the Humanities at the University of Queensland, and it has been a delight to work within that fine institute under Peter Harrison's directorship. I have learned a great deal from Peter about the intimate theological backstory of modern science (thanks, Peter!). From 2018 to 2021 Peter and I ran a Templeton World Charity Foundation (TWCF) funded research project called the After Science and Religion Project (ASR). I am very thankful to the TWCF for making that research possible. ASR also received some financial assistance from the Issachar Fund and a couple of private donors, including my father-in-law Mr. Karl Wiethoff (many thanks again, Pop!).

This book is one of the outputs of the ASR project. Seventeen top-ranking philosophical theologians,[1] two outstanding historians of modern science,[2] and four scientists with deep interests in Christian theology and natural philosophy[3] participated with me in the ASR project. While none of these wonderful thinkers should be held responsible for my own thoughts, I have gained enormously from reading their work and talking with them about Christian theology and our understanding of the natural world. I owe a deep debt of gratitude to these twenty-three remarkable scholars.

Directly in relation to the production of this book, I am somewhat overwhelmed by David Bentley Hart's very kind foreword. Dave Nelson and Alexander DeMarco at Baker Academic have been super helpful in panel-beating the manuscript into shape. Many thanks! Of course, Annette—my better half—and our four daughters have been very gracious to me as I have juggled so many book projects, including this one, over the past three years.

I am thankful to that very fine journal, *Communio*, for permission to herein reproduce my understanding of the epistemological implications of Plato's divided line analogy, which they published while I was writing the manuscript for this book.[4]

And it always goes without saying—but this time I will say it—that I am thankful to the divine *Logos* for intelligibility itself, and for gifting me the embodied joy of being a thinking, perceiving, communicating participant in the singing cosmos that accompanies the eternal love dance of the Trinity. What a privilege and joy!

1. Knut Alfsvåg, Andrew Davison, William Desmond, Michael Hanby, David Bentley Hart, Pui Him Ip, Simone Kotva, Nathan Lyons, John Milbank, Sotiris Mitralexis, Michael Northcott, Simon Oliver, Catherine Pickstock, David C. Schindler, Janet Soskice, Charles Taylor, and Rowan Williams.
2. Peter Harrison and Bernard Lightman.
3. Spike Bucklow, Keith Fox, Tom McLeish, and David Wilkinson.
4. Chapter 7 in this book expands on the argument about Platonically inflected Christian epistemology that was first published in Paul Tyson, "What is Music? On the Form and Performance of Beauty," *Communio: International Catholic Review* 48, no. 2 (Summer 2021): 355–74. Specifically, pages 361–69 are, in part, reproduced and expanded on in this book—again, with *Communio*'s permission.

Introduction

A Christian Theology of *Science*

The Difference between *And* and *Of*

Because truth is a unity, incommensurate truth frameworks never really work. If you are a rationalist, somehow you have to incorporate the body into your rationalism. If you are an empiricist, somehow you have to define the mind in empirical terms. The very idea of **truth**[1] implies a unified field of knowledge and meaning. Such a unified field also implies the practical need for some explicit or tacit **first truth discourse** that enables us to organize disparate types of knowledge into a single framework of meaning. This does not, of course, imply that we can master the true field of knowledge and meaning with our tiny minds. At the level of immanent reality, our knowledge constructs are inherently incomplete, contingent, and contextual. And blessedly so. For, as Leonard Cohen might put it, it is the cracks in our pretension to complete knowledge mastery that enable the light to get in.

Even so, we try to fix the cracks. To make knowledge mastery viable in at least a limited way, we tend to divide knowledge up into smaller and more controllable silos. Specialization and domain limitation give our aspirations to know and control reality a semblance of plausibility. Essentially, we give ourselves smaller bowls to swim in—which can make us feel like bigger fish than we actually are. Discrete knowledge silos have great advantages for linear knowledge development down narrowly defined branches of interest. However, the sheer number and size of our silos has now seriously problematized the

1. Bolded terms are defined in the glossary at the back of the book.

integration of knowledge itself.[2] Trying to think how different silos relate to one another in a coherent manner becomes increasingly difficult over time. This challenge generates a range of interdisciplinary knowledge adventures, usually defined by the conjunction *and*. Here we get inter-silo bridging enterprises like "philosophy and psychology," "culture and technology," and, notoriously, "science and religion."

Whenever the *and* is in play between knowledge silos, some form of first truth unification discourse is also in play. For example, with "culture and technology," the two silos can be mutually causal—culture causes technology at the same time that technology causes culture—and yet what both culture and technology themselves *are* will need to be understood within a single discourse of meaning if each silo is to genuinely contact the other. In the philosophy of technology, for example, materialists will understand what both culture and technology *are* in instrumental and mechanical categories. Today, this need not be the linear and unvaryingly determinate regularities of Newtonian physics and may incorporate, say, quantum indeterminacy at a micro level while still presupposing probabilistic and statistical determinacy at macro scales. However, some theologically daring French theorists—like Jacques Ellul and Paul Ricœur—think of materialism itself as a function of theology and myth, but this puts them outside the first truth discourse of naturalistic materialism.

There are, then, competing first truth discourses bubbling away merrily on the enormous cooktop of human knowledge production. And yet—as signaled above by the word *daring*—there are dominant and peripheral first truth discourses in any given milieu of meaning. In our present times, the functionally materialist knowledge categories of science act as the dominant first truth discourse of Western modernity's overarching framework of academic meaning. When "science and . . ." is in play, the reductively naturalist first truth discourse of our academy tacitly disciplines whatever is on the other side of science (say, religion) to be commensurate with its own functionally materialist first truth commitments.

Science has not always been our academy's first truth discourse. Indeed, up until less than two hundred years ago, Christian theology was Western modernity's first truth discourse. In early modernity, "science" (then called "natural philosophy") not only sat within the first truth discourse of Christian theology but also had its very birth and dynamic youth within that discourse.

---

2. This is the problem of the fragmentation of knowledge that increases in proportion to advances in siloed knowledge. For an attempt to address this problem from the grounds of Christian theological metaphysics, see Tyson, *De-fragmenting Modernity*.

But things changed. From about 1870 to 1970, Western modernity underwent a broad cultural transition out of the first truth discourse of Christian theology and into the secular and naturalistic first truth discourse of science. This was a cultural mutation of unparalleled significance. But whether science can really bear the weight of being our first truth discourse is another matter. And whether Christian theology has any meaning at all if it is not understood as a first truth discourse by Christians is now an unavoidable question.

What you are about to read is not a "science and religion" book. This book does not allow the *and* to tacitly reduce the first truth claims of Christian theology to the knowledge categories of naturalistic science. I appreciate that many highly intelligent secular and religious thinkers are entirely comfortable with science as our tacit first truth discourse and often think that religion is safe in its own specialist silo. To such an outlook, religion can reach happily (if carefully and respectfully) into the domain of science without being defined by "scientistic" truth categories. Indeed, such thinkers would find the idea that Christian theology should wish to be the first truth discourse for modern science deeply offensive. This they would see as the inversion of "scientism"; perhaps they would call it "religionism." But I think the history of what has actually transpired during the de-Christianization of Western culture, which is the same time period when science became our first truth discourse, makes any happy interdisciplinary "science and religion" outlook wishful thinking, at least for the Christian. This book, then, seeks to understand science theologically; it seeks to presuppose Christian theology as a first truth discourse when thinking about science; it seeks to recover and reimagine the theology *of* science. Oh, brave new world . . .

We are used to the idea of the *philosophy of science*. Philosophy here incorporates science into itself and purports to be in a position to stand, in some sense, above science and to explore the validity of the warrants of scientific truth that science itself must simply assume. However, we are not used to the idea of the *theology of science* doing the same thing. There is a reason for this. Modern philosophy itself is usually compatible with the reductive naturalism and functional materialism assumed by modern science, but traditional Christian theology is not. Which is to say that the *of* in the "philosophy of science" is not a genuine *of*. Actually, science *and* philosophy (which we tend to call "philosophy of science") is much the same enterprise as science *and* religion. The first truth discourse of naturalistic materialism defines both philosophy and science in most of what passes for the philosophy of science today. Put another way, the empiricist, rationalist, and materialist understandings of modern philosophy that have raised science itself to the status of a functional first philosophy mean that contemporary science and philosophy are already harmonized; secular philosophy and naturalistic science have long since combined to form the first truth discourse of Western modernity.

The theology of science, then, *does* purport to function on a higher plain of truth than naturalistic science. This is an impossible stance if one is committed to the dominant scientific first truth discourse of the contemporary secular academy. Yet—as I hope to demonstrate in this book—natural knowledge must sit within a theological account of reality if Christian theology itself is to be taken as a genuine first truth discourse, at least by Christians. Conversely, any participation in the "science and religion" discourse on the terms of the prevailing first truth discourse of secular naturalism will buy epistemic credibility at the price of selling the theological and metaphysical soul of the Christian faith. Not a good deal for the Christian.

Swooping down from the lofty conceptual atmosphere of the above paragraphs, the rest of this introduction will outline how we might move from an assumed outlook of "science *and* religion," where science tacitly defines truth itself, to a "theology *of* science" outlook, appealing to the long traditions of Christian thinking about nature and knowledge that predate the past two hundred years.

Naming the Uneasy History of Science *and* Christian Theology

Christian theology has a complex and intimate relationship with modern science. This text seeks to describe, explain, and encourage change in this relationship. What is unusual about this account is that it is written from the standpoint of Christian theology; it is not "a view from nowhere," nor is it naturalistic science thinking about the credibility or otherwise of Christian theology.

The nub of the complexity of this relationship is that, while Christian theology is the historical womb of modern science, science gradually displaced Christian theology as the West's primary public truth discourse. This displacement was anything but intentional at the outset. Even so, modern science initiated an approach to demonstrable truth within a practical understanding of physical reality that, over time, became radically incommensurate with the core metaphysical and miraculous truth claims of Christian theology.

Significantly, this development started out being strongly religiously motivated. Harking back to the Reformation and to the various religious uses to which the recovery of ancient skepticism were put, the high authority of established truth in matters theological and metaphysical gave way to the practical and down-to-earth claims of demonstrable evidence. The seventeenth-century motto of the Royal Society of London for Improving Natural Knowledge is *"nullius in verba"* (take no one's word for it). This motto exemplifies a strongly Protestant rejection of any unconditional obedience to institutional religious authority, a firm commitment to the "plain meaning" of reality as grasped by sensible people, and it is an overt defiance of the metaphysical book learning of natural philosophers in the universities.

Between the seventeenth century and the nineteenth century, the primary truth warrants of Western European culture noticeably shifted from the doctrinal authority of Christian theology to the demonstrable proofs of modern science. By the late eighteenth century, some theologians were keenly aware of this shift. In response, liberal Protestant theology adapted itself to the credibility criteria and knowledge modes of the new learning. After this, the metaphysical and miraculous truth claims of Christian theology became increasingly incredible to leading Enlightenment figures of the European intelligentsia. Through the nineteenth century, a growing discontent with traditional Christian outlooks on truth and reality steadily matured in Western academic circles. By this time the scientific secularization of Western European knowledge was firmly in motion.

By the early twentieth century, religious agnosticism and open disbelief toward traditional Christian truth claims were picking up serious momentum in the academy. The physical resurrection of Jesus of Nazareth, as a historical fact, started to noticeably shift from being a common-sense public truth to being a hard-to-believe personal conviction. With the likes of Herbert Spencer and Bertrand Russell, serious attacks on the credibility of traditional Christian theology were launched in earnest by agnostic and atheist science advocates. Over the twentieth century, Western scientific knowledge increasingly became public truth at the cultural expense of the wisdom, morality, social organization, and metaphysical meaning framework of creedal Christian theology. Science was replacing Christian theology as the modern Western world's first discourse of public truth. By the 1960s this process was pretty well complete, and we see a steep decline in the cultural influence of Christian theology on Western modernity in general thereafter.

Backing up to the early twentieth century, Christian theology was then responding to the transfer of its public truth standing to science in three main ways: **adaptation, withdrawal,** and **appropriation.**

Adaptation

The progressive trajectory forged by liberal Protestants sought to adapt Christian theology to the credibility parameters, knowledge methodologies, and functional materialism of modern science. This often involved jettisoning (or privatizing or mythologizing) the miraculous and the metaphysical from modern theology. Even so, more nuanced forms of adaptation that endeavored to hold fealty to both modern science and orthodox Christian doctrine were certainly being put forward. These largely operated by making some sort of Chalcedonian-style attempt not to confuse the two natures of science and religion in the one hypostatic unity of the Christian scientist. Whether this really worked is a complex question.

Withdrawal

The conservative trajectory in Christian theology withdrew from the public sphere and retreated into the discretely "religious" domain of systematic theology. This transformed traditional creedal Christianity into a hermetically sealed personal-salvation religion that had no real bearing on the natural sciences or on public knowledge in general. Here orthodoxy within "religious freedom" is bought at the high price of being in a bubble apart from the secular world.

Appropriation

The fundamentalist, anti-Darwinian tendency in—largely American— evangelical circles started up in earnest in the 1920s. This trajectory is continuous with pre-Darwinian natural theology, such as William Paley's divine watchmaker apologetics (from the eighteenth century), and with the biblical positivism of Bishop James Ussher's six-thousand-year biblical chronology (from the seventeenth century). This is a conservatively modern movement seeking to read Genesis as a natural history text while maintaining that the Bible—as revealed—has greater authority than the reconstructive speculations of secular natural historians. In cosmology, this stance views creation as being, though originally harmonious and peaceable, now sinful, violent, and evil due to a world-reordering fall. Salvation history shows God's redemptive intervention in the order of the world via the incarnation and passion of Christ, though this intervention is yet to be fully consummated in the eschaton. This early modern creation cosmology holds that death, evil, and violence are aberrations in God's originally good created order and that divinely caused catastrophic upheavals in the natural world are prominent features of recorded human history. In the nineteenth- and twentieth-century trajectories that are continuous with Ussher and Paley, the epistemic modes of modern science, guided by divine revelation, are employed against Charles Lyell's geological uniformitarianism and Charles Darwin's violently competitive evolutionary biology. This is an appropriation of modern science for a theological purpose that uses the inductive methodologies, evidential positivism, and rationalist assumptions of modern scientific proof but without accepting an agonistic and uniformitarian cosmology, or a reductively materialist philosophy of nature. In the Reformed positivist tradition that is so important in early modern science, this stance maintains a "plain meaning" biblical hermeneutic, with deference to the epistemic authority of divine revelation. Thus "creation science"—note the explicit appropriation of the word *science* here—is set against the mainstream of twentieth- and twenty-first-century secularized and functionally materialist biological science. However, the opposition of creation science to Darwinian evolution fed neatly into an already existing "conflict" understanding of science and religion, which had been promoted in the late nineteenth century by advocates of secularized and functionally materialist science. Thus, appropriation advanced the historically fictitious "conflict myth."[3]

Failed Strategies of War and Peace between Science and Religion

From the standpoint of Christian theology, it could be argued that the strategies of adaptation, withdrawal, and appropriation employed over the past two centuries have done little other than entrench an inherently dysfunctional relationship between Christian theology and modern science. The basic truth commitments of creedal Christianity have become harder for modern Western people to believe as Christian doctrine has become isolated from public truth and quarantined within religion. At the same time, science has become firmly secularized; its scope has been universalized to include ethics, politics, religion, the psyche, and more; and our public knowledge culture has become increasingly and reductively materialist.

It is significant that adaptation, withdrawal, and appropriation are all rear-guard responses. None of them have put forward a serious critique of the distinctive theoretical underpinnings of modern science that have eroded Christian theology's public truth standing: modern empiricism, modern rationalism, and modern reductive physicalism. The reason why Christian theology has not yet produced a well-accepted first-order critique of the scientific secularization of Western intellectual culture is so obvious that it is hard to see.

---

3. No serious contemporary historian of modern science finds the late nineteenth-century idea that Christian theology and science are intrinsically at war remotely believable. Yet popular tropes from this fully discredited "conflict myth" not only persist but are routinely replicated. For a representative collection of myth-busting historians on this topic, see Numbers, *Galileo Goes to Jail*.

The truth is, Christian theology gave birth to modern science and thus has a deeply ingrained maternal loyalty to its offspring.[4] Further, the story of this intimate relationship between Christian theology and modern science goes much further back than the modern era. Certain late-medieval forms of Christian theology—nominalism, voluntarism, the corpuscular doctrine of pure matter, and religiously motivated skepticism[5]—are the deep sources of the preconditions for modern scientific knowledge. Modern Christian theology would have to critique its own tacit knowledge assumptions if it were to find a way of thinking outside the truth categories of modern science. Many modern Christians have no interest in rethinking their own outlook on knowledge and nature, and those who are trying often have a hard time reworking their own presuppositions back far enough to undertake a serious first-order rethink of modern approaches to the knowledge of nature.

The Challenge of Making a New Start

So how does the contemporary relationship between Christian theology and modern science look from the perspective of Christian theology? In many regards one would have to say it looks pretty damaging, even though modern science is the love child of Christian theology and a devotion to the Creator by means of understanding the wonders of creation. But perhaps the more interesting question is, What could the future of the relationship between Christian theology and science look like? There are growing indications that the dominant modes of adaptation, withdrawal, and appropriation, which have been with us since the late Victorian era, are increasingly being abandoned by Christian theologians, and some rather interesting alternatives are emerging.[6] The relationship is changing, and—so this text will argue—changing for the

---

4. See, for example, Harrison, *Bible, Protestantism, and the Rise of Natural Science*; Thomas, *Religion and the Decline of Magic*; Webster, *Paracelsus*; Hooykaas, *Religion and the Rise of Modern Science*; Shapin, *Scientific Life*; Gaukroger, *Emergence of a Scientific Culture*; Gaukroger, *Francis Bacon*.

5. These terms will be unpacked further on in the text.

6. One example of an interesting emerging endeavor is the After Science and Religion Project (2018–2021) run through the Institute for Advanced Studies in the Humanities at the University of Queensland, Australia. Here world-class philosophical theologians (such as John Milbank, David Bentley Hart, and Rowan Williams) have settled down with top historians of modern science (Peter Harrison and Bernard Lightman); first-rate, theologically sensitive philosophers (William Desmond, David C. Schindler, and Charles Taylor); and high-standing, theologically engaged scientists (Andrew Davison and Tom McLeish) to do some first-order rethinking of how we understand science and religion themselves. The two central publications of this project are Milbank and Harrison, *After Science and Religion*; and Harrison and Tyson, *New Directions in Theology and Science*.

better. There may yet be a very interesting future for Christian theology and science. Perhaps, even, Christians will start to move away from the past two centuries of "science and religion" discourse and make the attempt to recover a *theology of science*. But such an enterprise is not simply the overcoming of existing problems; it is the redefining of the problems themselves. This is a very difficult process. We cannot go from the deeply engrained assumptions of science-and-religion thinking to a theology-of-science outlook in one jump. We need to start with what is familiar to us and from there move to what is unfamiliar. In order to do this the argument that follows will open by seeking to define Christian theology within the truth categories of modern science. This exercise is important for a number of reasons. It will set up starting categories of thought that lead quite convincingly to the death of Christian theology as a viable first truth discourse. Once we can see where those categories take us, if we are interested in Christian theology coming back to life as a first truth discourse, then obviously we may have to reconsider the categories that got us into such a mess. This will entail—as we go—reconsidering the very ideas of "science" and "religion" as we currently know them. Once we can get to that point, we can start to think about what a Christian theology of science might actually look like. But to get started, it will be helpful to first sketch out working definitions of Christian theology and modern science.

Starting Definitions of Christian Theology and of Science

Decisive and true answers to the questions "What is Christian theology?" and "What is science?" are far harder to come up with than one might think.[1] There are reasons for this that we will explore as we go, but in order to sidestep major questions in meta-theology, the philosophy of science, and the history of "science and religion"—at least at the outset—this book is going to open with provisional definitions of Christian theology and of science.

1.1 What Is Christian Theology?

The word *theology* is derived from two Greek words: *theos*, meaning God, and *logos*, meaning reason. Theology is reasoning about God. **Christian theology** is reasoning about God as underpinned by the most foundational belief commitments of the Christian faith. Hence, to find out what Christian theology is, one must first know something about what the most foundational belief commitments of a Christian are. What do Christians take to be the primary truths of their faith?

---

1. The case against essentialist definitions of science and religion is very strong and largely appreciated in the field of scholarship that is concerned with the nature and history of modern science and modern religion. For an excellent recent text in this trajectory, see Reeves, *Against Methodology in Science and Religion*.

For a minimal starting definition of Christian theology, I am going to stick with what most obviously makes Christian reasoning about God distinctive: Christology. Here I am going to define a Christian as someone who is committed to the truth of these five claims: (1) the historical person Jesus of Nazareth was God incarnate, (2) he was born of a virgin, (3) he was crucified and died under the Roman governor Pontius Pilate, (4) he physically rose from the dead, and (5) he then ascended to heaven. This way of defining Christian theology as reasoning about God from its core doctrinal belief commitments is, again, only a minimal and starting way of defining what Christian theology is, and yet I think it is an inescapable starting point. I take it that while one can be a scholar *of* Christian theology without being committed to these five orthodox Christological truth claims, one cannot *be* a Christian theologian without holding that these claims are really true.

It is important to note that four out of five of these core Christian truth claims are of a miraculous or metaphysical nature. I take a **miracle** to be a singular act of God within nature that cannot be explained by our understanding of the regular operations of nature. I take **metaphysics** to pertain to transcendent realities that are the grounds *of* observable physical nature, rather than being truths directly discoverable "within" nature.

It is also important to note that Christian theology takes the idea of revelation seriously, viewing revelation as the primary basis for true theological knowledge. That is, the Christian understanding is that the source of theological truth lies ultimately beyond the normal limitations of human sensory perception and logic, even though those limited faculties partially mediate divine truth to us.[2]

1.2 What Is Science?

The oldest currently active scientific institution of the modern world is the Royal Society of London for Improving Natural Knowledge. It was granted a royal charter in 1662. Well before the word *science* was in common use,[3] this society was set up as a college for "the promoting of physico-mathematical

2. Christian theology—particularly in its patristic expression—upholds an apophatic sensibility concerning the inherent limitations of the creature in trying to understand the Creator. See Dionysius the Areopagite, *Divine Names and Mystical Theology*. This is also well represented in Roman Catholic theology. See Nicholas of Cusa, *Of Learned Ignorance*; and Pieper, *Silence of St. Thomas*. Lutheran theology appreciates this line of reasoning also. See Alfsvåg, *What No Mind Has Conceived*.
3. Harrison, *Territories of Science and Religion*, 147–48.

experimental learning."[4] Let us start with the idea that **modern science** is physico-mathematical, experimental, natural knowledge.

The experimental component of this new (in the seventeenth century) type of learning concerns what we now call **empiricism**. This is the "look and see" approach to natural knowledge. The idea here is that carefully calibrated, accurate observation provides us with the best means of understanding the physical world. This is because sense perception is taken—by modern empiricists—to be the *only* grounds of our knowledge of the world. After we have observed and accurately measured natural regularities, we can then mathematically and imaginatively formulate theories about how nature works. Then, once we have a theoretical idea about what we expect will always happen in nature, we can rig up a controlled experiment that will enable us to "see" if what we think should happen actually does happen. Observation then either confirms or refutes our theories about natural causal necessities. Here observation is the first measure and ultimate test of the validity of our theories about nature. Modern science, then, is characterized by the empirical interrogation of natural phenomena via controlled experiments.

The physico-mathematical part of the Royal Society's approach to natural knowledge is what we might call its rationalist theoretical inclination and its physically reductive methodology. Let us look at mathematical **rationalism** first.

Way back in classical times, Aristotle produced some fascinating thinking on the relationship between mathematical points, lines, and geometrical objects, on the one hand, and real bodies in the physical world, on the other.[5] What type of relationship there really is between mathematics and physical bodies is still a complex and genuinely hard problem, but that there *is* a relationship is a very old idea that has proved enormously helpful in all sorts of practical and theoretical arenas of human knowing and making. Of course, this idea did not start with Aristotle. Going back further in time—as seen in the civilizations of Mesopotamia, the Indus Valley, Egypt, and every archaic people group—the careful study of the regular movements of heavenly bodies integrated mathematics with observable phenomena. Mathematics, in other words, is a language that often very successfully describes necessary and causal relationships in nature.

4. On November 28, 1660, a committee of twelve prominent scholars, physicians, and members of the English royal court convened at Gresham College in London to inaugurate the formation of a new college. The minutes of its first meeting record that the purpose of this college was "the promoting of physico-mathematical experimental learning." This college became the Royal Society of London two years later. See Hunter, "Founder Members of the Royal Society."

5. Aristotle, *Physics* 193b23–194a12.

However one understands the *meaning* of the regularities we can observe in nature, the *fact* is, most natural systems can be mathematically modeled in one way or another. For this reason, the precise quantification and careful spatiotemporal measurement that provide data for the mathematical modeling of physical phenomena are central features of the modern scientific method. Modern science is a mathematically rationalist enterprise. But unlike the mystical mathematical rationalism of the ancient Pythagoreans, for example, modern science is also a physically reductive enterprise.

The "physico" part of the Royal Society's guiding purpose reduced its knowledge scope to a practical and physical understanding of how nature works. Before the late nineteenth century, nature (*physis*) was seldom seen as reductively material.[6] However, a functional materialism was latent in modern science, as dropping medieval ideas about matter gave at least two great boons to the new learning. The first boon granted by a purely physical (**pure matter**) conception of nature is that this outlook greatly simplifies nature metaphysically. Purpose, theology, essence, and value can be bracketed out from a "nature" that is simply "material." The second is that, once theology and metaphysics are no longer the concern of the observer and user of a purely material nature, curiosity and technological power can be liberated from sacred and moral constraint.

Metaphysically, the seventeenth-century idea of "pure matter" entails the idea that the material domain, as distinct from the supernatural domain, is entirely autonomous from divine grace and can be fully comprehended without recourse to any notions of transcendent essence or divine energy. This modern idea of pure matter is a decisive break with medieval **hylomorphism** ("matter" and "form" integrated conceptions of physical reality). To medieval Aristotelians, the moral and intellective form of any existing being ("form" here concerns essence, structure, purpose, and value) is not material, but form is just as surely a part of nature (*physis*) as matter is. To a modern, pure-matter outlook, matter itself—not form, not essence, not purpose, not value—is all that really exists in nature. Things are complex and involved when trying to follow the changes in the metaphysics of matter from the sixteenth to the seventeenth century, but certain sixteenth-century theological ideas paved the way for a de-gracing (full naturalization) of nature that made a new metaphysics of matter viable from the seventeenth century onward.[7]

6. From its founding, the Royal Society was often interested in observation-based experimentation and theorizing in astrology, witches, occult phenomena, and the like.

7. For a quick look at the de-gracing of physical reality in the sixteenth century, see Dupré, *Passage to Modernity*, 171–89.

Once nature is thought of as purely material, this gives a distinctive license to the new natural knowledge to be focused on use. Knowledge becomes instrumental power for the improvement of humanity's lot. Further, once the natural world is thought of as being at least functionally theologically neutral—that is, as able to be meaningfully understood outside the domain of theology—then Protestant and Catholic natural philosophers could agree on *what* was observed in nature, even if they could not agree on the *meaning* of nature. It is important to recognize that this idea of a purely material reality did not imply atheism in early modernity and that modern science was largely embedded within modern Western theology up until the late nineteenth century.

The complement to the seventeenth-century idea of a purely material physical reality was the invention of an entirely spiritual idea of **supernatural** reality. Here reality itself had two carefully separated stories. But the autonomous yet complementary understanding of a two-storied reality did not stay complementary. By the late nineteenth century, a functional physical reductionism in the purely material bottom story of reality was changing its relationship with a purely supernatural upper story. Increasingly, functional physical reductionism was evolving into a theoretical reductionism, presupposing a materialist outlook on reality itself. The supernatural upper story became seen as the domain of make-believe. The social sciences, for example, were born in the nineteenth century out of reductively materialist thinking about politics and economics as put forward by Karl Marx.[8] Sigmund Freud's psychological science, equally, presupposed that all human meanings are poetically generated out of instinctive and socially conditioned necessities that are reducible, in the end, to material reality.[9] By the early twentieth century, the knowledge generated by our academic culture—particularly in the human sciences—largely assumed that science itself must be reductively materialist in its theoretical commitments, and that the physical world is the only reality we *can* know about.

Modern science today is knowledge of the natural world that is derived from at least these three foundational philosophical and methodologically applied commitments: empiricism, rationalism, and **physical reductionism**. This will be our core, though admittedly un-nuanced, starting answer to the question "What is science?"

8. Marx is regarded as the first of the three great thinkers in modern classical sociology, the other two being Max Weber and Émile Durkheim. See Kimmel, *Classical Sociological Theory*; and Singer, *Karl Marx*.
9. Freud, *Future of an Illusion*.

1.3 Prescriptive Theology and Descriptive Science

A significant issue regarding the operational differences between Christian theology and science within the public norms of Western modernity concerns description and prescription. The usual story is that science is descriptive of "simply" what is physically "there," whereas Christian theology is prescriptive.

Theology concerns how Christians *should* live and how they *should* make sense of the world in the light of revealed first-order truths. There is a **normative** aspect at the very heart of the Christian theological enterprise. Here first-order truths are the foundational premises of the Christian way of life, which can be lived well (as enabled by the Holy Spirit, in accord with the revelations given to the church, in the fellowship of believers) or not so well. There is a perfect model for the Christian to both emulate and participate in—namely, the life of Christ. For this reason, the imperfect Christian in the church militant can always be encouraged to do better.

Science, on the other hand, is seen not as prescriptive but as descriptive. Science—we tend to assume—is not interested in telling anyone how they should live, or in making normative judgments at all. Science simply tells us what is physically there and how it physically works.

A highly significant consequence of seeing science as descriptive and Christian theology as prescriptive is that we have corralled metaphysical and normative concerns (first-order beliefs and prescriptive qualitative judgments) into the *personal* territory of religion (or, perhaps, philosophy), and we have corralled matters of fact and instrumental know-how into the *public* territory of science and technology. Here, first-order beliefs and normative commitments are not seen as matters of public knowledge. Matters of public knowledge are not, in themselves, seen as carrying any metaphysical, prescriptive, or normative freight.

In reality, applied science can be every bit as prescriptive as Christian theology,[10] and applied Christian theology should be just as concerned with accurately describing reality and with understanding instrumental power as is science.[11] The mismatch between our assumptions about autonomous, objective description and subjective prescription, and how we actually integrate

10. For example, if you want to stop the spread of a pandemic by translating a scientific understanding of its transmission and cure into enforceable and implemented policies, then science will be integral to the normative objective of controlling the pandemic and saving human lives.

11. For example, accurate and factual knowledge—of both political realities and scriptural meanings—is required if the believer is to discern under what circumstances loyalty to God requires disobedience to civil authorities.

the two, need not concern us yet. But at this tentative definitional outset, a significant sociological feature of the way we typically define Christian theology and science is that the former is presumed to be prescriptive and the latter is presumed to be descriptive. The separation of meaning, value, and transcendence, on the one hand, from facts, use, and working knowledge, on the other, is a very significant feature of how Christian theology and science have developed within the modern Western way of life, at least over the past two hundred years.

1.4 Christian Theology and Science?

Using our starting definitions, we can say that Christian theology is prescriptive thinking about God and reality as done by people who hold that Christ is God incarnate, was born of a virgin, was crucified, rose from the dead, and ascended into heaven; and science is a rational, empirical, and reductively physical form of descriptive natural knowledge.

As sketched in the introduction, science has come to displace Christian theology as the first truth discourse of the modern scientific age. This is important to understand. When Christian theology was the first truth discourse of the broadly Western lifeworld, the meaning of natural knowledge was interpreted and situated within Christian theology. When things are the other way around, the meaning of Christian theology is readily understood and interpreted as situated within the truth criteria of modern science.

The next chapter will show what happens when you take these core starting definitions and try to look at the truth claims of Christian theology through the interpretive lens of modern science. As should be obvious, this is not going to work well for Christian theology. This is by no means the end of the matter concerning the relationship between Christian theology and modern science. Even so, there is nothing to be gained by pretending that Christian theology has nothing to be concerned about under the cultural conditions wherein modern science is the first truth discourse of our public knowledge culture.

2

Viewing Christian Theology through the Truth Lens of Science

George MacDonald famously said, "Seeing is not believing—it is only seeing."[1] It is clear from the context of the quote that MacDonald is not here offering us a defense of "only seeing." Rather, he is drawing our attention to the intimate and unavoidable relationship between *what* we see and *how* we see.[2] That is, there are always prior beliefs (and prior unbeliefs) that are the interpretive lenses through which we understand our experience of the world and its meaning.

If we think of modern science as an empirical, rational, and physically reductive approach to an at least provisionally valid knowledge of the natural world, then we are using science as an interpretive lens to give us a distinctive vision of the natural world. If we then look through this lens at the truth

1. MacDonald, *Princess and the Goblin*, 173.
2. In the story, the young hero, Curdie, is gently castigated for not believing the heroine, Princess Irene, simply because he could not see what she described to him. The story makes it clear that Curdie had every reason to believe that Irene would not lie to him, and every reason to believe that she had unusual virtue and insight. Had he trusted these high reasons, this would have relativized the fact that he could not see what she was describing to him with his own eyes. But seeing, on the spiritual plane, is a function of trust in higher truths than what ordinary sight can naturally grasp. MacDonald is explaining that in these high matters one must believe in order to see, and it is entirely the wrong way around to try to see in order to believe.

claims of Christian theology, anything outside the ambit of what that lens is ground to view will immediately become invisible—whether it is there or not, whether it is true or not. This is what MacDonald means by "seeing is not believing."[3]

But given that science is very good at knowledge construction within the ambit of what it *does* see, perhaps the interests of truth are well served by using science to examine foundational Christian truth claims. This seems sensible. Science aspires to giving us true knowledge about the natural world. Further, the Christian faith claims to be inextricably embedded in real historical events in the natural world; the Christian faith is lived out in the natural world; and "religion"[4] is, at least in some measure, a natural human phenomenon. If the Christian Gospels are real historical documents reporting real historical events, then surely the scientific knowledge tools of empirical evidence and rational analysis should happily substantiate the truth claims of Christian theology.

Before subjecting Christian truth claims to the knowledge criteria of modern science, an important historical point needs to be made: certain types of Christian theology were a driving force in the invention of modern science.[5] We will come back to this later, as the explicitly non-theological way of understanding what science itself is only really becomes something "in the air," so to speak, in the nineteenth century. But as we are historically situated after the nineteenth century, the manner in which "science" has become a terrain discretely cordoned off from "religion" and the manner in which "theology" has become discretely "religious" deeply shape the way we now think about what both science and Christian theology are.[6] In this chapter, we will start with contemporary "science and religion" assumptions, even though the situation is much more complex than their assumed definability and independence really allow.

So, provisionally bracketing out the important historical fact that modern science is profoundly indebted to Christian theology, let us think about what post-nineteenth-century science has to say about Christian theology. Let us look at our five core Christian truths through the knowledge lenses of scientific empiricism, rationalism, and physical reductionism.

3. Concerning all those things that science does not see (value, meaning, love, purpose, etc.), see Tyson, *Seven Brief Lessons on Magic*.
4. As already mentioned, there are good reasons to be uncomfortable with the idea that we can say what "religion" is. See Nongbri, *Before Religion*. But at this point of the argument, I am speaking *as if* "science" has valid grounds for judging "religion."
5. Harrison, *Fall of Man*; Gaukroger, *Emergence of a Scientific Culture*, 471–509.
6. Again, see Harrison, *Territories of Science and Religion*.

2.1 Empiricism and Christian Theology

David Hume is probably the most widely revered philosophical thinker in the modern empiricist trajectory. Hume explicitly thinks about whether miracles can be believed, and he argues that they cannot be.[7] As four out of five of our core Christian truth claims have to do with the miraculous, if Hume is right, then it looks as though Christian theology is incompatible with a modern empirical understanding of a meaningful knowledge of the natural world. If the modern evidential criteria of empiricism can establish only that it is historically reasonable to believe that Jesus of Nazareth was crucified under Pontius Pilate in the first century of the Common Era, then either the other core claims of Christian truth are false or they are simply outside the truth criteria of empiricism. In his famous "fork," Hume himself treats anything that is not a matter of rational tautology or probable empirical fact as tosh. He explains, "If we take in our hand any volume; of divinity or school metaphysics, for instance; let us ask, Does it contain any abstract reasoning concerning quantity or number? No. Does it contain any experimental reasoning concerning matter of fact and existence? No. Commit it then to the flames: for it can contain nothing but sophistry and illusion."[8]

Hume's reasoning is powerful. Empirical knowledge is, as philosophers say, *a posteriori*.[9] That is, we form an understanding of the physical world *after* we have sensory experience to reason about. Rigorously empirical knowledge does not presume to know what will happen before anything happens. The fact that my pencil falls when I drop it is not something I can indubitably and empirically *know* in advance of its happening, *if* I am relying purely on sensory experience. Even so, if I observe something happening the same way many times, and observe no exceptions to this pattern, this gives me reason to expect a probable natural tendency, and I may well be able to formulate probable natural tendencies into universal "laws of nature" that enable at least some degree of predictive and manipulative power over natural phenomena. Physical regularities seem to be how observable reality works. So, the idea of theoretically formulating scientific "laws" as universal predictions on the basis of repeated observations is a solid form of genuine knowledge about the

---

7. Hume, *Enquiry Concerning Human Understanding*, section 10, "Of Miracles" (70–85).

8. Hume, *Enquiry Concerning Human Understanding*, 107.

9. In philosophical jargon, *a posteriori* reasoning is inductive reasoning, which endeavors to move from the particular and tangible to the universal and the rational. The inverse of this is *a priori* reasoning, which is deductive reasoning, endeavoring to move from the universal and abstract to the particular and tangible. I say "endeavoring" very intentionally here, for, as Hume points out, neither approach, as tried in modern Western philosophy, has proved itself capable of realizing this endeavor so as to be able to produce certain knowledge.

natural world. By this pathway, however, any miraculous event—any singular, complete anomaly with respect to the probable and observed regularities of nature, particularly if learned about only by hearsay—cannot be believed if one is to maintain a commitment to reasonable empirical knowledge. Also, to this outlook any metaphysical speculation about the supposed unobservable preconditions of the observable world can never amount to empirical knowledge. So, in principle, the only thing that empiricism could judge regarding the five basic truth claims of Christianity would be whether Jesus of Nazareth really was a historical figure who was crucified under Pontius Pilate. All metaphysical and miraculous claims would be dismissed as inherently unbelievable by Hume.

I am going to side with Hume here—just at the outset, mind—and conclude that the defining features of Christology are either false or impossible to comment on by the criteria of empirical science. If this is the case, then it has serious implications for a striking tendency within biblical scholarship, particularly as influenced by German thought from the late eighteenth century to the present.

What can be loosely called the **historical-critical method** of biblical analysis applies the categories of empirical credibility in historical knowledge to the humanist linguistic- and textual-analysis traditions of early modernity in the **exegesis** and **hermeneutics** of the Christian Scriptures. Many fascinating insights about the larger historical, linguistic, and (speculatively reconstructed) textual history of the Christian Scriptures have been put forward by such scholarship, but the truth criteria of Humean empiricism are inherently incompatible with any miraculous and any metaphysical truth. We shall return to this matter later. But as a point of historical fact, this development in the modern scientific exegesis and interpretation of the Christian Scriptures is directly linked to the birth of modern atheism in the mid-nineteenth century and is a profound causal driver of the post-Christian secularism of European culture, which took the world by storm not long after World War II.[10] It seems

10. The manner in which David Strauss's *Life of Jesus Critically Examined* (1835–36) paves the way for Ludwig Feuerbach's *Essence of Christianity* (1841), which energizes Karl Marx's critique of the prevailing class-based social order in his "Contribution to the Critique of Hegel's Philosophy of Right" (1843), is but one clear link between German biblical scholarship and nineteenth-century radical atheism. The historiographical rejections of supernatural and metaphysical accounts of the life of Jesus by liberal Protestant biblical scholars is by no means the only factor producing post-Marxist atheism, but it is by no means insignificant. On the social and intellectual history of post-Marxist atheism, see Spencer, *Atheists*, for an excellent and very accessible account, in particular, of the development of atheism from the nineteenth century forward. For a dense scholarly analysis of the sixteenth-century backstory to modern atheism, see Buckley, *At the Origins of Modern Atheism*. See Jenkins, *God's Continent*, for a careful look at the collapse of Christianity in Europe after World War II.

historically hard to deny that trying to understand the nature and meaning of the Christian scriptural revelation in the categories of empirical science is tantamount to making orthodox Christian theology unbelievable.[11]

It looks like evaluating the truth claims of Christian theology by empirical science is going to lead one to the decisive either/or frontier of Hume's fork. If one goes down this path, then one must choose as a first truth criterion either empirical science and abstract reason or—if science *is* empirical knowledge after Hume's manner of thinking—an anti-science and irrational Christian revelation. One cannot be committed to the miraculous historical truth claims of orthodox Christianity and be a Humean empiricist.

2.2 Rationalism and Christian Theology

Mathematical and syllogistic logic is inherently tautological, universally valid, abstract, and *a priori* in nature. Every valid mathematical equation is true by definition and whichever way you say it. If $a = bc^2$, then $bc^2 = a$, and $c^2 = a \div b$. Mathematical truths are universally true. The relationship between the diameter and the circumference of a circle is always the same for any (perfect) circle. But in physical reality, there is no perfect circle, and every falling object in an atmosphere will fall in a particular rather than a uniformly universal manner owing to the contingencies of the aerodynamics of its shape, the movement of the medium in which it is falling, and the gravitational and other forces, fields, and interactive influences to which it is subject. But here is the interesting thing. On the basis of abstract universal and mathematically defined principles, enough contingent information will allow for a high degree of predictive accuracy in describing the trajectory of a falling object. So there is a relationship between the universal mathematical abstractions expressed in Newton's laws of motion and the highly contingent context of any particular real object in motion. Even so, we never "see" the universal abstract "law" itself; we only see its effects. This is troubling for the empiricist. How, from an empiricist standpoint, can something that we cannot directly perceive with our senses, something that is itself not physical (such as a mathematical "law"), be real?

Modern science is a curious beast that has its being within a strange, philosophically incoherent partnership between *a posteriori* sensory perception and *a priori* abstract reasoning.[12] The practical ideology of science is the means

11. David Strauss thinks that myth is the proper category in which to understand Christian truth. Yet he also does not believe in miracles and uses the tools of historical reconstruction, based on naturalistic categories, to isolate religious myth from historical fact.

12. Immanuel Kant's acclaimed attempt to unite rationalist philosophy with empiricist philosophy by reducing our knowledge of reality to the knowledge of phenomena is one of

by which this incoherence is bypassed: It works, so who cares if it doesn't make watertight philosophical sense? But leaving this curious philosophical incoherence and its pragmatic "solution" to one side for now, let us simply think about how a modern rationalist outlook might evaluate the basic truth claims of Christian theology.

Pre-Christian classical Greek theology is highly rationalistic. It appeals to universal, abstract, rational, immaterial, and eternally valid conceptions of divinity. For this reason—as Saint Paul noticed—the idea that God entered history and became flesh, that this paradoxical God-man was crucified, and that Jesus physically rose from the dead is foolishness to the Greeks. The Christian gospel is all too particular, too contingent, too historically em-bedded, too exotic to be taken seriously as rationally credible. Indeed, the very transmission of Christian doctrine is highly distasteful to the rational-ist. Accounts of miraculous events, transmitted through the prejudices and limitations of particular narrative-constructing communities, defy rational credibility. Theology should be universal, mathematically necessary, and logically coherent to be credible to a rationalist.[13] In contrast, orthodox Christianity is embedded in historical particularity and **contingency**, often in logical paradox; and Christology in particular is distastefully anthropocen-tric (God, indeed, becomes *human*). Further, the passion, crisis, existential commitment, and communal submission of Christian faith are offensive to the impersonally rationalist, religiously autonomous, and reductively analytic disposition. The eighteenth century saw the rise of rationalist **deism** among elite intellectuals, and it was decisively non-Christian, particularly as regards orthodox Christology.[14]

It seems that the rationalist face of modern science may well be just as unimpressed with the core truth claims of Christian theology as is the em-piricist face of modern science. Indeed, contemporary mitigated rationalists are usually highly averse to any metaphysical or theological use of reason. After Kant, the idea that we can't know any metaphysical truth about things

the most impressive achievements of modern philosophy. However, the history of the strong idealist reaction to Kant, followed by a strong praxis inversion of idealism and by the revolt against both rationalism and empiricism in those figures of the nineteenth century we now call counter-Enlightenment thinkers, would lead one to wonder whether Kant did really "solve" the relationship between rationalism and empiricism. I, for one, am not satisfied that he did.

13. See the fascinating rationalist natural theology book *The Mind of God* by the entirely nonreligious theoretical cosmologist Paul Davies.

14. Isaac Newton was an Arian (someone who does not believe in creedal Christology and trinitarian theology) at—ironically—Trinity College Cambridge. The rationalist spirit of the eighteenth century, particularly when applied to matters of primary belief in theological earnest, had a lot of trouble with orthodox Christology.

as they really are,[15] along with the rise of reductive materialism within the professionalized and secularized scientific culture, fostered by the likes of Thomas Huxley and Bertrand Russell, means that the pre-nineteenth-century rationalist and deistic trajectory has largely become today's analytic and atheistic trajectory. Here abstract reason is often paired with a commitment to reductive materialism. Reason is here firmly opposed to any metaphysical or spiritual reality. This sort of reason is certainly as opposed to the miraculous as Hume is.

If rationalism admits only of timeless, universal, necessary, and impersonally mathematical truths, then God becoming human within the contingencies of history, as well as all the miraculous violations of the necessary logical regularities of nature entwined in the foundations of Christian truth claims, makes it hard to see how Christian theology could be compatible with a scientific rationalist perspective. Here, too, we seem faced with an either/or choice between Christian theology and scientific rationalism.

2.3 Physical Reductionism and Christian Theology

This bit can be done very quickly. If science is concerned only with physical reality, then four out of five of the core Christian truth commitments must either be false or outside the ambit of science. Again, it seems that one must make an either/or choice between scientific reductive physicalism and Christian theology.

2.4 Are Modern Science and Christian Theology Incompatible?

If, in our secular age, science is defined as the empirical, rational, and physically reductive knowledge of nature, then it must judge the core truth claims of Christian theology as either false or outside its ambit (i.e., outside the ambit of a factual and rational knowledge of the natural world). The idea that one could be a Christian for scientific reasons seems impossible if science and Christian theology are defined in the way we have defined them. The idea that Christian theology—at least as regards the historical and meta-

---

15. According to Kant, we can know only "transcendental" (*not* transcendent) truths about how things *appear* to us, and we can know only "categorical" rational moral imperatives, again arising from within us. Faith, for Kant, is entirely separate from knowledge, such that if Christian faith is to have any respect as something reasonable (religion within the bounds of reason alone), it is only Christianity's upholding of what Kant considers to be rational moral imperatives that can be taken as valid. Following this sort of reasoning, being a good Christian often reduces to being rationally moral from Kant onward in high German thinking.

physical truth of core Christological claims—could even be compatible with modern secular and naturalistically reductive science seems hard to sustain.

In a context where science is the dominant public truth discourse, Christian theology is not only separated from a knowledge of the tangibly real world; it is inherently unbelievable by the truth criteria of the dominant knowledge culture. This, I think, Christian theology must recognize as the situation in which it is placed by the dominant knowledge and operational norms of our contemporary secular, technological, pragmatic lifeworld. In this context, when Christian thinkers too eagerly seek the imprimatur of science, or too completely accept the truth criteria of modern science as something that Christian theology needs to conform to if it is to have any real validity, it is curtains for Christian theology. Our recent crop of evangelical atheists are usually egregiously ignorant of Christian theology[16]—but there is a scientism that is empiricist, rationalist, and reductively physicalist, and so an avowed enemy of the truth credibility of Christian theology, that really does have a good claim to be the progeny of post-nineteenth-century science itself.

We have now very quickly run the foundational truth claims of Christian theology through the validity criteria of modern empirical, rational, and physically reductive science. This process has not had a positive outcome for Christian theology. But let us try this process the other way around and see where that ends up. In turning the tables in this way, we may discover that there are credible reasons to conclude that the distinctive knowledge outlook of modern science cannot carry the weight of being Western culture's first truth discourse.

But first we need to prepare the way in the next chapter, because to run the foundational truth claims of science through the validity criteria of Christian theology is much harder than it looks. It is hard because judging the basic interpretive commitments of contemporary science with orthodox Christian theology is to use Christian theology as a first truth discourse. This is something we are no longer accustomed to doing. We must therefore recover what Christian theology as a first truth discourse actually looks like before we can try the reverse of the process we performed so effortlessly in this chapter.

16. Dawkins (*The God Delusion*) is, for example, stunningly ignorant of Christian theology. David Bentley Hart provides the best antidote to this sort of polemic. See Hart, *Experience of God* and *Atheist Delusions*.

Christian Theology as a First Truth Discourse

3.1 Secularization and Interpretation

Since the late nineteenth century, Western intellectual culture has secularized to a remarkable extent.[1] In this period, **secularization** has demoted Christian theology as Western culture's primary public truth discourse, and it has set up science as its first discourse of public truth. It is, however, important to bear in mind that our presently assumed "science and religion" truth interpretation norms are not a function of modernity itself, for in early modernity Christian theology largely interpreted the true meaning of natural philosophy.

In the age of Bacon, Galileo, Descartes, Boyle, Leibniz, Newton—right up to Faraday in the nineteenth century—we can call early modernity's outlook on theology and natural philosophy a **religion-to-science interpretive dynamic**. That is, those whom we now call the pioneers of modern science were lay theologians as much as they were natural philosophers, speaking about the

1. See Chadwick, *Secularization of the European Mind in the Nineteenth Century*. The secularization of the intellectual culture of the West should not be confused with the "secularization thesis," which predicts that religion declines in direct proportion to advances in modernization. See Berger, *Desecularization of the World*, for a significant rebuttal of the secularization thesis. Even so, what John Milbank calls "secular reason" has indeed profoundly influenced Western intellectual culture, embedding our public truth discourse in a "methodological atheism" (*Theology and Social Theory*, 253) that is increasingly incompatible with any theologically orthodox Christian understanding of the world.

meaning of nature in the context of a deeply theologically inflected **lifeworld**.[2] But now, after the nineteenth century, science interprets the true meaning of religion within a theologically neutralized, secularized, and naturalized public truth culture, which assumes what we might call a **science-to-religion interpretive dynamic.**

Our present science-to-religion interpretive framework is a culturally assumed dynamic; it is now the taken-for-granted "wallpaper" of how we interpret public truth. You will notice this wallpaper only if you make a special effort to look for it. To do this, one has to be, as one sociologist describes it, "reflexive" about one's own meta-interpretive givens.[3] We can notice our interpretive assumptions only by trying to see what it is that we take for granted. For example, when we talk about "science and religion" now, we naturally say the word *science* first, and the truth claims of "science" are simply assumed by us to be what "religion" must measure its own credibility against. Something as assumed as word order reveals that we now live within a culture that takes a science-to-religion interpretive dynamic for granted as regards credible public truth. We do not talk of "religion and science" or of "theologically engaged science." Religion and theology are naturally measured by science, and religion must engage with the truths of science when it comes to our culture's tacitly assumed public truth commitments.

In our present context, the exercise of the previous chapter was easy. How the truth claims of Christian theology measure up (or not) to the truth ruler of science falls easily within the taken-for-granted science-to-religion interpretive framework of our secular and naturalistic times. Interpreting truth the other way around is going to be much harder.

To treat Christian theology as a first truth discourse and then interpret the truth claims of science in light of it is to try to think again within a religion-to-science interpretive dynamic. Such an attempt seriously rubs the

---

2. *Lifeworld* is a sociological term that refers to the assumed collective structures of valid belief and reasonable action in which we live. The German term *Lebenswelt*—particularly as used by Edmund Husserl—is usually translated into English as "lifeworld." Other sociological terms with the same basic meaning are *life-form* and *form-of-life*. The notion in sociology refers to the manner in which we only ever experience reality from within some distinctive culturally and historically situated "way of life" that we simply find ourselves born within, such that the obvious meanings, the normal practices, and the common experiences of our time and place deeply form the way we see and act in the world.

3. The sociologist Jason Josephson-Storm's fascinating book *The Myth of Disenchantment* seeks to think about the assumed interpretive dynamic of sociological analysis and to include that in his sociological analysis. This is a double reflexive movement. To do this one has to try to notice what it is that one is taking for granted. This is a skill one can develop. This is not hopelessly circular, but it is a recognition of the inescapable "entanglement" of all theoretical stances in culturally assumed interpretive commitments.

science-to-religion interpretive assumptions of our lifeworld the wrong way. It violates the private role that religion is expected to play in our secular lifeworld, and it violates the objectivity and universality of the public role that science is expected to play.

The sociological reality is that we now unconsciously presuppose a broadly scientistic first truth outlook that is functionally materialist and functionally anti-supernaturalist. This we think of as theologically unproblematic because our lifeworld norms simply assume that religion is a matter of personal conviction and individual belief and that it therefore has nothing to say to public truth. In this context, to make theology the truth lens through which science is viewed is to not "get" how the territories of science and religion now work, sociologically.

This chapter is going to uncomfortably butt up against the prevailing secularized truth-interpretation norms of our lifeworld. Indeed, in turning the normal interpretive telescope around and looking at our working definition of science through the truth lens of creedal Christian theology, everything is going to look strange, and wrong.

For the above reason, we cannot simply leap straight into judging the truth claims of modern science through the interpretive lens of Christian theology. For, frankly, we no longer know what Christian theology as a first truth interpretive lens actually looks like. Only after we have recovered what some of the basic interpretive commitments of Christian theology, as a first truth discourse, are will we then be in a position to evaluate how modern science itself stacks up as measured by Christian theology.

3.2 The Primary Interpretive Commitments of Christian Theology

As sketched above, the collectively assumed norms of our lifeworld concerning "science" and "religion" now make the primary interpretive assumptions of traditional Christian theology basically incomprehensible. We must start, then, with a summary of some of the primary traditional interpretive commitments of Christian theology, as a first truth discourse.

3.2.1 God

The starting point in grasping the interpretive commitments of a Christian understanding of reality and knowledge is the theology of God. Here, intangible metaphysical reality (God) is primary, and tangible physical reality (creation) is a derivative of primary reality. The New Testament upholds the traditional Christian teaching that the entire creation is made out of nothing by the Word of God (John 1:1–3), and, as Saint Paul notes (Acts 17:28), we, along with all of creation, live and move and have our being in God.[4] That is, the invisible and eternal is the ground of the visible and temporal. This order cannot be reversed. The temporal and visible is not the ground of the eternal and invisible.

Starting with the radical dependence of creation on the Creator, traditional Christian metaphysics has a long heritage of thinking about reality and human knowledge while presupposing the primacy of God. Christian metaphysics seeks to understand how everything that exists, including everything that our bodies can perceive and our minds can understand, depends on God for both its existence and its intelligibility. The dependency we are speaking of—derived from the primacy of God—is a complete dependence. Both nature and our understanding are derivative of God in a primary, undergirding, overshadowing, and continuous manner. In this context, where reality and knowing are divinely gifted, that which is real and known remains shrouded in the ineffable mystery of the divine Giver, which is always beyond our ken. That is, we live *between* the mysterious grounds of physical existence undergirding us (vanishing from our understanding into the divine gift of material existence itself) and the mysterious horizon of essential transcendence overshadowing us (vanishing from our understanding into the divine gift of intelligibility and, in the largest sense, speech). Both of these mysteries have their ground in God, and we will never fully understand either them or God, but we understand the middle order of our awareness between these mysteries, *through* these mysteries that are graciously given to us by God.[5]

In traditional Christian philosophical categories, the dependence of all created material beings on God for their concrete reality in matter, space, and time is a function of the dependence of created existence on God. Likewise, the ability of our minds to have an intelligible understanding of the world is a function of the dependence of all created intelligible essences on God.

These two terms—existence and essence—need to be explained in our times, for the larger cultural knowledge environment of our secular academies no longer assumes the primacy of God, or of any metaphysical or essential truth, when it seeks to understand nature. As Charles Taylor points out, our secular age now largely treats knowledge within a reductively **immanent frame**.[6] Within that frame, traditional Christian distinctions between essence and existence fall somewhere between quaintly outdated "prescientific"

---

4. In Luke's account of Paul's address to the Areopagus, he seems to be citing the poem "Cretica," attributed to Epimenides.

5. The great contemporary philosopher of this "between" zone of our actual human awareness is William Desmond. See any of his "between" books (*Being and the Between*, *Ethics and the Between*, and *God and the Between*).

6. Taylor, *Secular Age*, 539–93.

curiosities and completely incomprehensible baloney. But if God *is* the primary truth undergirding all created existence and all intelligible essence, then these categories need retrieving if we are to use the primary interpretive commitments of Christian theology to evaluate the manner in which "science" now sees the natural world, the nature of human knowledge, and the truth claims of Christian orthodoxy.

What, then, are essence and existence?

3.2.2 God as the Source of All Created Essence and Existence

In patristic and medieval Christian thinking, **existence** refers to any tangible being's particular and concrete reality, as expressed in matter, space, time, and energy. **Essence** here refers to any tangible being's intelligibly ordered nature such that the being is identifiable to our minds as (to at least some degree) knowable. It is a creature's essence that allows us to know that it is a distinctive kind of being (a flower, not a cat); a creature's essence is the source of the qualitative and purposive attributes of its kind. That is, created beings all have *essential* attributes that are intelligible, qualitative, and purposive, because they are the creations of God. For God is the cosmos-ordering divine *Logos* who gives intelligible natures, essential qualities, and meaningful purposes to all the beings of creation. This gifting of essential meanings and intrinsic values to nature from God remains true even though some aspects of creation have been "subjected to futility" by the fall, according to Saint Paul (Rom. 8:20 RSV). God is the source of all intelligible essence and is completely good. All the qualities of reality—in particular the intrinsic values of life, light, love, and goodness—are gifted to the cosmos, and continuously upheld, by God. God is also the undergirding source of all temporal and physical existence. Essence and existence are not their own grounds and do not determine their own purposes; for this reason, creation—correctly perceived—always displays the glory of the Creator, even in its fallen state.

To the Christian, both existence and essence are donated to all tangible beings from the limitless superabundance of the Ground of Being, the "I Am," who is God, who is love. To the Christian, the fullest knowledge we can have of any creature is the knowledge of love, as enabled by the Spirit of God transformatively and redemptively renewing our minds. In the present age our sin is epistemically degrading, but in the final restoration of all things we shall know fully, just as we are fully known by God (1 Cor. 13:12).[7] That is, **intrinsic**, essential, empathetic knowing—attuned to and aligned with the

---

7. See Kierkegaard, *Concluding Unscientific Postscript*, for a profound Christian theological epistemology. The manner in which sin and faith are always epistemically present is explored here with superb theological dexterity.

God-given purposes of natural flourishing and doxological fulfillment—is God-enabled knowing. In contrast—but not necessarily in conflict—**extrinsic,** calculative, and instrumental "knowing" is normative for fallen knowledge.

To Christian theology, without God's originating and ongoing creative activity, we would not exist and would not have essential natures. That is, as creatures we are—completely and at all times—ontologically, existentially, essentially, and substantially dependent on God. Created space-time had an origin, but God's act of creation is continuous and present as the existential and essential ground of created being. The relation of Creator to creation is one of continuous divine creative gift. Significantly, while creation is foundationally dependent on the Creator, the Creator is not dependent on creation. That is, the tangible and physical is a dependent derivative of the intangible and spiritual reality of God, as far as a Christian understanding of the nature of reality is concerned; this does not imply any dependence of the spiritual reality of God on tangible creation.

The prologue to John's Gospel proclaims that the created and ordered cosmos is a medium of communication between God and us. The divine Word makes the world, and the world continues to speak of the Word that made it, whenever its true meaning is comprehended. Creation, then, is a communicative gift of divinely originated order, purpose, love, and value, from God to us. God speaks to us through the normal operations of the natural world, though this is not the only way that God speaks to us. Hence, the knowledge of nature is a communicative and **doxological** enterprise for Christian theology (as any Christian scientist and any spiritually attuned nature lover knows). The essential meaning of creation is to express the goodness, truth, mind, beauty, and love of the Creator. This outlook was largely taken for granted in medieval natural philosophy and in early modern science, because in both cases "science" was deeply embedded in certain forms of Christian theology. We shall come back to this. But, as signaled a couple of times already, a **remarkable reversal**[8] happened in the nineteenth century such that the meaning of sensory data (empiricism), the meaning of the rational ordering of observable and intelligible reality (rationalism), and a practical interest in the effective control of nature (a functionally reductive physicalism) became increasingly incompatible with a traditional Christian understanding of creation.[9]

8. Harrison, "'Science' and 'Religion,'" 87. This is the nineteenth-century switch where religion fades from being the primary public truth discourse that sits in judgment on the meaning and truth claims of science, and science increasingly becomes the primary public truth discourse that sits in judgment on the meaning and truth claims of religion.

9. See again Taylor, *Secular Age*, for a fascinating, if epic, account of the rise of "the immanent frame."

A crucial aspect of the remarkable reversal is the manner in which the first basis of a valid understanding of nature shifts from one of *faith* in God—who undergirds and sustains all being, all existence, and all human knowing—to one of *doubting* everything other than the proofs or reasonable deduction and practical inference produced by human sense and logic alone. This is a profound shift from faith-based **theocentric ontological foundationalism** (**TOF**) to skeptical **egocentric epistemological foundationalism** (**EEF**). If we are to evaluate modern science from the interpretive commitments of Christian theology, we need to understand how TOF works in traditional Christian theology and *not*, supposedly in the service of Christian theology, assume EEF approaches to truth.

It may seem like a digression here, but unpacking how both TOF and EEF interpret reality is particularly important in understanding how EEF-situated post-Victorian rationalism, empiricism, and reductive materialism actually look to any traditional TOF-situated Christian theology.

3.3 Theocentric Foundations versus Egocentric Foundations

A key feature of Enlightenment philosophy is the desire to replace every partial understanding of revealed metaphysical truths, and every authoritatively reported miraculous truth that one must *trust*, with a demonstration of natural facts and rational formulations that anyone can indubitably *prove* for themselves. Whether such ambitions are realizable is one question, but, more problematically, the very attempt to *replace* trust regarding that which theologically and metaphysically stands over us and beyond us with proof concerning what we epistemologically stand over undermines crucial modes of truth transmission that are indispensable for Christian theology. The remarkable reversal signals a first-order interpretive transition concerning where the locus of truth itself lies: it shifts from the divine Creator to the human knower. This is a profoundly important difference, as the very idea of what counts as truth is radically inverted when one moves from one locus of truth to the other.

Before proceeding any further with TOF and EEF, we should clarify terms. Ontology is the branch of philosophy concerned with understanding the nature of being. Thinking about "being" is now hard for the modern mind to grasp, but this used to be what metaphysics was primarily concerned with; it sought to understand the divine ground on which existing things depend in order for them to "be" what they are.[10] In more familiar terrain to the modern mind,

---

10. On recovering the notion of being in our times, see Tyson, *De-fragmenting Modernity*.

epistemology is the branch of philosophy that seeks to understand the nature of human knowledge. **Foundationalism**[11] seeks some sure foundation on which to build a valid system of reasoned understanding. **Egocentrism** in epistemology places the locus of knowledge within the individual knower. **Theocentrism** in ontology and epistemology places the loci of both being and knowing in God.

I will here argue that modern EEF is inherently opposed to traditional Western TOF and that, since the turn of the nineteenth century, EEF considers itself to have replaced TOF. There is some controversy about the lineage of modern EEF that I will need to clear up before unpacking the meaning of this term, as the question of whether early modern thinkers—like Descartes—were epistemological foundationalists is historically important but theoretically unimportant as regards my argument.

Questions about which modern thinkers are, and which are not, epistemological foundationalists are confusing for the following reason. Early modern thinkers, who usually had a keen interest in Christian or deist or Arian theology, have been appropriated by high modernists in the nineteenth century, who typically have a complete *disinterest* in any sort of theology or traditional metaphysics. This late nineteenth-century secularized and "purely" philosophical approach to doubt and knowledge produced what I will call **PHIL100** representations of what epistemology itself is.[12] This nineteenth-century epistemology produced the three modern so-called truth theories that were so fashionable in Anglo-American philosophy in the twentieth century: the correspondence theory, the coherence theory, and the pragmatic theory. The historical reality is that egocentric and rigorously secular epistemological foundationalism (which has never actually worked philosophically) is an invention of the nineteenth century rather than of the seventeenth century.[13]

11. In philosophy *foundationalism* has become a word tied tightly to modern egoistic positivist truth stances, such that any rejection of those truth stances is considered "anti-foundationalist." I am using the word *foundational* here in such a way that it can refer not only to proof-based modern EEF endeavors but also to trust-based pre-modern truth grounds that are now not usually considered viable options in our reductively naturalistic and religiously secularized academic contexts.

12. PHIL100 was the timetable code for the first-year Introduction to Philosophy class I took as an undergraduate student at university. Peter Harrison usefully identifies Kuno Fisher (1824–1907) as one of the dominant proponents of reading Descartes as advocating a rationalistic epistemological foundationalism as the grounds of any viable modern philosophy. Harrison notes, "Many introductions to modern philosophy still follow this line, and undergraduates are typically introduced to the subject through [Descartes's] *Meditations*" (*Fall of Man*, 9). This was certainly the case in my own undergraduate studies in philosophy. It is also how Bertrand Russell proceeds in his immensely influential 1912 text *The Problems of Philosophy*.

13. See Pasnau, *After Certainty*, 1: "The very term 'epistemology' goes back only to the middle of the nineteenth century."

In what follows I will use Descartes and Sextus Empiricus to describe EEF, and while this is not contextually fair to Descartes himself, it is fair to the form of EEF that has replaced TOF in the dominant discourse of modern Anglo-American academic philosophy since the late nineteenth century.

Here, in a sketch, is the PHIL100 story about the foundations of valid knowledge. Supposedly following Descartes, the first aim of a modern philosophy is to establish at least one indubitably true article of *knowledge* that does not rely on any unproven premise that one must believe. If this Archimedean point of certain knowledge can be secured, then the promise of building a demonstrably valid understanding of reality might be realized. Aiming at doubt-free certainty, Descartes came up with a rationalist epistemic foundation—his famous *cogito*: "I think, therefore I am." Whatever else Descartes could not be sure of, he had indubitable knowledge that, because he was thinking, he must exist. Descartes searched for this sure epistemic foundation to counter the late classical skeptic Sextus Empiricus, who had been recently recovered in Descartes's intellectual milieu. Empiricus had pointed out the many problems with attempting to establish decisively demonstrated truth by means of the senses, by pure reason, or by accepting the authority of any received opinion. Yet even though the ancient skeptics were skeptical about *every* claim to know truth, they preferred sense over reason, and they rejected divine revelation and metaphysical speculation outright as inherently indemonstrable.

Of course, the seventeenth century had a very different "faith and reason" tenor to the nineteenth century. In reality, what we now think of as scientific atheism was hardly conceivable in the seventeenth century. Even so, there really was something of a crisis in knowledge going on in early modernity. Late classical skeptics were being recovered, Aristotle's authority was being fundamentally questioned or simply bypassed by the new mathematico-experimental natural philosophy, and the tradition-questioning spirit of the Reformation was alive and well. In this context the desire to demonstratively prove truth, rather than to accept authority, was in the air among the innovative natural philosophy thinkers of the seventeenth century.

The late classical skeptical attack on every form of proof was every bit as troubling to the new learning in the seventeenth century as was the notion of accepting the authority of Aristotle or the church in matters of natural philosophy. Trying to make sense perception and reason demonstrably true—without appeal to authority or "speculative" metaphysics—was a big challenge. By the nineteenth century—and particularly in radical progressive circles—the search for entirely materialist rational and evidential proofs that were able to withstand every reasonable doubt increasingly came to define the purpose of academic philosophy itself. Reductively secular modernity must have true knowledge to replace blind faith in tradition-grounded authority and to counter a revived ancient form of rapacious and intellectually omnivorous doubt.

So the basic idea of egocentric epistemological foundationalism is that by rational or perception-based modes (or a Kantian combination of the two) the knowing subject (the ego) comes to find an indubitable foundation for knowledge, and on that foundation a philosophically true understanding of the world can be built.

EEF is easy for us to understand—or, at least, it is familiar to anyone who has studied philosophy. And it is rather assumed in our knowledge culture in general. It is now time to take a closer look at the traditional Christian alternative to EEF—that is, theocentric ontological foundationalism (TOF).

Let us start by unpacking the word *ontology* a little. A useful way of understanding ontology opens up when we think about the distinction between being and doing. For a job, I might practice law or dig ditches. *What I do* can be understood by looking at my external actions, the constructions I make, the way I present myself in those actions; and we often look to the metrics of financial remuneration (positive or negative) that signal the relative status of my actions as determined by our financialized valuations.[14] But *who I am* is a different sort of concern. **Being** is an essential and relational category.[15] To say "*I am* a lawyer" is to confuse what I do with who I am. We tend to do this a lot because our language is now ontologically degraded so that we tend to assume that who I am is a construction in the same way that the things I do are constructions. And while there is *some* truth to this, it really is a false conflation to equate doing with being.

Being human is prior to "being" a lawyer; being is firstly a category of essence, not of action. Action flows from essence (a cat does what a cat is), but essence does not flow from action. I am not human because I am a lawyer or a nurse; an AI answering machine is not human because it does (in a limited way) what a human does. To be human is to have the essence of humanity gifted to you (I *am* human) prior to any particular shape that you and others mold that essence into, which then gives you a distinctive and unique essence (I am *Paul*). After our essential humanity, the most fundamental and unique identity molders are not actions but relations. I am the child of these two people, bonded to this extended family, in this place and time, speaking this

14. See Gay, *Cash Values*, for a very interesting look at how money has come to define our values within the sociological lifeworld of contemporary consumer society.

15. See Buber, *I and Thou*. This text explores the deep links between essence and relation when it comes to grasping who we are.

language, belonging to these communities. Ontology is about being; it is about essential natures and primary meaning-giving relationships.

In TOF, human knowledge is never foundational in itself, as it is embedded in and complexly derivative of divine being, which gifts meaning both to the world and to minds. Here one cannot establish truths of being from the human knowing that is its derivative. The secondary cannot generate the primary. Yet one *can* have a reasonable trust in normal human knowledge, which is never epistemically indubitable, on the basis of *confidence* in divine grace. For it is not unreasonable simply to accept that as an existing and sensually aware being in an intelligible cosmos, one's epistemic abilities are a divine gift. And indeed, denying the demand for indubitable proof, via empirical skepticism, was often embedded in theological foundationalism in early modern approaches to natural philosophy.[16] That is, if one has theocentric ontological reasons to *trust* sensory awareness, the fact that sense is not indubitable in its own terms reinforces the theological grounds of an empirical approach to the natural world. While early modern empiricism was embedded in a religion-to-science interpretive framework, it was compatible with Christian theology. It is only as the lifeworld embedded in religion-to-science assumptions comes unraveled that empiricism becomes transformed into a species of doubt-defined egocentrism. Once this happens, then modern empiricism itself becomes incompatible with Christian theology. Kierkegaard was extremely astute in noticing this methodological and egoistic epistemic shift to doubt in the 1840s, which happened in bizarre concert with the idealist desire for the dialectical transcendence of "pure" thought. In his *De omnibus dubitandum est* (Everything must be doubted) of 1843, Kierkegaard recognizes the theological hubris and self-defeating epistemic dynamic in what he calls "modern philosophy." Empiricist doubt, as a purely naturalistic exercise, as *not* underpinned by theological faith, is not a viable knowledge methodology that can deliver truth.[17]

But the nineteenth-century secular philosophers have a point. The modern philosophical enterprise, to some extent, is indeed born out of the ambition to enable knowledge and technology to *escape* the controlling grip of institutionally governed Christian theology and university-controlled Aristotelian metaphysics. This escape requires "liberation" from traditional Western ontology. Starting with that escape impetus, things evolved over time. From the seventeenth to the nineteenth century, Western philosophy seems to undergo

---

16. See Hooykaas, *Religion and the Rise of Modern Science*, 44–52.

17. The full title of this extended essay is *Johannes Climacus, or De omnibus dubitandum est*. See Kierkegaard, *Philosophical Fragments, Johannes Climacus*, 113–72. See in particular "I. Modern Philosophy Begins with Doubt," "II. Philosophy Begins with Doubt," and "III. In Order to Philosophize, One Must Have Doubted" (133–59).

a generalized shift. Things move from TOF, where reason and sensation are not indubitable but *can* be trusted, to an empirically skeptical (pragmatic) and mathematically rationalist EEF, where both sensation and reason are ultimately *not* truth revealing. We moderns have told ourselves that the TOF-presuming late medieval church and early modern university were the enemies of intellectual and religious freedom, the enemies of a true knowledge and governance of the natural world, and the bastions of superstition and blind authority. By now it is culturally assumed that the modern age is an obviously good liberation from pre-modern intellectual and religious darkness. However, without denigrating the modern world or downplaying its astonishing achievements, and without asserting that early modern institutionally controlled Christian theology and university-governed scholasticism were not seriously problematic in many regards, whether EEF was ever a viable philosophical project is another matter altogether.

Actually, EEF does not work. We will look more closely at how it fails in both its secular empiricism and secular rationalist forms below. But here, what needs to be pointed out is how careful any thinking coherent with creedally orthodox Christian theology must be to avoid EEF if it wishes to uphold the interpretive commitments consistent with the primacy of God. Assuming EEF in either attacking Christian truth or (worse) defending it is to become lost to truth itself and unable to see knowledge and the world through Christian theology as a primary truth lens. But it was not just Christians who avoided EEF in the West's deep heritage of high intellectual traditions.

The dominant Platonist and Aristotelian streams of classical, Neoplatonist, patristic, and medieval philosophy in Western intellectual history are theocentric and ontologically foundational up until the modern era.[18] Here, to draw on Plato's famous cave analogy, the ultimate ground of reality is divine; it is intrinsically qualitative and intellective; it is eternal; and it is essentially Good, True, and Beautiful. Moral reality is derived from this divine fount, and all beings within spatiotemporal reality are dependent on "the Goodness Beyond Being" (God) for both their existence in time, space, and matter and their (at least partially) intelligible essence. To Plato, true knowledge—*noēsis*—is not reducible to either human rationality or sensory perception. Rather, in the Christian Realist metaphysical tradition indebted to Plato,[19] analogically true

18. See Gerson, *Ancient Epistemology*. Epistemology was always embedded in ontology and theology in the Platonist and Aristotelian mainstream of Western philosophy. Robert Pasnau (*After Certainty*) points out that epistemology was never foundational in itself until the nineteenth century.

19. I use *Realism* and *Realist*, with a capital *R*, to distinguish classical and medieval Realism (according to which the eternal and essential are the Real) from modern realism (according to

knowledge is the gift of the self-disclosures of God to the human creature, *through* revelation, as transmitted by Scripture, perception, creation, reason, language, imagination, poetic construction, and culture. Here, ordinary perception-based understanding of the natural world is not simply a natural process; it is an ontologically embedded and spiritually transformative process for the knower. To both Plato and Augustine, conversion and illumination are necessary for true knowledge.[20] Like the skeptics who came after him, Plato maintains that both perception and sophistic rational argument are shadows that do not reveal truth in themselves. But unlike the skeptics and the sophists, Plato ventures to look hopefully upward, in an act of good faith in the Reason and Goodness that is the ground of reality, to a receptive and partial understanding of divine truth.

Moving into a more Aristotelian register, this basic commitment to the ontological reality of a divinely sustained, meaningful cosmos means that our scrupulously careful sensory perceptions and our genuinely logical reasonings can be trusted, even if they do not provide the warrants of their own foundation. Here, the light of reason in the mind illuminates the perceived world with some measure of its true meaning because there is a great chain of being that, at its far distant top, is the intellective and causal fount both of all essential meanings in the perceived cosmos and of human intellectual illumination.

Where ontology is the grounds of epistemology, one must believe in order to understand and then know truth; but in egocentric epistemological foundationalism, one must know the truth before one can understand the nature of reality. And here is the essential point: modern EEF aspires to *replace belief with knowledge*. EEF is about humanly taken knowledge rather than divinely received revelation. Thus the aspiration of secularized modern philosophy has been to attain a self-justifying epistemic stance that can act as a foundation for true knowledge, not just in what we now call the natural sciences, but in metaphysics, theology, ethics, aesthetics, politics, economics, semantics, and so on. Where this egocentric conception of validly proved knowledge cannot be established, belief, faith, art, and prejudice can *replace* truth, but such convictions cannot *be* true.

To sum up, when we now seek to evaluate contemporary notions of empirical, rational, and reductively physical science through the primary interpretive commitments of Christian theology, we will be presupposing TOF—the view

---

which only the temporal and existential are real). Note, modern *realism* is not capitalized in this book.

20. See Schumacher, *Divine Illumination*, for a fascinating exploration of the transformative illumination approach to knowledge in Augustine and its viability today.

that God is the ground of all created existence and essence and the ground of all human knowledge. These interpretive commitments will enable us to treat Christian theology as a genuine first truth discourse. With this interpretive apparatus in place, let us now turn to the question of how Christian theology evaluates modern science.

Viewing Science through the Truth Lens of Christian Theology

We are now able to look through the interpretive lens of traditional Christian theology—as a first truth discourse—at the core interpretive commitments of contemporary, secular scientific knowledge. Christian theology is not antagonistic to natural knowledge, but—as we shall see—its understanding of the meaning of sensory knowledge, reasoned logic, and methodological reductionism is distinctive. Indeed, traditional Christian theology *is* incompatible with the interpretive commitments of post-Victorian science that led us to reject key Christological truth claims in chapter 2. Further, there are reasons to think that the interpretive commitments of modern science, as a first truth discourse, are self-defeating. As we unpack this situation, it will become clear that there is no persuasive reason why Christian theology should allow modern science to play the role of first truth discourse or why Christian theology should accept the impossibility of its own primary truth commitments. If this can be established, then we will be led to consider how science would look if Christian theology were recovered as our first truth discourse.

So, then, let us ask how Christian theology judges the truth viability of today's empirical, rationalist, and reductively materialist scientific knowledge.

4.1 Christian Theology and Empiricism

Christian theology has a high regard for embodied life and for sensory perception. Material creation is—at its fundamental origin—good,[1] and Christ's incarnation is a profound affirmation of the dignity of the human body. The ability of the senses to reveal truth and construct knowledge is an implied good within a theology of the reality and goodness of creation, the dignity of the human body, and the providential love of the Creator. Thomas Aquinas, with Aristotle, affirms the dignity of the senses as the indispensable door to understanding: "Nothing is in the intellect that was not first in the senses."[2] There is *confidence* (literally, "with faith") in the truth-carrying power of sensory perception for Christian theology. The Christian does *not* require indubitable proof from sensation, for the ground of epistemic trust is not sensation itself but the God who has created both our senses and the world they perceive. Of course, the senses and our understanding of sensory perception can be in error, but the warrant of truth itself is God, not our senses and understanding. The Christian approach to sense is one of reasonable second-order trust. This being the case, it might look like Christian theology is going to affirm empiricism. But actually, a Christian theological affirmation of sensory perception is not compatible with either ancient skeptical empiricism or its modern egocentric and proof-aspiring children.

Philosophically, it is crucial to recognize that the conception of perception-based "knowledge" as propounded by Sextus Empiricus in the third century does *not* affirm the truth-carrying power of the human senses and does *not* presuppose the senses as gifts of God to humanity. It does not even believe that the world itself is intelligible, as—being a skeptical stance—it refuses to *believe* anything at all. Recent empiricism, as developed in its decisively modern direction by Hume in the eighteenth century, is quite consistent with the skeptical and rigorously agnostic outlook of Sextus Empiricus. This unbelieving and

---

1. The doctrine of the fall is indispensable for the narrative arc of salvation history as told by the Christian Scriptures. See J. Smith, "What Stands on the Fall?" Even so, according to Augustine, an Edenic ontology remains the most fundamental truth about nature; creation is, in its true being, good. See Augustine, *On Genesis*. An originary ontology of cosmic harmony, rather than one of cosmic struggle, is what distinguishes the doxological focus of the City of God (the peaceable love of God and neighbor) from the doxological focus of the City of Man (warrior self-love, the pursuit of contest-based and violent glory). See Augustine, *City of God*. Simone Weil's stunning essay "The Iliad, or the Poem of Force" draws out the agonism, tragedy, and fatalism of the ancient warrior culture's search for glory, which is the outlook contrasted by Augustine with a Christian understanding of the goodness at the fount of creation. See Weil and Bespaloff, *War and the Iliad*, 1–37.

2. Aquinas, *Quaestiones disputatae de veritate* q. 2, a. 3, arg. 19: "Nihil est in intellectu quod non sit prius in sensu."

unknowing approach to sensory experience is phenomenologically tweaked by Kant in order to put an end, once and for all, to speculative metaphysics. According to Kant, we *cannot* know things as they really are (**noumena**); we only know how they *appear* to our own consciousness (**phenomena**). Metaphysics as the exploration of reality itself (noumena), hence, becomes redundant. The knowledge of truth about reality itself—and the very meaning of the idea *of* truth, as truth *about reality*—becomes radically unknowable. After Kant, this supposedly post-metaphysical stance eventually matures into British analytic empiricism and American **pragmatism** in the twentieth century. After Kant we now have a skeptical, instrumental, and formally logical approach to sensory experience where value, meaning, and truth are eviscerated from the sensory manifold itself, and the world of perceived physical objects is deemed only functionally "real," and descriptive sentences about physical "reality" are deemed to "obtain" logical validity in entirely linguistic and materialist categories. Somehow this analytic-empirical epistemology is deemed to be non-metaphysical—as if, *per impossibile*, reductive functional materialism and deflationary, semantically constructivist accounts of language are not metaphysical stances. To hold that one truly *cannot know* that the world is real, that reality is outside human knowledge, is to presume to know something about the nature of reality (that it is unknowable) and to maintain a *metaphysical* commitment to **skepticism**. Skeptical empiricism—refusing to trust the Creator when it comes to a reasonable confidence in sensory experience as truth revealing—is now entirely incompatible, metaphysically, with Christian theology.

But it is not simply the case that Christian theology finds post-nineteenth-century empiricism to be an inherently unbelieving (i.e., bad faith) approach to sensory knowledge. Theologically, modern empiricism indeed does functionally occlude the metaphysical source of both knowledge and reality (God), and then it thinks of the world and our knowledge in fabulously abstracted and unreal ways—without intrinsic qualities, meanings, and purposes. But the philosophical reality is that modern skeptical empiricism rejects the possibility of ever knowing truth. Hence, empiricism itself *cannot be true* in the terms of its own philosophical commitments. This warrants further unpacking, but the terrain is complicated because of the relationship between naive and skeptical empiricism within modernity.

Naive and skeptical empiricism are both species of egocentric epistemological foundationalism. Naive empiricism is not skeptical but maintains that the evidence of the senses is the proper foundation for a true knowledge of reality. Here sensory perception, and only sensory perception, produces a true understanding of reality. Anything that has no perceivable physical manifestation and cannot be quantified or observed via some sort of perception-enhancing apparatus does not—as far as a naive empiricist understanding of reality is concerned—exist. Naive empiricism is, in practice at least, reductively materialist. Every science textbook that I have looked at for the general education of school children or the training of scientists at university assumes naive empiricism and functional materialism (and tacit metaphysical materialism).

The above is a naive stance because, philosophically, it cannot be taken seriously. Sensory perception is an astonishingly complex thing.[3] The generation of human meanings out of sensory perception in the production of knowledge is, indeed, enmeshed in the wondrous, unified awareness manifold produced by physical sensations. But the interpretation of sensory perception is also inextricably enmeshed in the culturally complex, linguistically structured, and inherently philosophically, theologically, imaginatively, interpersonally, and historically situated dynamics of "normal" human understanding.[4] You never get "simple" positivity from such a complex process as perception-based understanding.

Philosophically, few contemporary empiricists would be so skeptical as to seriously doubt that there is an external world, and few thinkers would hold that there is no intimate relationship between the human sensory manifold and "reality" (whatever that is). But thinking after Kant and without reference to any theological warrants, the notion that the "merely" measurable, tangible world as anyone "simply" perceives it correlates directly to how things really are cannot be taken seriously; such naivete would be eviscerated by even the most casual engagement with the writings of Sextus Empiricus.[5]

Naive empiricism and skeptical empiricism are, however, related. They both share EEF interpretive commitments and the epistemic privileging of sensory perception. But unlike **naive empiricism, skeptical empiricism**—which is deeply indebted to the late classical philosopher Sextus Empiricus—is a very sophisticated philosophical outlook. And, strange as it may sound, skeptical empiricism as a philosophical stance readily produces naive empiricism as a practical stance.

This is a little tricky to describe, for while modern skeptical empiricism is a philosophy of knowledge, it is premised on the impossibility of knowing

3. See Chalmers, *What Is This Thing Called Science?*, 1–17. For a fascinating introduction to a phenomenological analysis of the richness of perception, see Merleau-Ponty, *World of Perception*.
4. Zimmermann, *Hermeneutics*. This little book is a wonderful introduction to the interpretive aspects of human meaning, but see the last chapter in particular: "Hermeneutics and Science," 116–32.
5. Empiricus, *Outlines of Pyrrhonism*.

whether or not one's knowledge is true. At this point let us say that sense perception does not give the skeptical empiricist *true* knowledge, but sense perception is the most *useful* form of knowledge we can have, and hence the only sort of knowledge one can build a *useful* philosophical foundation on. Modern empiricism replaces truth with use as the only valid grounds of viable sensory knowledge. This move carries with it a tacitly instrumental normativity and functionally materialist metaphysics. But can such a stance be reasonably believed? And how does Christian theology view such an epistemic stance?

Replacing truth with use is philosophically compelling only if one's thinking is already embedded in the interpretive commitments of naturalistic egoism as regards knowledge. And the complex truth is that while sophisticated empiricism denies true knowledge of the external world, it does so on the grounds of a tacit egocentric epistemological foundationalism. The ancient skeptics were prepared to believe practically useful things, even though they were not prepared to call their beliefs true knowledge of how things really are. Here sense is *practically* valid, and that is as good a proof as you are going to get. What this does *in practice* is elevate sense and use above reason and revelation. But reason and indemonstrable belief can still be subservient to sense if they are practically useful and if they do not contradict sense. So both ancient and modern skeptical empiricism provide us with a sensory-based *functional* truth foundation (a pragmatic reframing of "proof"), even though they deny that any philosophical (or other) truth foundation can be shown to be indubitably true. The effect is that useful sense perception displaces reason and revelation as the first "truth" warrant, even though empiricism in the shadow of Empiricus is a stance that is skeptical about *all* truth warrants.

You can see how a PHIL100 pragmatic anti-metaphysical interest in sensory "knowledge" would seem entirely compatible with an early modernist, like Francis Bacon, who wants to do something *useful* with natural knowledge and who doesn't have any interest in scholastic metaphysics.[6] For this reason, the

6. Contrary to the PHIL100 outlook, scholastic philosophy and theology contains some of the most exciting and profound intellectual achievements of the Western intellectual tradition. See Pieper, *Scholasticism*, for a fine introduction to the thought world of the Middle Ages. Indeed, Aristotelian scholastic philosophy was vigorous right into the seventeenth century. See Schmitt, *Aristotle and the Renaissance*. And yet it is also the case that scholastic philosophy in the seventeenth-century universities was something of a high-flying intellectual bubble world, locking out those with a new and more practical interest in observation-based experimental knowledge. Such a dynamic is pretty normal in the historical rise and fall of various knowledge discourses. Indeed, its highly specialized skeptical arcana make contemporary materialist philosophy an excellent example of a discourse bubble that seeks to lock out promising new expressions of philosophical theology from the secular academy today. We have yet to see what

reality of Bacon's deep embeddedness in Christian theology, and the profound links between his theology and his approach to what we would now call science and technology,[7] did not come into the PHIL100 story about the birth of modern philosophy and science as it was conveyed to me and my cohort in my undergraduate days.

Even so, there *are* strong links between ancient skepticism and modern philosophy. There really is an important sense in which Descartes's rationalist epistemic foundation (as profoundly theologically motivated as that was to him) is of a kindred spirit to classical Greco-Roman empirical skepticism. For both Sextus Empiricus and René Descartes, the first and only locus of any system of human meaning, practice, or knowledge is a conscious awareness of *the self*. Egocentrism is basic here. For Empiricus, the self experiences sensations, which may or may not (who knows?) indicate an external, real world. For Descartes, it is the self that knows its own existence through reason, independent of sense. The self, then, is the locus of awareness to both modern rationalists and ancient Greco-Roman skeptical empiricists. To all stances that egocentrically privilege epistemology as philosophically primary, the establishment of valid individual human knowledge is the only reasonable foundation for a valid understanding of truth in all fields on knowing. Equally, the *failure* to establish an indubitable egocentric epistemic foundation is functionally philosophically foundational. That is, if one believes that there is no demonstrably indubitable epistemological truth but remains a *functional* egocentric epistemological foundationalist nonetheless, then one is committed to the *impossibility* of demonstrably true knowledge, and this itself becomes the foundation for a functionally materialist and pragmatic philosophy. What is not typically even contemplated by a PHIL100 modern thinker is that making epistemology primary and egocentrically pinning truth to human consciousness is not the only way one can approach truth. Theocentric ontological foundationalism (TOF)—the mainstream of ancient Platonist and Aristotelian philosophy and of patristic and medieval Christian theology—is not even contemplated in post-Victorian empiricist philosophy.

Further, EEF, as Plato and the ancient skeptics pointed out long ago, just doesn't work as an epistemic proof. You cannot get to a self-authenticating epistemic warrant for indubitable truth by epistemology alone, whether by a rational egoist or a sensory egoist route. Neither route can escape solipsism, for they make the internal field of human consciousness the center of

---

will come of this. Contemporary materialist philosophy may well go the way of late scholastic Aristotelianism.

7. See, for example, these excellent texts on Francis Bacon: Henry, *Knowledge Is Power*; Gaukroger, *Francis Bacon*.

knowledge (or useful opinion), and try as they might, they can never be sure that the internal field of knowledge provides indubitable accesses to truths about external reality. Hume's rather touching account of how he comes to terms with the inherent frailties of our epistemic powers goes like this:

> The *intense* view of these manifold contradictions and imperfections in human reason has so wrought upon me, and heated my brain, that I am ready to reject all belief and reasoning, and can look upon no opinion even as more probable or likely than another. Where am I, or what? From what causes do I derive my existence, and to what condition shall I return? Whose favour shall I court, and whose anger must I dread? What beings surround me? and on whom have I any influence, or who have any influence on me? I am confounded with all these questions, and begin to fancy myself in the most deplorable condition imaginable, inviron'd with the deepest darkness, and utterly depriv'd of the use of every member and faculty.
>
> Most fortunately it happens, that since reason is incapable of dispelling these clouds, nature herself suffices to that purpose, and cures me of this philosophical melancholy and delirium, either by relaxing this bent of mind, or by some avocation, and lively impression of my senses, which obliterate all these chimeras. I dine, I play a game of back-gammon, I converse, and am merry with my friends; and when after three or four hours' amusement, I wou'd return to these speculations, they appear so cold, and strain'd, and ridiculous, that I cannot find in my heart to enter into them any farther.[8]

The greatest thinker of the Scottish Enlightenment and the father of modern empiricism counsels us to play backgammon and try not to think too much about where the modern failure to achieve egocentric epistemic certainty leaves us. But not everyone has taken his ironically sage advice. It is the failure of both empirical and rational EEF that gives postmodernism its intellectual opportunity.[9]

The philosophical failure of the modern epistemic project produces two main types of intellectually serious, yet failure premised, alternatives: a pragmatic replacement of truth with use, which ultimately reduces knowledge to power,[10] and an irrealist rejection of the very idea of truth itself, which often seeks to assert pluralistic constructed freedom against conformist instrumental power.[11]

8. Hume, *Treatise of Human Nature*, 268–69.

9. Lyotard embraces the collapse of EEF and with this the rejection of all truth meta-narratives as both impossible and oppressive. See Lyotard, *Postmodern Condition*.

10. The end result of this reduction is post-truth instrumental egotism. Here, projection and interest entirely replace any awareness of the very possibility of objective truths of both quantity (facts) and quality (right and wrong). There is no distinction between a lie and the truth here, as the *effect* of assertions are seen as the only real significance of language. See Taibbi, *Griftopia*, for an exploration of this dynamic in relation to the 2008 financial crisis.

11. See Foucault, *Order of Things*.

Scientists are generally naive empiricists, so they tend not to take either an anti-realist philosophical stance that reduces knowledge to power or an irrealist philosophical stance that makes "science" just one fable among every other knowledge construct. Scientists tend to *believe in* science as the pursuit of a true knowledge of natural reality, even if their senior university administrators may believe only in personal career advancement and the profitability or otherwise of their institution. Scientists tend to uphold a progressive idea of the advancement of knowledge in which scientific truth is pushing back the frontiers of ignorance, even though it looks like our technological powers are going be the undoing of the globe's ecological viability and modern civilization as we know it. Which is to say, again, that scientists are usually pretty naive and incoherent, philosophically speaking, and that they are often not directly involved at the pointy end of decision-making power or at the intellectually crunchy end of philosophy. So even though the technological application of knowledge native to modern science can reduce knowledge to power, it is not often scientists who take that approach. Amoral pragmatism in finance, commerce, and political economics is where the reduction of entirely constructed knowledge to power is now abundantly conspicuous.[12]

Back to the philosophers. To the modern empiricist, science may give us useful and manipulatively effective power, but what the real truth about the physical world actually is, science cannot tell us. That is, philosophically serious modern empiricists are pragmatists. Properly "understanding" some property of nature, on the basis of carefully measured and rationally theorized scientific observation, is useful. Magical or religious views about nature are—so the argument goes—not so useful. Therefore, science is superior to magic and prayer. In this manner "realism" is a function not of truth but of use. Of course, non-philosophically aware functional empiricists may assume that because something works it is true. But this cannot be philosophically substantiated, and it is easily refuted. Ptolemaic navigation, for example, still works even though it is theorized out of a geocentric natural philosophy.

Broadly along Plato's line of reasoning, I think it reasonable to hold that if one is not prepared to have good faith in a divinely ordered and meaningful cosmos, and if one is not prepared to find the locus of cosmic meaning and truth outside one's ego, then one should give up any pretense of being seriously interested in philosophy, meaning, truth, quality, and purpose and concern oneself only with effective instrumental power.[13] But as far as Christian theology is

---

12. For a significant description of such power, see Varoufakis, *And the Weak Suffer What They Must?*

13. Thrasymachus is a good model here. See Plato, *Republic*, book 1, in *Complete Works*, 972–98.

concerned, the warrant of truth is not going to be found in the human mind, as if the locus of truth were our own consciousness; the fount of truth is, rather, the divine *Logos* who both orders and actualizes the cosmos. To Christian theology, it is God who creates the world and who is also communicatively active within our own minds. It is God who bridges the human object-subject epistemic divide, thereby allowing us to have some partial knowledge of real truth.

In philosophical categories, Christian theology has a TOF truth stance. With Plato, I am inclined to think that this is the only way one can reasonably *have* a truth stance. And if someone wishes to persuade me that I am deluded when they really have a pragmatic rather than a truth-based conception of reality, then they are not really interested in truth but only in what use they can make of my beliefs. If one responds to the failure of EEF in either a pragmatic or an irrealist manner, then Foucault is right about power being what "philosophy," "science," and "religion" are *really* about. But what is not tried within secular modern philosophy or the postmodern philosophy premised on the failure of secular modern knowledge as truth is looking for truth along the lines of the TOF heritage of the pre-modern West. This is not tried because, with astonishing hubris, we modernists are deeply formed by the myth of progress, as measured by scientific and technological achievement. We cannot fathom that we may have made a mistake, and we do not countenance the possibility that the best way forward may be to go back to where the mistake was made.

For sure, modern science and technology have far better observation tools, far greater instrumental power, and far more mathematically sophisticated theoretical models of the fundamental mysteries of material reality than pre-modern natural philosophy ever had. For sure, there is great good that we can now do for the betterment of the human condition that we could not do before the modern scientific age. But all this is about power; it is not—for a strict empiricist—about truth. And the other side of modern scientific pragmatism is that we now have power for catastrophic evil in ways that we never had before. Whether modernity will usher in an Atlantean apocalypse of global destruction, a wonderful new step in the progress of humanity, or an incoherent maelstrom of both is still—at the very least—an open question.

If the *Logos* of God became flesh and miraculously entered our human world, died, rose again, ascended to the Father, and then established his church on earth, sending the Holy Spirit, then the fact that an egocentric, skeptical modern empiricism cannot believe any of this is not surprising. But this unbelief is—for a Christian theologian—not because empiricism is (or could be) true but because modern empiricism, through a strange ontological blindness and a dogged commitment to epistemic egocentrism, cannot understand the nature of truth that the human condition *does* allow. For this reason—so

Christian theology maintains—post-Humean empiricism misunderstands the partial truth-revealing nature of sensory perception, and post-Kantian rationalism misunderstands the partial truth-revealing nature of human reason.

The Christian theologian, then, has good reason to dismiss contemporary empiricism as a truth stance, for it could never be truth revealing in any egocentric epistemological foundational sense. This does not mean the Christian theologian dismisses sensory knowledge as a means of understanding nature. Far from it! But a Christian theological approach to sensory-dependent natural knowledge can no longer be called empiricism. To Empiricus, the modus of a useful epistemic outlook is doubt, where "knowledge" is never true. There is—in the end—no true knowledge available to the empiricist, but skeptical pragmatism replaces truth. In contrast, to Christian theology, the modus of a partially true sensory-based appreciation of creation is faith in the working of the divine *Logos*. The *Logos* gifts real essential meanings to the external world—however partially and transiently expressed—and the same *Logos* is operative within the human mind to be partially truth revealing as regards essence. Truth, real truth, can be partially known only by trust in the reality and illuminating work of Christ, who is the Truth. This is the stance put forward by Augustine in his powerful refutation of ancient skepticism (*Against the Academicians*) and in his positive account of how the mind knows truth (*The Teacher*).

Going back to our original definition of science, the experimental and physically reductive side of the original purpose of the Royal Society no doubt has some relationship to modern EEF. For the Royal Society wished to pursue natural knowledge independently of the ontological foundationalism and the received truths of ecclesial and university authority structures (and to be protected from them by the king). Certainly, observation-based experimental natural knowledge was of pragmatic interest to the king because new technologies could be invented with this knowledge that would advance the military and commercial power of the English Crown. So a pragmatic interest in natural knowledge at the birth of modern science may indeed be intimately entwined with what we now call an empiricist scientific outlook and methodology. And yet it is also clear that Christian theological warrants were very important to the birth of modern science. That nature is God's creation, that the advancement of natural knowledge and the increase of human power over nature are forms of participation in a divinely ordained eschatological enterprise,[14] and that human knowledge in some manner escapes the skeptical trap because we as knowers are the handiwork of the omnipotent, omnibenevolent God all remained firmly active beliefs in early modern times. Remnants of Christian

14. See Henry, *Knowledge Is Power*.

ontological foundationalism are still strongly present in science, even today.[15] Equally, the isolation of the physical from the metaphysical by the Royal Society did not imply an anti-metaphysical empiricist stance from the outset; it implied only the rejection of various medieval Aristotelian metaphysical stances and their modified university progeny.

In sum, modern empiricism—in the skeptical and pragmatic trajectory of Sextus Empiricus, in the EEF trajectory of high modernity, and in the anti-metaphysical and anti-miraculous trajectory of Hume—is not a defendable account of truth in its own terms, and it is incompatible with revealed truth when viewed through the truth lens of Christian theology.

The relationship of sensory perception to truth is never proven by the ego-centric epistemic warrants of sense alone. For this reason secularized empiricism can be in no position to say anything at all about truth. The Christian, then, should in no manner submit to a truth evaluation structured in terms of the supposed truth warrants of secular, post-nineteenth-century empiricism. The Christian has excellent reasons to reject the suitability of pragmatic empiricism to be a first truth discourse. A Christian judgment about the truth claims of any form of egocentric and reductively naturalistic empiricism is that such a stance must fail as a truth stance, but such failure—to the Christian—does *not* imply resignation either to the pragmatic replacement of truth with use or to a postmodern constructivism toward all meanings. Indeed, to a Christian, sense can be genuinely (if always partially) truth reveal-ing only if one first has good faith that the perceived world is divinely given, divinely ordered, divinely intelligible, and hence practically reliable. Such a stance seems, actually, quite sensible.

Let us move on from sense to reason. How does Christian theology evaluate modern rationalism?

4.2 Christian Theology and Rationalism

We start again with the problem of egocentric epistemological foundationalism.

The *Theaetetus* is Plato's dialogue on knowledge. Plato does a devastatingly convincing job of showing that if you want knowledge that is "justified true belief" about reality, you will have serious problems getting it if you try either the pathway of sense or the pathway of mathematical logic.[16] Yet when you

15. The naive empiricist attitude toward perception adopted by most modern scientists presupposes an inherently meaningful, perceivable cosmos—in which case it either has no real relation to skeptical empiricism or it is an incoherent expression of pragmatic anti-realism.

16. Indeed, the *Theaetetus* is arguably the most important founding document of ancient academic skepticism. After Plato died, the academy he set up became almost synonymous

get to the end of the dialogue, and every avenue to decisively prove justified true belief has been tried and carefully rejected, this does not end in skeptical resignation. To the contrary, we have now attained the lofty achievement of Socratic ignorance—we now know that we don't know what true knowledge is or how one might get it—and this is taken as the necessary entry point to a more pious appreciation of the mystery of knowledge. Plato seems to be implying that really, rather than a mundane sensation-based approach, or even a cunning linguistic approach, one will need a spiritual and divinely enabled approach if one is going to grasp true knowledge.[17] But interestingly, while Plato does not have a high opinion of what we would now call an empirical approach to truth, he is some sort of Pythagorean—with a spiritual, even mystical, love of mathematics.

Mathematics *is* a form of true knowledge, according to Plato, and yet what we might call pure mathematics is, to him, a low form of truth. Mathematical theorems about right-angle triangles really are true, and they indirectly tell us something fascinating about the operation of intelligence within our minds and about the ratios and necessary logical relationship we can observe in nature, indicating indirectly that the cosmos itself is embedded in reason. But mere mathematical dexterity cannot directly say anything about the true knowledge of reality that Plato is after. The high truths of *noēsis* that Plato seeks—the only truths about which he thought one could have genuine knowledge—are eternal and divine truths regarding the sources of goodness, beauty, and truth both in the human soul and transcending the human soul at the ground of being itself.

Plato thinks that you cannot leap from being good at geometry or science,[18] or simply winning a rational debate, to understanding the truths of high wisdom that the philosopher seeks. That is a process that requires the purification and conversion of the soul, and it requires the revelatory disclosure of the divine Good itself. This is not something that simply being smart or having astute powers of sensory observation is going to be any help with. Plato advocates philosophy—particularly as it concerns truth—as a spiritual enterprise.[19] On this the early church fathers and the great theologians of high

---

with brilliant intellectual justifications for the suspension of all beliefs regarding truth. Middle Platonism revived the religious emphasis of Plato's dialogues in the first century BC, and after this the skeptics of the late classical Greco-Roman world increasingly looked to the pre-Socratic atomists and pursued their own naturalistic skeptical arguments, but Plato's analysis of the impossibility of egocentric epistemological foundationalism via the *Theaetetus* was understood to be very powerful in ancient times.

17. On how "religious" Plato's philosophy really is, see Burkert, "Philosophical Religion."

18. By "science" here, I mean the kind of natural philosophy that Aristotle did, not modern science.

19. See again Burkert, "Philosophical Religion." On the transformative illuminationist approach to knowledge within the Augustinian tradition, see again Schumacher, *Divine Illumination*.

medieval times fully agreed with Plato. In this regard it is fair to characterize Christian theology as Platonist. But Christian theology firmly disagrees
with Platonist religious philosophy concerning the particular actions of God
within the contingencies of space and time.[20] This is outside Plato's thought
world, but it is essential for Christian theology.

In the latter part of book 6 in the *Republic*, Plato defines the realm of
appearance, about which one will have opinions, as being concerned with
particular and tangible things that are partially and unstably good, partially
and unstably beautiful, etcetera. The person who loves these things will have
some inkling of the Good and the Beautiful that is eternal and unchanging.
That is, opinions about the apparent world of spatiotemporal things are
not complete ignorance to Plato, but neither are they true knowledge. The
lover of apparent things deals in the realm of opinion (*doxa*), whereas the
lover of wisdom—the philosopher—is concerned with the eternal realities
of Goodness and Beauty, the realm of true knowledge. For Plato, both what
we now call "science" and "religion" are located within the realm of appearance and opinion concerning contingent and changeable things, rather than
within the high realm of true knowledge. Yet Christian theology maintains
that *doxa* is the manifest (apparent) glory of God through the medium of
contingent historical time, particular people and places, and ever shifting
and evolving cultural and linguistic meaning contexts. The doctrines of the
church are derived not from Plato's understanding of pure high knowledge
but from the *doxa* of the acts of God manifest to us within time and space.
With Plato, Christian theology is committed to the notion of a transcendent
and eternal high reality in which our world of apparent things participates,
but Christian theology has a much higher opinion of opinion (and hence of
"religion" and "science") as the truth-carrying media of the divine *Logos* than
does Plato. According to Christian theology, God is partially revealed to us
through our tangible apprehension of creation and history, and this revelation
is transmitted by the community of believers through the very human and
contingent media of inspired writings and doxological practices embedded in
human institutions. This would be far too tangible and contingent a notion
of divine Truth for Plato.

As already noted, modern (and ancient) rationalism has serious trouble
with the idea of eternal and divine revelation being situated contingently
within history. And yet, while purely logical reason and immediate sensation
are both inadequate as true knowledge foundations, as Plato outlines in the
Theaetetus, how else is the divine *Logos* to reach us if it does not condescend

20. See Tyson, *Returning to Reality*, 90–125.

to the limited categories of human experience and understanding? The Christian revelation unflinchingly teaches that God *is* revealed to us in terms that we humans can actually understand.[21] God is an excellent communicator who can make himself clear both to elite theologians like Saint Paul and to uneducated fishermen like Saint Peter. God, then, speaks to us through tangibly apprehended revelations, and through sense and reason as embedded in space and time, even though sense and reason are not adequate truth foundations in their own terms.

If one is too empiricist for any miraculous and metaphysical work of God in nature, too rationalistic for any humanly framed and contingently expressed historical account of God's words and actions among us, too academic for the hearsay stories of common people about miraculous goings-on, then one is too epistemically proud, too inclined to worship one's own supposedly autonomous and self-validating mind, to receive the Christian revelation. Knowledge itself, if grasped in pride and in bad faith toward God, is a sin.

Kierkegaard makes much of the epistemic and existential offense of the gospel: only the humble can receive and live within divine truth.[22] The Christian gospel is not an exercise in perfect tautological logic. Indeed, all the key doctrines of Christian theology contain inescapable logical paradoxes.[23] And Christian theology is not expressed in repeatable scientific proofs, as if God were a controllable and demonstrable part of nature. It is expressed in historical narratives recounting the words and act of God made flesh among us, as passed on by the community of faith. And it is expressed in the personal encounters with God that are held within the orthodox understanding and practice structures of the living community of faith.

A purely mathematical, tautological, logically necessary truth criterion is unable to speak to the contingent historical world in which we actually live—a world in which, perhaps, the dangerous invasion of our tiny lives by divinity cannot be rationally ruled out. But then what of the way the operational norms of the physical world are in fact dependably logically

21. Jesus and Paul explain that God has a special interest in making revelation accessible to those outside the social spheres of power and established knowledge (Matt. 18:3; 1 Cor. 1:20). As Walter Brueggemann points out, the prophetic revelation of hope is—in the Hebrew and Christian traditions—usually given to those who are crushed and marginalized by the prevailing "royal consciousness"; it is given "precisely to those ill-schooled in explanation and understanding. It comes to those who will settle for amazements they can neither explain nor understand." Brueggemann, *Prophetic Imagination*, 104.

22. Kierkegaard, *Practice in Christianity* and *Philosophical Fragments*.

23. One of the most profound and beautiful books regarding one of the most astonishing paradoxes of Christian orthodoxy that I have read is *The Suffering of the Impassible God* by the Orthodox theologian Paul L. Gavrilyuk.

ordered? Christianity accounts for this as the providential inner governance of nature by the divine Mind for our benefit (among other things). And this Christian assumption of a divine cause to a nature that is rationally dependable and intellectually comprehensible is where modern scientific rationalism comes from. So again, while Christian theology rejects a "pure" rationalism that has no place for singular divine revelations in contingent human history, it upholds a commitment to reason governing the normal operations of the natural world, and it upholds faith in the intelligibility of reality and the connection of our intelligence to that reality. But human reason does not come with its own truth warrant any more than perception is its own truth warrant. Egocentric rationalism cannot establish itself. The divine *Logos*, as the source of both creation generally and of our own minds, and as the truth connecting subjective human consciousness with objective reality, makes an intelligible cosmos reasonable to believe in.[24] Egocentric and "pure" *a priori* human rationality can no more be a first truth discourse than egocentric empiricism can.

Once again, while there is no compelling reason to accept a rationalism that rejects—on egocentric epistemological grounds—the revelation of God in human history, Christian theology does not reject reason. Christian theology has its own TOF-framed rational understanding of nature, but such an understanding is not the religiously anti-religious analytical rationality of, for example, logical positivism.[25]

We have now given quick attention to why post-nineteenth-century empiricism and post-nineteenth-century rationalism cannot function well as first truth discourses, and why Christian theology need feel no obligation to submit itself to the supposed truth criteria of either of these interpretive frameworks for natural knowledge. But the most prominent thing that makes post-nineteenth-century empiricism and rationalism so theologically different from various pre-nineteenth-century approaches to sensory knowledge and reasonable truth is physically reductive naturalism. The acceptance of the validity of a purely physical view of natural reality is at the center of the incompatibility of Christian theology with post-nineteenth-century empiricist and rationalist accounts of the knowledge of nature. This physical reductionism is really the matter that requires the closest attention if we are to argue that it is still justifiable to reject the "scientific" disbelief in the truth claims of Christian doctrine, and to revive traditional TOF approaches to a viable first truth discourse when approaching natural knowledge.

24. Augustine, *Against the Academicians.*
25. See Ayer, *Language, Truth and Logic.*

4.3 Christian Theology and Physical Reductionism

Given that the basic starting premise of Christian faith is the ontological primacy of God and the ontological dependence of all creation on God, Christian theology has no place for the belief that only material things and measurable natural forces constitute reality (metaphysical materialism). For—apart from the mystery of the incarnation—God is not a material being existing within the cosmos. "God is spirit," Jesus explains, "and his worshipers must worship in the Spirit and in truth" (John 4:24). Paul explains to the Roman Christians that unbelief in God arises from a willful disregard of the obvious truth of God's grandeur as expressed through the material cosmos: "What is known of God is manifest among them; because God made it manifest to them. For from the creation of the cosmos his invisible things are clearly descried, understood from the things made:[26] both his everlasting power and his deity; so they are without defense" (Rom. 1:19–20). That the tangible created order is entirely dependent on the uncreated Creator—who is himself in no manner dependent on the tangible created order—is basic to the doctrine of God, and to the doctrine of creation, in all three of the Abrahamic faiths. So, holding to the revelation, accepting the five main tenets of orthodox Christology (four

26. I have used David Bentley Hart's *The New Testament* translation here because Hart is sensitive to the manner in which we easily misread the New Testament through philosophically and culturally modern eyes. Romans 1 should decisively *not* be read as a modern scientific apology for deism. The Greek phrase "τοῖς ποιήμασιν νοούμενα καθορᾶται" has a distinctive meaning in its first-century context that is continuous with Greek philosophical views of how a degree of spiritual understanding is achieved *through* perception, rather than with the modern positivist assumption according to which all understanding is *derived from* perception.

Here Paul notes that that which is "clearly descried"—obviously, via the senses—is "understood" (νοούμενα) by the mind. Understanding here explicitly concerns the insight of the mind into the realm of spiritual and eternal truth. The word Hart has translated as "clearly descried" (καθορᾶται) does not here simply mean "seen" in any reductively physical sense; rather, as qualified by "νοούμενα," what is descried is the *in*visible theological meaning of the cosmos. So, when Paul says that we can descry God's "invisible qualities" (as the NIV puts it) and that God's (non-material) "everlasting power and his deity" are "understood from the things made," the tangible experience of creation, in itself, is not the *cause* of this understanding. Rather, the tangible world as a derivative of divine reality is a catalyst for spiritual insight in each person's mind.

This is exactly *not* a nineteenth-century natural theology "proof of the existence of God" in which there is a presumed linear progression from demonstrable empirical observation and mathematical necessity to a rationally and scientifically demonstrated "proof" of a "supernatural" truth. The eternal and divine is always prior to the temporal and material in both the orthodox Hebrew thinking of the first century and the classical Greek thinking of Platonist and Aristotelian lineage; one cannot prove the primary (God) from the secondary (creation). But the reality of the secondary (the temporal and material) cosmos is, in effect, proven by the primary (eternal and divine) Reality of God, so that a perverse and merely naturalistic theory of the world is, as Paul discerns, theologically inexcusable.

of which are entirely incompatible with physical reductionism), Christian
theology is simply *a priori* committed to the stance that the physical reductionism of modern science is false. But can this commitment be justified?
And even if physical reductionism as a metaphysical stance is incompatible
with Christian theology, is there any real problem with physical reductionism
as a methodological stance, as long as metaphysical agnosticism is upheld?

We come now to the complex knot of the relation of methodological to
metaphysical physical reductionism. Early modern physical reductionism,
as an experimental and conceptually limited methodology, was invented by
Christians. But things readily get blurred over time because, while a *functional* methodological materialism—that may purport to have no opinion
about metaphysical materialism, or may strongly uphold a supernaturalist
metaphysics—need not imply metaphysical materialism, there is a clear sociological relationship between practice and belief. What can start out as
a methodologically reductionist interest in "merely" physical things easily
(perhaps inevitably) evolves into a tacit, culturally situated *metaphysical* materialism over time.

Actually, it is more complex than practice producing tacit metaphysics,
for metaphysics and theology produced a reductive and instrumental practice toward nature in the first place in the West. The roots of this process
are deeply embedded in medieval times. First, after the fourteenth century, a
nominalist revolution in metaphysics promoted a disinterest in the intangible
categories of being (we shall unpack this below). Second, after the fourteenth
century, a voluntarist theological revolution promoted a more extrinsic and
instrumental conception of humanity's ruling relationship with nature (we
shall also unpack this). Third, a splintered Western Christendom in the seventeenth century readily found itself situated within a metaphysical cosmology
in which there was a supernatural "second story" to reality that was fully
discrete from a now functionally autonomous physical nature. Between the
seventeenth and the nineteenth century, this two-story cosmology evolved
into an increasingly hardened physical reductionism in the "natural" sphere.
In these centuries, advances in entirely "natural" knowledge through what
we now call modern science made the supernatural second story simply irrelevant to an instrumental and mechanical understanding of nature. By the
nineteenth century, we had landed firmly in the cultural terrain of reductive
metaphysical naturalism, and modern scientistic atheism rose naturally, as
it were, from there.

It is important to unpack this process in a little more detail. We will not
appreciate how deep our formation in functional-cum-metaphysical physical
reductionism is without quite a sophisticated appreciation of the medieval

preconditions of Western modernity. For these medieval preconditions have never gone away and rule the lifeworld in which we live unchallenged, precisely because they are now invisible and assumed. Assuming (falsely) that medieval thought categories are now completely irrelevant to the modern age, we have allowed these preconditions to become the unseen wallpaper to our cultural outlook on reality.

Two Western theological developments that occurred well prior to both the Reformation and the seventeenth century are highly significant for the emergence of a functional physical reductionism as integral with the rise of modern science. They are nominalism and voluntarism. These developments made it easy for the seventeenth-century revival (suitably baptized) of pre-Christian Democritean[27] atomism to produce what I will call the notion of pure matter.[28] The credibility (or otherwise) of post-nineteenth-century and secularized physical reductionism depends on the credibility (or otherwise) of these three developments. As we have already seen, Christian theology, as defined by orthodox Christology, becomes impossible if methodological physical reductionism carried to a tacitly metaphysical register is both credible and true. For this reason, it is vital to obtain a careful and critical understanding of this passage from the high medieval conception of a spiritually embedded cosmos in the thirteenth century to the late nineteenth-century secularized cosmos of pure matter. Let us explore this terrain briefly now.

4.3.1 Nominalism and Physical Reductionism

Nominalism is the idea that abstract qualities (such as *beauty*) and universals ("species" or "types"—such as *cat*) do not exist in concrete reality,

27. Democritus was a pre-Socratic ancient Greek philosopher who believed that there were only three realities: matter (as atoms), motion, and void. Ancient atomism was understood—in early modern times—as a pagan and atheistic perspective. The historical reception of atomism in Christian Europe is a fascinating example of the way in which late-medieval theological categories were carefully bracketed out of a more instrumental and abstractly physical conception of observable nature (atomism). Pierre Gassendi—a Catholic priest—was a key figure who made atomism a practically useful theory of matter that was acceptable for Christian use among the new physico-mathematical experimental natural philosophers of that era.

28. I am aware that, as Robert Pasnau points out, terms like *nominalist* are of questionable utility because they are used by different scholars to describe profoundly different philosophical commitments. Even so, these terms are not totally useless, as, however one describes it, there really is a shift from the thirteenth century to the seventeenth century—which is a shift from an Augustinian metaphysics of ontological participation (a love-centric theology of God and an ontologically dependent notion of creation) to a world of individual things, to will being the central defining feature of divinity, and to a self-standing, non-supernaturally dependent idea of nature. The terms *nominalist*, *voluntarist*, and *pure matter* will do to describe this overarching shift. For a far more fine-grained look at this enormous transition in medieval metaphysical thinking, see Pasnau, *Metaphysical Themes 1274–1671.*

for only material and particular things actually exist. Hence, qualities and universals are considered by nominalists to be "only names" (the Latin word *nomen*, from which we get *nominalism*, means "name"). Such "names," according to nominalists, signify no essential reality that transcends individual things. This sounds self-evident to us because we modernists are nominalists by default. But prior to the fifteenth century, the dominant streams of Western Christian metaphysics were of an Augustinian inflection, and here there is a strong heritage of **ontological participation**. That is, while the church certainly was a tangible collection of individual Christians, the church was also thought of as a transcendent and spiritual reality—the body of Christ—that was not simply reducible to the sum total of individual Christian worshipers in different locations at any one time. The sacrament of the Eucharist is also the body of Christ, yet there is only one church. So different physical things—a piece of bread, a living Christian, a departed saint—in spiritual unity with Christ himself can be "one" in some sense that is not reducible to the realm of tangible, temporal, locational specificity. The church was thought to be gathered in its fullness—in some manner transcending space, time, and the barriers between the church militant on earth and the church triumphant in heaven—whenever and wherever the eucharistic feast was being partaken of.

It was not only explicitly Christian theological "things"—like the church—that were thought to transcend physical particularity; the medieval *transcendentalia* (Goodness, Beauty, Truth, Unity) were immaterial qualities and ideas from the domain of eternal essence that were thought of as *realer* than temporally and physically existing bodies. To a medieval **Realist** of this nature, individual physical bodies partially participated in transcendent, immaterial, qualitative, and intellective forms. Nominalism is a broad metaphysical development that—over time—rejects high medieval ontological Realism in favor of thinking of reality in reductively particular, non-transcendence-participating terms.[29] We shall not delve further into this complex terrain at present, but for now it is important to understand that sixteenth-century Protestantism was largely born nominalist, as it was fourteenth-century Franciscans who got

29. In the fourteenth century William of Ockham, with his famous principle of ontological economy (Ockham's razor), continues a long process of critiquing Platonist-inflected medieval Realism, a process that starts in the early twelfth century with Peter Abelard. But even with Ockham, the notion of ontological participation is not totally elided. Nominalism is more of a process than a set doctrine. In this process the early to high medieval notion of the ontological participation of particular temporal physical beings in immaterial intellective forms becomes increasingly backgrounded to an interest in self-standing physical things. This process is not fully completed until around the seventeenth century. For a very helpful introduction to Ockham, see Keele, *Ockham Explained*.

nominalism up and running in earnest in Western Christendom's universities. In continuity with the great Franciscan intellectuals of the fourteenth century, early modern Catholics also largely accepted nominalist "corrections" of the older, high medieval Realist tendencies—as found, for example, in Aquinas.[30] What this means is that by the seventeenth century there was a more or less assumed tendency to reject pre-fourteenth-century ontological participation and to treat every tangible physical thing as ontologically self-standing and self-sufficient.[31] But whether nominalism is really compatible with a Christian metaphysical understanding of individual physical beings, or of spiritual realities in which physical beings ontologically participate (most fundamentally, God), is an important question to ask.

I cannot see how one can really adhere to key Christian doctrines about the ongoing ontological dependence of creation on the Creator if one is a nominalist. Within a pre-nominalist outlook there is nothing reductively natural about nature. Nature is dependent on supernature *to be* natural. To orthodox Christian belief, the soul, the church, the sacraments, and being itself—as participated in by all creatures—are ontologically derivative and dependent realities, relying continuously on divine grace. The "two story" isolation of heaven from earth and belief in the self-sufficiency of earth that a nominalist rejection of ontological participation entails are incompatible with an orthodox Christian theology of God as Creator.

Further, a significant problem with post-Aristotelian nominalism is not only that it rejected any natural participation in transcendent forms but also that (certainly in non-sacramental Protestantism) it eventually dropped the notion of intellective essence as integral with any physical body. One then had no way of thinking about significant features of a being's essence—its quality, purpose, intrinsic value, and meaning—as *real* aspects of the natural world. Consequently, by the late nineteenth century, all meanings and values

30. The profound impact of the brilliant Jesuit theologian Francisco Suárez on late sixteenth- and seventeenth-century Roman Catholic thinking moderated Aquinas in a nominalist direction, producing the modern trajectories in neo-Thomist thinking. The thought of Suárez is central to the "second scholasticism" in Roman Catholicism in the early modern era.

31. The Lutheran philosophical theologian Knut Alfsvåg challenges my stance on Protestantism being born nominalist by pointing out that Luther was deeply indebted to the Augustinian tradition that was vehemently opposed to Aristotelian scholasticism, but—claims Alfsvåg—for largely Platonist metaphysical reasons. This objection has credibility in that certainly Hamann in the eighteenth century and Kierkegaard in the nineteenth century show a face of Lutheranism that has strong ontological participationist signatures. To Hamann, language participates in the divine Word; to Kierkegaard, the self is ontologically defined by its participatory relationship with God. However, more broadly, modernity itself largely finds participationist ontology incomprehensible, as the fourteenth-century Franciscan revolution in nominalist metaphysics had a far-reaching impact on Western theology before the Protestant Reformation.

were thought of as constructs of culture, and strangely separate from (though derivative of) nature.[32]

There are philosophical and theological reasons why nominalism arose in the Middle Ages, but when—over time—nominalism came to entail the complete loss of ontological participation, it departed from a Christian vision of creation as ontologically upheld by God. That creation is fully dependent on God, at all times, in all places, implies that from the largest cosmic structure (a galaxy cluster) to the structure of empty space-time itself, everything *is* and has its ongoing *being* only because God calls it into being out of radical nothingness, only because God continually sustains all of creation in being.

Simon Oliver's very helpful book *Creation: A Guide for the Perplexed* points out that it is a profoundly impoverished conception of creation that thinks of God as making the natural world a self-standing thing and then going off to a supernatural heaven from which he can watch us from a distance and intervene in nature on occasion. In significant doctrinal regards, this is *not* an orthodox Christian understanding of creation. This sub-Christian outlook on creation is now so widespread among Western Christians because of the impact of nominalism in our assumed account of reality.

Contemporary physical reductionism is a descendent of the medieval nominalist understanding of nature, according to which material things are singular objects that do not participate in universal forms. That is, both medieval nominalists and we modernists take it for granted that there are no metaphysical essences that are shared by species of the same kind and that individual beings do not participate in spiritual realities that are not tangibly apparent.[33]

Nominalism makes essential meanings partially expressed in contingent space and time, transcendently originating value, all genuinely spiritual higher purposes, and the divine ground of created being—as real features within and

---

32. C. S. Lewis notes, "If you take nature as a teacher she will teach you exactly the lesson you had already decided to learn; this is only another way of saying that nature does not teach" (*Four Loves*, 23–24). That is, when we decide that values and meanings are cultural glosses thrown up by nature, then the *real* meaning of value and meaning becomes amoral and non-semantic, which is very convenient if you wanted to act in an amoral and merely power-concerned way in the first place.

33. In other words, spiritual essence is here thought of as residing entirely within material existence, with no "extra-existential," extra-material ontological remainder. Natural being is thus fully existentially concretized; all material reality is particularized such that any thought of a non-concrete, spiritual ground of material being becomes incoherent. Material nature here becomes fully discrete from spiritual supernature. This is the complex sixteenth-century doctrinal terrain of *natura pura* (pure nature), and the notion of a "pure" supernature also arises from this intellectual movement. Thus are heaven and earth first strongly disentangled from each other within Western Christendom. This will eventually result in the discrete territories of science and religion in the nineteenth century.

upholding created reality—disappear. But actually, meaning, value, purpose, and God have *not* disappeared, and the traditional Christian doctrine of creation as ontologically dependent on the Creator remains indispensable to creedal Christian theology. Could it be that nominalism was a serious medieval theological mistake leading to a seriously deficient modern view of nature?

4.3.2 Voluntarism and Physical Reductionism

Voluntarism is the theological idea that the most defining truth about God is that his will is sovereign and free, and that the most defining truth about us humans is that, since we are made in the image of God, our wills are also sovereign and free (*voluntas* is Latin for "will"). By the seventeenth century, this sovereign liberty was seen as gifted to humanity by God in Eden, granting us complete dominion over all the earth. Entailed in this outlook is the assumption that human will—the engine of ruling power and sovereign freedom—lifts us above inert creation and makes us in some sense separate from nature. Hence, voluntarism justifies an instrumental and extrinsic approach to nature.

Once physical nature is seen as purely natural and ontologically self-sufficient, and once one has adopted a voluntarist approach to humanity's rulership of nature as an expression of our unfettered will, the door is open for an entirely utilitarian and desacralized understanding of a reductively physical nature.[34] The instrumentalism of the seventeenth-century approach to the study of nature—where nature is simply the set of material objects that exists for us to use as we see fit—is grounded in late-medieval voluntarist theology. But again, whether such voluntarism is valid within Christian theology is another question.

In a terrifying simplification, I am going to posit a clean opposition between the fourteenth-century Franciscan voluntarism of Duns Scotus and William of Ockham, and Thomas Aquinas's thirteenth-century Augustinian **intellectualism**. According to Augustine and Aquinas, it is love and goodness, rather than omnipotence, that first defines God's nature; and, consequently, it is love and goodness, rather than sovereign free will, that define human nature (since

---

34. In this way, voluntarist Christian theology was key to de-magicing the natural world and opening the door for modern science. For a detailed exploration of the role that Christian theology and practice have played in this long and complex process more broadly in Western intellectual history, see Thomas, *Religion and the Decline of Magic*. For a brief look at how disenchantment has taken moral and metaphysical truths out of our understanding of reality, but how value and high meaning have not disappeared even so, see Tyson, *Seven Brief Lessons on Magic*. For an interesting eco-feminist exploration of pre-modern Western accounts of magical nature, see Merchant, *Death of Nature*.

humans are made in the image of God). Note that love is also seen as a function of will by Augustine and Aquinas. But these two are not voluntarists because, in their view, it is not unfettered freedom that defines the rightly ordered will; rather, the will is determined by *reasons* of love. For example, on Scotus and Ockham's voluntarist view, a moral rule given to us by God is not given to us because it is a truth in its own right, one that God himself is subject to; rather, we are subject to the moral rule simply because God's will designates it a moral truth. (Five-point Calvinists use much the same argument to explain why double predestination is just.) But to Aquinas, if God's primary nature is love, then there are *reasons* why some things are moral and other things are immoral, reasons that even God himself could not simply designate as otherwise. That is, love gives a defined logic to morality, and God himself, as supremely good, is bound by the moral rationality of love. But this, Scotus argues, would limit God's omnipotence. Now, this is highly complex terrain. And I mean no disrespect to one of the greatest thinkers and most deeply pious friars of Western Christianity. But I think that Aquinas, in the final analysis, is right and that Scotus's advocacy of primal moral relativism, making the good relative to the divine will, is wrong. For it is not only the case that God has supreme power, but God is also good (Ps. 100:5). God's goodness is the very definition of reliable, even—seeing through a glass darkly—to our small and fallen minds, and this divine faithfulness is the *reasonable* grounds of trust in him.

If voluntarism, defined by the sovereign freedom of powerful action alone, is the template for anthropology (if mere will is central to our true nature, and we are created, firstly, to rule over God's creation), then, as mentioned above, an extrinsic instrumentalism toward nature naturally follows. Physical reductionism is a conceptual act (the cutting out of value, purpose, meaning, pious taboo, etc.) that is consistent with the merely voluntarist anthropology that Augustine and Aquinas reject. To an Augustinian intellectualist anthropology, the voluntarist act of physical reduction is an offense against the meaning and value of real things. This instrumental reduction is at the root of the post-nineteenth-century separation of nature from culture. Values and meanings are no longer deemed to exist in nature but are thought of as strangely unnatural artifacts of culture. But if Augustine and Aquinas are more right than Scotus and Ockham, then physical reductionism is a derivative of an extrinsicizing **utilitarian** voluntarism that the Christian should find both abhorrent and false.

4.3.3 Pure Matter and Physical Reductionism

But now we come to the real heart of the matter for modern physical reductionism. Once one adheres to the nominalist metaphysical assumption of ontological singularity,[35] once one assumes a voluntarist anthropology that justifies an extrinsic and utilitarian relationship with nature, one has need of a theory of matter that fits a reductively physical view of reality. At this point Aristotle will not do. The revolt against an Aristotelian metaphysics of matter in the seventeenth century was not simply an accident of history; it was a *requirement* of the nominalist and voluntarist revolutions of the late Middle Ages. But it was also the corollary of some inherent difficulties with the medieval Aristotelian understanding of matter.

In order to understand the revolution that took place in the metaphysics of matter in the seventeenth century, we first need a working knowledge of the understanding of matter that it was revolting against.

Aristotle—and the medieval scholastics who gave us the Western university—held to what is called a hylomorphic view of substantial beings. That is, every concretely existing creature was a composite of matter (*hylē*, which is the Greek word for "wood," here means just material stuff) and form (*morphē*). Notably, the *form* bit of this matter-and-form outlook is problematic for physical reductionism because form is an intellective category, not a physical category. The most significant difference between an Aristotelian understanding of informed matter and our modern atomistic understanding of matter is that we can't see intellective, purposive, and qualitative things in physical nature, whereas an Aristotelian can. Some examples will help explain this distinction.

Aristotle thinks that any substantial thing in the world has **four causes**: material, efficient, formal, and final. Let us start thinking about this with the production of a human artifact. A chair, for example, might owe its *material cause* to the wood out of which it is made. But matter is not enough for it to be a chair. It has an *efficient cause* as well: a carpenter uses shaping tools and fastening devices on the wood. But the carpenter does not randomly shape and fasten the wood; he is guided by an idea in his mind, the form of the thing he is making. So the design of the chair is the *formal cause*. But the chair exists for a purpose, and it is the purpose that has stimulated the creative ideas in the mind of the carpenter. The purpose of the chair is to be sat on, to aid human flourishing. This is its *final cause*.

The same four causes—in a more complex and intrinsic manner—can be said to apply to living beings as well. Consider a duck, for example. The material cause of the duck is whatever stuff there is inside its egg. The efficient cause of the duck is its parents. The formal cause of the duck is the essential

35. "Ontological singularity" here refers to the view that any existing thing is itself alone, that it is self-standing. This denies the more Platonist outlook of *ontological participation*—in which a thing's "being" can be more complex than its unique physical particularity.

duck nature that every duck in its own way expresses. This formal nature is a set of distinctive characteristics shared by all naturally flourishing ducks, an intellectual quality that is recognizable by any suitably able mind (animal, human, demonic, or divine) as qualifying the duck as a being of a specific kind. This essential nature equips the duck for certain characteristically duck-like behaviors: swimming, eating duckweed, flying, quacking, socializing, reproducing, and avoiding predators. And the duck has a purpose consistent with its essence: flourishing. When a duck can do all the things its nature equips it to do, it is fulfilling its (final) purpose in life and is a good duck. If, for any reason, it fails to be able to do what its essential duck nature urges it to do, its purpose in life is frustrated, and this is bad. Notably, on this outlook, morality—the concept of "good" and its frustration, "bad"—is a feature of nature itself. Here, purposes and the intellective distinctives of essence are also features of nature itself. Further, natural beings exist firstly for their own flourishing and have essential natures; hence a purely extrinsic and utilitarian perspective on natural beings and nature is not possible for an Aristotelian, or for an Aristotelian Christian like Aquinas (but it *is* possible for Descartes).

According to an Aristotelian, these four causes apply to humans as well. Indeed, this outlook remains, to this day, embedded in the long natural law traditions of English jurisprudence. We are—in this Christian natural law tradition—fallen, and yet human flourishing remains defined by the still-good natural *telos* originally gifted to us by God in our primeval state of innocence. Here, what is good is what is natural, and harmonious flourishing is its corollary. Equally, that which is evil is unnatural, and an agonistic and destructive futility is its corollary. Nature itself is now also subjected to futility because of the fall of humanity. However hard it is for us fallen creatures to now discern the original natural good, the echoes of Eden are by no means impossible to hear because the self-correcting limits of flourishing are easily reached when human norms become too unnatural. By a process of natural equilibrium, the workable extreme boundaries of sustainable human flourishing are discovered, and societies develop norms (albeit fallen ones) governing power and behavior that have at least some of the attributes of sustainable human flourishing. Here there is something objective, not culturally relative, about right and wrong. Human law attempts to mirror natural law such that those things that frustrate true human flourishing are outlawed and those things that enable true human flourishing are protected. To this outlook there is both reason and science in *discovering* (rather than simply generating) moral truths. Culture is not a mere construction, and morals are not merely about power. Ethical norms are, of course, embedded in culturally relative customs and imaginatively inflected meaning constructs, but these norms and constructs must partially express *natural* truths that express essential formal and final purposes if they are to facilitate genuine human flourishing. Alasdair MacIntryre's revival of virtue ethics, Charles Taylor's critique of the subjective "ethics of authenticity," and John Finnis's revival of natural law in jurisprudence show us that the science of traditional Catholic moral philosophy is far from a spent force, even today.[36] Notably, natural law finds nature itself undergirded by meaningful purposes, overshadowed by essential meanings, and ontologically sustained by God, who is the Goodness Beyond Being.[37] This is the moral Realist universe of Shakespeare, and this is *not* the utilitarian and reductively constructivist culture that is a strange byproduct of a purely natural nature.

In the history of Western ideas, it is the medieval Aristotelian conception of **informed matter** that must be dispensed with if the abstraction of physical reductionism native to modern science and technology is to get into the air. Modernity, thus, had to produce a new theory of matter. This was not that hard to do, as Aristotle's theory of matter ran into increasing difficulties from the fifteenth century onward.

The concept of unformed matter (**prime matter**) is both impossible and implied by the concept of hylomorphism. That is, matter-and-form composites must have matter as the medium of form, so matter must be something in itself to be this medium. Yet, to Aristotle, matter is *always* formed, and form never exists autonomously from matter in some Platonic heaven. The conceptual search for prime matter while upholding firm hylomorphism was a stunningly complex feature of late medieval metaphysics. Also going on at this time were complex theological debates about *natura pura* (pure nature)— the idea that natural things, once gifted with concrete existence, do not need any ongoing grace from God to be what they are.[38] We cannot explore these complexities here, but by the time we arrive at the early modern period, the revival of **Democritean atomic matter** looked very metaphysically attractive.[39] Here—in contrast to both prime matter and hylomorphic matter—was a genuinely pure matter. Matter was composed of indestructible and indivisible atoms, in motion, in void, out of which everything was made. And this

36. See MacIntyre, *After Virtue*; Taylor, *Ethics of Authenticity*; and Finnis, *Natural Law and Natural Rights*.

37. See Rist, *Real Ethics*, for a sophisticated contemporary defense of a theistic and Platonist conception of the Good as the ground of ethical truth.

38. See Dupré, *Passage to Modernity*, 170–89.

39. The rise of ancient atomism in the seventeenth century is a highly significant feature of what makes the new natural philosophy that became modern science metaphysically distinct from medieval natural philosophy. See Joy, *Gassendi the Atomist*, for a fascinating exposition of one of the key transmitters of ancient atomism into the context of early modern science.

idea was embraced as a logically coherent medium for material bodies. But if material bodies are made only out of atoms of pure matter, this renders form and purpose strangely extrinsic to material reality itself (as Democritus well understood). Thus the natural operations of material bodies were then conceived in entirely mechanistic terms. For example, Descartes thought of animals as machines. Drawing on Democritus again, the notion of random motion on a minute, sub-detectable scale producing probabilistic meta-effects at the level of sensory perception is eventually enlivened as well.

With modern atomism we turned to a concept of matter in which only material and efficient causation were needed to explain force and motion in the world. In this way, Aristotle's formal and final causations became redundant in explanations of the material world. This hugely simplified the metaphysics of matter and material bodies, liberating calculative and instrumental reason (concerned with the practical, material world) from moral and **teleological** constraint. Intellective essence, moral quality, and purpose could be removed from nature and dropped from our understanding of the material world. As a result, a mathematically and mechanically pure vision of reality could escape from the moral and essential constraints of theologians and philosophers. Thus was the modern world born.

As with nominalism and voluntarism, "pure matter" sounds self-evidently true to most modern Christians, because we *are* modern. But this was, in point of fact, an astonishing departure from the way Christian metaphysics understood creation prior to the sixteenth century. As outlined above, in a Christian Aristotelian cosmos, divine grace donates intelligible forms and moral purpose to all created beings, for matter itself is always formed and purposive. But, dispensing with Aristotle, we have taken all the intellective, moral, and teleological color out of nature and are left with Locke's stark black-and-white world of primary qualities: solidity, extension, motion, number, and figure.[40] This is the morally and teleologically impoverished world of objective scientific facts.

Rejecting the Aristotelian understanding of informed matter, the seventeenth-century Christian fathers of modern science started to embrace a firm operational separation between the natural (the material) and the supernatural (the immaterial) such that one could explore nature as *purely* natural, rather than as intimately enmeshed—ontologically, morally, and teleologically—in the ongoing operations of divine grace.

From the early modern period it became possible to think that the intellective and the moral could be dropped from "nature" such that modern

40. See Locke, *Essay Concerning Human Understanding.*

"objectivity" could get into the air.[41] We now needed to understand causation only in reductively material and efficient terms. "Objectivity"—a stance that suspends ethical, theological, philosophical, and aesthetic judgment and simply seeks to accurately observe and logically describe whatever it is that is present to sensory awareness—becomes, over time, equated with factual truth. The anti-Aristotelian metaphysical assumption here is that form and value are not actually intrinsic to the material world but "exist" only as superimposed, prejudicial human glosses. The modern war between objective, factual nature and subjective, interpretive culture (and, by our day, between the sciences and the humanities) starts here.

Central in the development of pure-matter thinking was the notion that physical reality is gifted with its own fully self-standing existence by God. At the start of this way of thinking, the being of physical creatures was thought to be not *ultimately* autonomous from God—the Creator—but entirely naturally full, even though nature was originally made and set in motion by God. Creating was seen as an extrinsic act of divine making rather than as an intrinsic and ongoing ontological sustaining of physical reality by God, on whom all created reality at every moment depends. Christian theology had always had an appreciation of the miraculous and the metaphysical, but what we see here is the development of the idea of a self-standing natural reality that can be isolated from a distinctly supernatural (and external) order of reality.[42] God, heaven, angels, spiritual realities—these were externalized from nature and placed in a supernatural category of reality that was distinct from ordinary, mundane nature. This development made Christian theology irrelevant to natural philosophy and politics, in the eyes of most Western people, as time went on. It turned miracles into some sort of inter-reality event in which immaterial supernature is thought to causally intervene—momentarily—in natural, physical reality. But this outlook denies the intimacy between Creator and creation. It makes God out to be an external, causal, and occasionally intervening agent rather than a fundamental ontological presence, internal to the natural reality of nature itself as well as transcendent of nature. It removes the natural appreciation of the miraculous in everyday life; the wonder of birth, the beauty of nature, and the sense of justice are all "naturalized" as no longer miraculous.

The rejection of Aristotelian informed matter in the seventeenth century was a very important precondition for the physical reductionism of nineteenth-century secular scientists. But if meaning (intelligible form) and

41. See Gaukroger, *Objectivity*.
42. De Lubac, *Mystery of the Supernatural*.

purpose are in fact features of nature and not just constructs of culture, then the pure-matter view of reality is blind to that which is most important to us as knowing and valuing beings. That is, pure-matter reductionism renders the meanings of culture as fictitious untruths, and it also renders nature meaningless. Since natural facts and cultural meanings were sundered in the nineteenth century, culture has inexorably become the product of meaningless nature. Those who really know and understand the true meaning of reality now know that meaning itself is merely a natural function of purely objective material facts. Qualities, purposes, essential meanings, and intellectual truths do not actually exist. But as human knowledge is itself a cultural artifact, even facts about nature (science) end up becoming meaningless constructs of instinct and power. Thus science itself goes down the post-truth gurgler[43] of a reductively pure-matter account of nature and culture.

But this is inherently self-defeating. If nature is pure matter, then thought, value, and purpose don't exist; and thinking that they don't exist is also an illusion. The conviction that values and meanings cannot be true features of natural reality because there is no value or meaning in a purely material nature not only mocks all those things we value in culture; it also effectively denies the truth value of natural facts.

4.4 Physical Reductionism Is a Useful and Dangerous Abstraction

Substantively, I see no reason to believe that a nominalist- and voluntarist-formed conception of pure matter gives us a realistic understanding of physical reality as we actually experience and understand it, or that such pure matter is compatible with a Christian understanding of the intimate ontological, moral, and essential dependence of nature on God. I see no reason why a Christian should presuppose that the abstract idea of pure matter—which would deem obvious value, meaning, and purpose as somehow unreal—should be treated as if it were true and that immediately grasped qualitative and purposive truth should be treated as if it were a fantasy. This is Thomas Nagel's problem with reductive materialist understandings of mind and cosmos too, even though Nagel—unlike myself—has no theological commitments.[44]

---

43. My linguistically superlative American editor informed me that *gurgler* is not a word in common use in the United States (as also *spanner* and a few other words that I have discovered are distinctly of an Australian, and perhaps British, idiom). However, he thought the term delightful, so I have kept it in. The common North American expression "going down the drain" translates into Australian as "going down the gurgler."

44. Nagel, *Mind and Cosmos*.

There are serious theological pathologies associated with the modern pure-matter outlook. As Simon Oliver argues, modernists tend to think of God as extrinsic to nature and as acting on nature from outside of it in the same way that we act on nature when we make something.[45] This is an astonishing idolatry, a making of God in our own image as an artificer. Eighteenth-century deism is the high-water mark of this divine watchmaker understanding of a discretely supernatural, externally initiating, engineering God who is entirely separated from a self-sustaining and self-enabling natural world. The death of this eighteenth-century fabricating deity, first at the hands of Hume, then at the hands of nineteenth-century dark iconoclasts (such as Nietzsche), and finally at the hands of Darwin (who was enamored with this deist "natural theology" in his younger years) did everyone a favor—be they new atheists or orthodox Christian theists. It is only those deeply attached to the idolatries of *Homo faber* who have not let go of this Supreme Fabricator, made in the image of scientific and technological humanity. Various forms of this outlook still remain relatively healthy in Christian circles today, as seen in some corners of the intelligent design camp.

Substantively, "pure matter" has more than one mortal wound, looked at from more than one camp of first commitments. Even so, the matter remains methodologically subtle. To Christian theology, the notion of reductive physical reality can be seen as a useful and partially truth-revealing abstraction. *As* God's creation, and *as* defined by *Logos*-infused natural "laws," truths about nature can indeed be grasped by viewing creation through the abstraction of a reductively physical lens. Even so, the history of modernity shows us that there are dangerous instrumental pluses and perilous formational minuses that come with such an abstract reduction.

On the dangerous plus side, a complete indifference to ontologically layered religious taboo enables curiosity to explore realms that an understanding of nature more infused with the sacred would simply not permit. Modern scientific humanity has no awareness of epistemic hubris. To a functionally physical reductionist stance, a physical entity is just a physical entity. So chopping up dead human bodies and digging into the secret places of the earth, for example, can be done to "pure nature" seen through a physically reductive and pragmatic lens. Religious taboos would hinder such work. Such taboo-free "objectivity" has facilitated astonishing advances in, for example, medical science and geology. And then if nature is simply there for us to rule, for us to bend to our will however we will, then instrumental mastery becomes the first aim of our relationship with nature. This can render science a servant of

45. Oliver, *Creation*, 61–89.

technology, valuing it first as a provider of powerful human tools that can be put in the service of commercial exploitation and military advantage. This is seen in the Industrial Revolution, in modern colonial and economic conquest, and in modern warfare.

On the cultural formation minus side, What if nature is not simply there for us to use? What if, as God's creation, it exists not only for our sake but for its own sake? What if an unbridled exploitative and reductively physical attitude toward nature leads to the technological subjugation of nature to our commercial will to such an extent that we actually make much of the planet uninhabitable? What if nature is never, actually, purely natural from the ontological perspective of Christian theology? Technological society and its pragmatic realism make these very questions seem increasingly unrealistic. Yet, as the psalmist warned long ago, we become like what we worship (Ps. 115:8). Should we worship merely material power, we will become lifeless in our basic outlook on reality. Over time, this reduces justice to power, law to "black box" parliamentary sovereignty, people in the workplace to human resources, citizens to consumers, and the entire world becomes a calculative grid of merely physical objects and forces to be manipulated and used. The meaning and purpose of reality is occluded, knowledge becomes a mere means to power, and the self-serving will of the powerful becomes the only "truth." Under such conditions, instrumental mastery plug up the spiritual porosity of nature, divine light can no longer get to our minds through nature, and a profound moral, metaphysical, and theological darkness settles down on us.

Christian theology, then, rejects physical reductionism as impious, dangerous, and false. This physical reductionism leads to the bizarre idea of the non-physical meanings and values of human culture being in some manner separated from purely physical nature.[46] And yet it really is possible to study chemical reactions, for example, as entirely determined physical processes that can be carefully and scientifically described. And the greatest "advantage" of physical reductionism—at least from the perspective of modernity—is the idea of the autonomy of science from metaphysics and theology. This bears a little more thought.

If nature is treated as merely physical, and if physical reality is understood as metaphysically self-standing, then metaphysics and theology can be cordoned off from science. Getting all those pre-defined and speculative philosophical and theological grids out of the way of "simply" looking at how nature works, and then mathematically and theoretically forming functional

46. Latour, *We Have Never Been Modern*, 1–12.

models of how natural necessities work, has astonishingly liberated our scientific understanding of the physical world and given us a universal idea of what scientific truth is (at least methodologically). Hindu, atheist, and Christian scientists can all agree about the science of a chemical reaction, whatever their metaphysical and theological commitments may be.

While physical reductionism is the single most problematic feature of modern science as regards the truth claims of Christian theology, and while Christian theology has strong reasons (and not just theological reasons) to reject physical reductionism, in a carefully regulated manner this reductionist abstraction really can have an operational place within a Christian theological approach to natural knowledge. But it must be understood as a useful (yet dangerous) methodological abstraction that cannot amount to a genuinely true understanding of nature. Further, the thought is simply laughable that such an instrumental artifact of the human mind could be used as valid grounds on which to judge the substantive truths of Christian theology. That would be to judge the most primary and real truth by what we know is a useful fiction. Put more seriously, in terms of theology, to accept the reductively physical outlook of modern science as the ultimate truth about reality is to deny the four premises of orthodox Christology that cannot be reduced to the merely physical; it is, therefore, to deny the faith. More broadly, should reality itself be understood in entirely physically reductive terms, one has to deny all meaning and value in nature as well; and then science becomes merely a tool of power and propaganda. You cannot value scientific truth itself if you have a metaphysics of pure nature.

———————

When one looks through Christian theology's truth lens at modern empiricism, modern rationalism, and the pragmatic outlook on nature defined by physical reductionism, serious defects with the natural philosophy of modern science become apparent. Bearing this in mind, there seems to be no compelling reason why Christian theology should allow itself to be judged in the court of modern science. Let us take it that if the "science and religion" conversation is to begin again—from the point of view of Christian theology—the time has come to stop pretending that post-Victorian science is a viable first truth discourse.

So where do we take the argument from here?

First up, we need to explore a little more closely how science became the dominant public truth discourse of Western modernity. To that end we will now try to get a handle on the most important lifeworld transition in the historical relationship between Christian theology and modern science: the "remarkable reversal."[47] As Peter Harrison has pointed out, somewhere in the late nineteenth century modern science displaced Christian theology as the dominant public truth discourse of Western European knowledge. Before this reversal, the meaning of modern science was largely interpreted within a cultural framework in which the truths of Christian theology were taken for granted and were hermeneutically primary. This is something historians of modern science have intimate familiarity with. It is difficult to explain, historically, how it is that Christian theology, which was foundational to modern science itself, became so extrinsic to modern science that it could even be polemically opposed to modern science in the late nineteenth century. This can look like an inexplicable and titanic transition that simply appears out of the blue.

Historians make us aware of some deeply baffling features about contemporary "science and religion" normality. For while—theoretically—the empiricist, rationalist, reductive, and instrumental features of modern science *could* have been used against Christian truth claims from the outset, this was, in practice, seldom done. Further, just about all the founding fathers of modern science were Christians or deists of some stripe, and they typically integrated their scientific knowledge with their faith commitments, without apparent difficulty. That is, the type of empiricism early modern science employed was not a vigorously skeptical Humean empiricism; it was a naive empiricism premised on Christian theological warrants that made perception truth carrying. The type of rationalism early modern science employed was not reductively immanent; it still presupposed some transcendent and cosmic divine Reason (again, usually embedded in Christian theological warrants). The type of physical reductionism early modern science employed was explicitly functional, and it did not have metaphysically materialist implications. Again, this is because it was typically embedded in tacitly Christian theological warrants. The instrumentalism of early modern science was deeply defined by eschatological theology where the recovery of the Adamic mastery over nature through applied natural knowledge would bring on the end of the fallen age. Instrumentalism and technological progress in early modern science were theologically justified. Modern science is the child of Christian theology.

After the nineteenth-century reversal, things changed rapidly and radically in the relationship between Christian theology and modern science. Increasingly, from the late nineteenth century on, a new naturalism defined by Humean empiricism, immanently framed rationalism, and a metaphysically materialist reductionism became the dominant truth discourse of the Western academy. In this context, Christian theology is increasingly decommissioned from public knowledge and quarantined within the discretely religious arena of non-scientific personal belief convictions.

The terrible open secret is that Christian theology was itself profoundly implicated in the rise of a reductively naturalistic science as the West's first truth discourse. We need to understand how Christian theology largely produced its own demise as the West's primary truth discourse if we are to properly evaluate the relationship between Christian theology and science, as it stands now, and to—hopefully—begin again on better and more theologically viable footing.

5

The Remarkable Reversal—
Revisiting History

The famous "historical" exposition of a perpetual war between science and religion dates back to the late nineteenth century.[1] It is significant that this happens shortly after the publication of Darwin's *Origin of Species* and at the same time that Thomas Huxley is creating a new group of academic professionals we now call scientists. But this context is not as significant as it seems. That is, this overt and antagonistic rupture between science and religion is the *end* of a long process; it is only the *beginning* of something new by default. What really is new, however, is that once the tide finally turns, once Christian theology no longer provides the truth warrant for science but, rather, science provides the truth warrant for Christian theology, the age of the progressives has arrived.

The **progressive** age has been with us since the 1870s. This age has been characterized by the most zealous upheavals in education, sexual and familial mores, social institutions, politics, law, commerce, exploitation of nature, employment, secular attitudes toward "religion," "religious" attitudes toward secular knowledge and society, and so on. This continuous upheaval and re-making of the old, **conservative** ways (i.e., of the European lifeworld norms

1. John William Draper published *History of the Conflict between Religion and Science* in 1874, and Andrew Dickson White published *A History of the Warfare of Science with Theology in Christendom* in 1896.

embedded in pre-1870s Christian theology) shows no signs of abating. This truly *is* a remarkable reversal in terms of its cultural impact.

I do not mean to say that there was anything static about Western European cultural norms before the progressive age. Conservativisms are always evolving and always attract reformers, and today's conservatives are often yesterday's reformers. But a noticeable shift in the cultural assumptions of public and final truth warrants from Christianity to science in the 1870s really is significant. Even so, this final turning of the tide had been coming—usually without deliberate orchestration—for a very long time.

As sketched in chapter 4, nominalist and voluntarist outlooks on physical reality, which lead to the seventeenth-century conception of pure matter, long predate the modern age and are largely taken for granted by the founders of the new scientific learning. These matured fourteenth-century theological outlooks start science off as functionally autonomous from ontological theology and Aristotelian philosophy and will unwittingly lean the development of science toward its decisive rupture with theology and metaphysics in the nineteenth century.[2] The shift from ontological foundationalism to epistemological foundationalism de-theologizes one's basic outlook on knowledge and truth, even if one does not notice it for the first few centuries. The eschatological instrumentalism of seventeenth-century pioneers in the new learning—such as Francis Bacon—can become secularized over time such that excitement with scientific advances and the promise of a human-made technological and rational utopia can give a secularized salvific sheen to science itself. These features of modern science are in the very DNA of the Royal Society from its inception, and they are harbingers of the 1870s rupture. But there are two other critical transition points that happen between the mid-eighteenth and the mid-nineteenth centuries that we need to understand if we are to see why the early modern synthesis between Christian theology and natural knowledge broke down so decisively in the late nineteenth century. I refer here to the scientific conception of history that developed in the eighteenth century and the scientific conception of society that developed in the nineteenth century.

2. Actually, knowledge is never autonomous from theology and metaphysics. But the nineteenth century certainly saw a rejection of modern *Christian* theology and *transcendent* and *substantive* metaphysics, and these have often been falsely equated with the rejection of theology and metaphysics themselves in progressive Western intellectual traditions. F. H. Bradley's comment is still valid: "The man who is ready to prove that metaphysical knowledge is wholly impossible . . . is a brother metaphysician with a rival theory of first principles. . . . To say that reality is such that our knowledge cannot reach it, is to claim to know reality; to urge that our knowledge is of a kind which must fail to transcend appearance, itself implies that transcendence." Bradley, *Appearance and Reality*, 1.

5.1 Modern Scientific Historiography and Christian Theology

History, as we have already noticed, is not strictly amenable to rational and objective analysis. Which is to say that history concerns unique, non-repeatable events, an uncontrollable array of contingencies, multiple and shifting interpretive options, and the creative surd of human indeterminacy. And the historian herself is never outside of history. This is why historians tend to be very shy about claiming to know any decisive and monocausal explanation of why things in history happen. Yet modern historians now like to deal only in reasonably provable historical facts, biasing any causal categories toward reductive naturalism. This is curious in that history is replete with reports of the transcendent breaking into the immanent.[3]

Modern historians can accept a *report* of such an inbreaking as a fact of history, but—at least in contemporary academic historiography—they functionally treat such a report as a fact of pure nature (i.e., not a genuine inbreaking of the transcendent). Clearly, any epiphany of transcendence is inherently troubling to the modern outlook on naturalistic factual credibility. A modern historiographical account of the reported transcendence-inbreaking experiences of, say, Meister Eckhart, Julian of Norwich, Martin Luther, Blaise Pascal, John Wesley, Billy Graham, and Mother Teresa must be understood—as Max Weber put it—under the sign of methodological atheism. Which is to say that these experiences are understood to be culturally informed interpretations of subjective states of consciousness that do not have any real transcendent referent. This methodologically atheistic "objectivity" is far from interpretively neutral. Is this interpretive bias against God himself reasonable? Why should all of human history be brought into the ambit of functionally and methodologically materialist scientific knowledge?

Without doubt, a careful and critical interest in historical facts is important. History performed under the banner of modern scientific credibility

3. See Chesterton, *Orthodoxy*, 130:
   My belief that miracles have happened in human history is not a mystical belief at all; I believe in them upon human evidences. . . . Somehow or other an extraordinary idea has arisen that the disbelievers in miracles consider them coldly and fairly, while believers in miracles accept them only in connection with some dogma. The fact is quite the other way. The believers in miracles accept them (rightly or wrongly) because they have evidence for them. The disbelievers in miracles deny them (rightly or wrongly) because they have a doctrine against them. . . . If you reject [the cataract of human testimony in favour of the supernatural], you can only mean one of two things. You reject the peasant's story about the ghost either because the man is a peasant or because the story is a ghost story. That is, you either deny the main principle of democracy, or you affirm the main principle of materialism—the abstract impossibility of miracle. You have a perfect right to do so; but in that case you are the dogmatist.

has its benefits. It is possible to discern broad developmental tendencies in ideas and practices in time, and it is possible to be careful about tracing as many different sources as one can to establish historical facts with a high degree of certainty. Good historians indeed do draw generalized developmental conclusions about factually accurate accounts of the things that have really happened. But history became a natural science of the past (and arguably the first modern natural science) in the eighteenth century. This changed history's nature considerably from what was previously understood as valid historical truth, particularly as it concerns miracles and any transcendent meaning expressed in religion.

In the eighteenth century Voltaire, Hume, and Gibbon were great Enlightenment literary pioneers of a supernaturally skeptical, anti-clerical, and naturalistically factual approach to history.[4] This broad type of history is not, in itself, new—indeed Thucydides is a model for this sort of skeptical realist approach to history in ancient times—but what is new in eighteenth-century Christian Europe is a quietly ironic and intellectually sophisticated skepticism toward any notion of high Christian meaning being actively expressed in history. Kings may believe they have divine rights, and reformers may believe God is on their side, but in reality—so these giants of eighteenth-century letters implied—these beliefs are themselves integral with historically situated political dynamics. History, then, shows us that the ambitions of power competitors must be managed with power and ambition in the natural course of political events. The histories these brilliant eighteenth-century men produced were masterful works of literature that attracted a very wide readership among the leisured classes in the English- and French-speaking worlds of their day.

These pioneers of naturalistically realist and ironically skeptical sociopolitical histories set the mood of high Anglo/Franco thought in the eighteenth century. Yet what is going on in the Protestant Germanic world at this time is even more significant for Christian theology. The higher criticism of Christian theology's biblical sources is developing into a sophisticated modern science of historical and textual analysis. This development happens via a complex merging of philosophical, scientific, and theological scholarship.

Christian Wolff was the most famous Germanic rationalist philosopher of the early to mid-eighteenth century.[5] In 1723 Wolff induced a vociferous Lutheran pietist reaction against his comparative study of Moses, Christ, Confucius, and Muhammad, which resulted in his being dismissed from his chair at Halle. Much

---

4. Voltaire, "History," in Diderot's *Encyclopédie* (1751–72); David Hume, *The History of England* (1754–61); Edward Gibbon, *The Decline and Fall of the Roman Empire* (1776).

5. See Christian Wolff, *Reasonable Thoughts on God, the World and the Human Soul, and All things in general, communicated to the Lovers of Truth* (1720).

ink was then spilled over this matter, and Wolff came out of the process as something of a hero of free-thinking Enlightenment intellectual virtue.

The influence of Wolff on Immanuel Kant is considerable, and the shadow of Kant looms large over nineteenth-century Protestant German theology.[6] In the Germanic kingdoms, the relationship between theology and philosophy was intimate in the lifetimes of Wolff and Kant. But this intimacy has more strongly Protestant roots than the pietist expulsion of Wolff from Halle might immediately indicate.

Gerhard Ebeling argues that the German Protestant tradition's emphasis on Scripture alone as its source of authority and Lutheranism's "plain meaning" approach to hermeneutics—as distinct from tradition-constrained, scholastically integrated, and institutionally authorized Roman Catholic biblical interpretation—gave rise to the early categories of the historical-critical method of biblical scholarship in the seventeenth century.[7] And indeed, over the past two millennia, no other historically situated text has been subject to anything like as much intense interpretive scrutiny, detailed textual analysis, and historical interest in Western culture as the Christian Scriptures. For the Protestant Reformation was born out of the Catholic humanist interest in the original sources of the Christian Scriptures that took Western Christendom by storm with Erasmus's Greek New Testament. Careful study of the Bible plays an enormous role in the intellectual life of Western Europe from the sixteenth to the eighteenth century.

In eighteenth-century Germany, a number of intellectual streams meet up to form a powerful river. Enlightenment rationalist deism, scientific biblical scholarship, the love of the new natural philosophy, disbelief in miracles, and skeptical empiricism applied to historical analysis all become blended in the

6. Kant is rapidly eclipsed by Hegel in the early nineteenth-century Germanic thought world, but Kant's post-metaphysical move never goes away and remains powerfully influential in both Continental and Anglophone thought to this day.

7. Ebeling, *Word and Faith*, chap. 1, "The Significance of the Critical Historical Method for Church and Theology in Protestantism." I am making a very broad point here. To add a little nuance, the relationship between the contemporary historical study of Scripture and the historical-critical method within Christian theology is by no means only destructive of Christian theology. Some of the most powerful Protestant biblical scholars working within Christian theological orthodoxy today, such as Walter Brueggemann and N. T. Wright, make excellent use of the best historical scholarship in the exegetical studies of the Christian Scriptures without any compromise to the miraculous and metaphysical truth commitments in hermeneutics that are necessary to uphold if one is to retain compatibility with creedal Christian theology. But, in keeping with the powerfully argued thesis of Brad Gregory (*The Unintended Reformation*), I think it really is the case that Protestant innovations from the sixteenth century are the womb of what eventually became a post-Christian, secular, functionally materialist "West." Protestant attitudes to Scripture and ecclesial authority are deeply formative of the modern world, including its understanding of natural knowledge.

exhilarating new thinking of the likes of Hermann Reimarus[8] and Gotthold Lessing.[9] This, in turn, results in the new theology and the new interpretive science of the Christian Scriptures in thinkers such as Friedrich Schleiermacher.[10] By the turn of the nineteenth century, an increasing number of the most intelligent and influential theologians of liberal Protestantism had profoundly reinterpreted orthodox creedal Christian theology on the basis that the educated and rational modern scientific person who is concerned with truth can no longer believe in miracles and can no longer believe that a genuinely historical reading of the New Testament concurs with creedal orthodoxy. From here the *true* meaning of the Scriptures must be located outside any naive faith commitment to the actual truth of creedal doctrine.[11] Sublime religious feeling, deep reverence for the higher intellectual life, the moral and intellectual fulfillment (and supersession) of traditional doctrinal Christianity in German intellectual life—these moves are necessary for the inevitable transformative evolution of Christianity under the conditions of modern rationalism and modern natural knowledge.

What we are seeing here is that, via a particular philosophical and theological route, the discipline of history itself becomes scientifically reductive and incompatible with Christian theology as we defined it in the first chapter of this book. But it doesn't stop there. Historical-critical biblical scholarship, as done by liberal German Protestant theologians, leads seamlessly to the nineteenth-century scientific conception of society, and on to the twentieth-century scientific conception of the human soul.

5.2 The Social Sciences and Christian Theology

By the turn of the nineteenth century, the sophisticated rationalist skepticism toward orthodox Christology of Reimarus had become intellectually compelling among a growing company of elite German philosophers and theologians. Kant, with his deep rationalist misgivings about orthodox

8. Hermann Reimarus, *Apologie oder Schutzschrift für die vernünftigen Verehrer Gottes* (An apology for, or some words in defense of, reasoning worshipers of God), published by Lessing as "Fragments by an Anonymous Writer" in his *Zur Geschichte und Literatur* (1774–1778). This is the first major naturalistic and rationalistic analysis of the "historical Jesus" in the German tradition.

9. See Lessing, "On the Proof of the Spirit and of Power (1777)." Here Lessing argues that miracles cannot be believed and that history—and the Christian Scriptures—must be understood naturalistically.

10. Schleiermacher, *On Religion: Speeches to its Cultured Despisers* (1799).

11. For a recent example of this long tradition, see Theissen and Winter, *Quest for the Plausible Jesus*.

Christian theology, is now enormously influential in German universities, and academic theologians do not want to be left out of the cutting edge of philosophical thinking. The first four decades of the nineteenth century show a deep engagement between Continental Protestant theology and first Kant and then Hegel, and over this time traditional Christian theology is becoming increasingly marginal to high intellectual culture.[12] Then, in 1835, comes the decisive break: David Strauss's *Life of Jesus, Critically Examined*. To Strauss, Jesus was a historical figure of great personal charisma, but he was not God incarnate, was not born of a virgin, did no miracles, and did not rise from the dead or ascend to heaven, and the *real* mythic meaning of religion is entirely incompatible with traditional Christian theology. Implicitly, anyone who now believes naively in the literal truth of the virgin birth and the resurrection is deluded and has misunderstood the true meaning of the historical Jesus and the myths integral with the cult and religion that grew up around him in pre-scientific times.

Strauss's work was embraced by intellectuals who no longer thought that Christian theology and scientific truth were compatible. Not long after *The Life of Jesus*, Ludwig Feuerbach published *The Essence of Christianity* (1841). This highly influential book argued that—given that the true meaning of Christianity is not factual but mythic—what Christianity has *really* done is create the myth of God in the exalted image of man. This reversal of the usual way of thinking about the dependence of anthropology on theology was the switch for a radically post-theological analysis of human meanings and social institutions. God is now poetically created in the *imago homo*. In 1845 Karl Marx's thesis on Feuerbach takes things further: the myth of religion is really about power. Theology is transformed into anthropology, which is then transformed into politics and economics. Marx argues that humanity can now throw off the delusions of religious belief and the human world can be best understood with the tools of political and economic science. Marx takes the historical materialism of his inverted Hegelianism and his critique of religion from Feuerbach and links up with the French application of science to society in the thinking of Saint-Simon and Comte, and the social sciences as we now know them are born.

---

12. Kierkegaard is one of the most keenly orthodox Christian thinkers of this period to notice how a scientistic approach to Christian faith is rendering orthodox Christian theological truth obsolete in Germanic high culture. His *Concluding Unscientific Postscript* is astonishingly astute. He also sought to think about what we would now call psychology (*The Sickness Unto Death*) and sociology (*Two Ages*) in explicitly theological terms. This became increasingly hard to do after the 1840s. On what I have called the 1840s fork, see Tyson, *Kierkegaard's Theological Sociology*, 31–40.

The modern social sciences are born with Marx's bold rejection of any theologically Realist understanding of Christian faith. Thus the social sciences presuppose that Christian theology, as we defined it in the opening chapter, is false, and that a true knowledge of human morality, religion, social organization, and meaning is revealed by rational, empirical, physical reductionism, with no mystical remainder. This same attitude births modern psychology as well. The human soul, no less, is now dissected on the table of rational, empirical, physical reductionism.

This erasure of the transcendent horizon is not simply a social and human science move, as history, before the invention of the modern social sciences, was also scientifically moving against traditional Christian theology. Clearly, what we now call the natural sciences are not merely objective and harmlessly neutral tools of knowledge with no theological bias. From the twentieth century our secularized academic culture could simply assume that knowledge has nothing to say about God, because credible human knowledge is concerned only with the rational, empirical, and physical characteristics of (purely) natural knowledge. Such "objective realism" firmly banishes religion, God, and metaphysics from the natural world. Here "God" can be studied as a cultural construct of the psychosis of religion. The only kind of belief in God that is acceptable to our knowledge culture now is a reductively naturalistic belief that can coexist with reductively naturalistic modern scientific knowledge. Here, religious faith is understood to be entirely subjective—a personal and private belief, in a God strictly separate from nature, defined by doctrines that are carefully limited to the discretely religious territory. This brings us to thinking about "science and religion" during and after the remarkable reversal.

5.3 "Science and Religion" and Christian Theology after the 1870s

Because of the central role that lay Christians, theologians, and clergy had in both the rise of reductively naturalistic modern science *and* the shift to science as our first truth discourse, Christian scientists have often been a bit bewildered by post-1870s "science and religion" relations. By the turn of the twentieth century, science had become solidly academically professionalized and had become an increasingly prominent feature of university life, and this had excluded many an amateur female naturalist and many a nature-loving clergyman from a seat at science's high table. Yet the idea that science is locked in mortal combat with religion is simply historically false, and Christians who were in the universities as scientists knew this. Indeed, science was born out of modern Christian theology, and many a modern Christian in the twentieth and twenty-first centuries has felt entirely at home in both science and religion.

And yet, the century of knowledge secularization that extended from 1870 to 1970 saw the rise of a vigorous ideology of scientific materialism as the tacit orthodoxy of the secular academy. The progressive social-transformation agendas that went with that scientific materialist ideology in turn produced a radical lifeworld upheaval away from the norms and assumptions that held sway in a Christianity-embedded European past. Twentieth-century universities became the incubators for radical progressive social transformation.[13] To the scientific rejecters of Christian theological truth claims, Darwin replaced the Genesis narrative, telling us where we came from; Bentham and Freud replaced Moses, telling us where morals come from; and Marx and de Beauvoir replaced the Sermon on the Mount and Saint Paul, telling us how we should reorganize power and sexuality in a post-Christian and scientific age. What need is there for God now in the liberated, progressive age of science?

As Peter Harrison points out, by the late nineteenth century, Western culture had developed the idea that there were two discrete territories: a territory of objective facts, valid public knowledge, and applied technological power called "science," on the one hand, and a territory of subjective convictions and identifiable behaviors, ritual ceremonies, personal freedoms, and moral and supernatural belief systems called "religion," on the other.[14] Here, science tells you facts; religion tells you meanings. While this demarcation seemed a good recipe for happy coexistence to many Christians in science, cordoning "religion" off from all matters of public factual truth and defining religious freedom as a matter of personal and private belief has been a godsend (irony intended) for progressive, secular social reformers. Progressive cultural remodelers and sanctity-disinterested pragmatists have had a very good run in bringing on the major post-Christian reform movements of public and individual life: the sexual revolution, hedonistic consumerism, neoliberal econometric pragmatism, and amoral political realism. It is naive to think that the displacement of Christian theology by functionally materialist modern science as our knowledge culture's first public truth discourse has not been central to the collapse of Christianity as a unifying truth narrative defining Western cultural metaphysics and normativity.

There have been three main ways of trying to nuance the "science and religion" dynamic in Christian circles since the 1870s: functional demarcation, autonomous overlap, and integration.

---

13. James Franklin's social history of the influence of professor John Anderson, the Scottish pragmatist atheist, on the intellectual climate at Sydney University from the 1920s on—flowering in the free love, anti-religion, peace activism, and anti-colonialism of the student movements of the 1960s—makes for fascinating reading. See Franklin, *History of Philosophy in Australia*.

14. Harrison, *Territories of Science and Religion*, 1–19.

5.3.1 Functional Demarcation

Professional scientists who are simply good scientists at work and pious Christians in their own time sit comfortably with a functional-demarcation outlook. Here the two worlds simply don't touch. They are complementary in the Christian scientists' own understanding, but this is a personal understanding that is irrelevant to the workplace. This approach is most easily applied by Christians who are already at home with a liberal Protestant commitment to adapting Christian theology to modern empiricism, rationalism, and reductive physicalism. But, as already outlined, liberal theology readily buys coherence with post-1870s "science" at the cost of jettisoning four out of five of the distinctive characteristics of Christian theology we are using in this text. This is not a viable choice from the perspective of orthodox Christian theology.

5.3.2 Autonomous Overlap

Autonomous overlap is John Polkinghorne's approach.[15] Here, science is understood in strongly modern mathematical and empirical categories and Christian theology is understood in strongly doctrinal and systematic categories (it helps if one is, like Polkinghorne, both a scientist and an ordained clergyperson). Dual competency provides a binocular outlook on reality by overlapping, without confusing, these two separate lenses; this overlap produces a sense of depth in the field of vision. To a Christian like Polkinghorne there is obvious coherence between the two outlooks, though he accepts that the warrants of religious faith cannot be (and should not be) proven on scientific grounds. But that a serious scientist can be an intelligent believer is an important counter-demonstration to the atheist scientistic notion that religion is for uneducated and unintelligent people who need a psychological crutch.

The difficulty with this approach for Christian theology is that the very way in which modernity separates a knowledge of the natural world from beliefs about supernatural, moral, and teleological reality—thus creating the territory of "religion"—is foreign to the integral reality vision of creedal Christian theology. Christ is to be the Lord not only of our souls within the discrete domain of private religion, but Christ is equally Lord of our minds, our bodies, our relations with others, and our actions, within the secular and objective world of public knowledge and action. Such an outlook is also foreign to the now-universal claim of science to be the first truth discourse for all aspects of reality—both physical facts and human meanings—not simply for non-human natural phenomena. Most seriously, the autonomous overlap approach does

15. See Polkinghorne, *Exploring Reality*.

not explore how both the factual and demonstrable "natural science" lens and the meaningful and believed "cultural religion" lens have come to take the shapes that they have taken in modernity. These lenses are pre-shaped by the late medieval theological categories that produced the remarkable reversal of the nineteenth century. These lenses now have deeply ingrained blind spots to what is most primary to Christian theology as a first truth discourse.

Aspects of the autonomous overlap stance are often done very credibly and are often very thoughtfully and admirably delivered. Performed within a science-to-religion set of interpretive norms, such Christian-overlap apologetics are usually constructed in broadly theistic categories, categories more amenable to secular philosophical discourse than to theological discourse. Here, discretely theological concerns have become decidedly "religious" and are deemed not relevant to "science." The way "science" views, for example, the resurrection of Christ is either left in silence or hotly denounced as an unallowable scientistic incursion into the domain of religion. Yet, given that we *do* live in a science-to-religion interpretive truth culture, this philosophically framed apologetic work is unavoidable, and it can be done well. The work of the Faraday Institute, at Cambridge, and the work of ISCAST, in Melbourne, come to mind as examples of this sort of apologetics being done well. And yet—often with an interesting nod to Michael Polanyi and Alvin Plantinga—the truth terms of the argument are still largely set by post-1870s secular and physically reductive science, which, as we have seen, cannot accept four out of five of Christian theology's core truth commitments as credible public knowledge claims.[16] (Try arguing that the physical resurrection of Jesus of Nazareth should be understood as a credible public knowledge claim within, say, the biology fraternity of the Royal Society.)[17] The valiant apologetics of fine thinkers like Polkinghorne has winsomely adapted itself to modern secular-knowledge truth categories, but this adaptation is premised on the credibility of discrete discourse territories that are science's proper domain and religion's proper domain. Such domains are happily normative to our lifeworld (though a

16. And, in the modern sense, they never *were* credible public knowledge claims. We cannot open up a very big can of worms here and pursue the question of what "faith" is in epistemological categories, but whatever it is, the reasons of faith and the proofs of modern scientific knowledge are not identical. See Kierkegaard's *Concluding Unscientific Postscript* for some very fine thinking on what faith as an existentially framed epistemological category actually looks like from within the truth categories of Christian theology. Christopher Ben Simpson's wonderful book *The Truth Is the Way* is an excellent introduction to Kierkegaard's theology.

17. Thomas H. Huxley, notoriously, argued the opposite in what was a bold, cunning, and victorious move against the established truth primacy of Christian theology. See his "Evidence of the Miracle of the Resurrection." Upholding the separation of science from religion, Huxley concludes that on the question of whether the "molecular death" of Jesus occurred, followed by physical resurrection around thirty-six hours later, "Reason reports 'No Evidence,' and Conscience warns that intellectual honesty means absolute submission to evidence."

known and artificial abstraction),[18] but they are obviously foreign to any religion-to-science interpretive context and are highly theologically and metaphysically problematic if one takes God to be the ground of all reality.

5.3.3 Integration

The third approach is far more problematic within the contemporary secular world than the other two, even though it is a deeply modern stance. This approach is a conservative early modern stance precisely because it pre-supposes a "religion-to-science" interpretive norm and does not respect the territorial boundaries of post-1870s "science and religion" innovation. This is the integration approach.

Trying to affirm, with equal seriousness, both a modern scientific approach to demonstrable truth and the miraculous and metaphysical truth claims of Christian theology and seeking to integrate them in one coherent outlook is the driving motivation behind Young Earth Creationism (YEC). This violates the hermeneutic safety barriers that were erected in the latter half of the nineteenth century that separated modern science from modern religion. The stubborn YEC refusal to abide by the late nineteenth-century interpretive safety innovation (the "science and religion" domain demarcation) makes many a scientist and many an advocate for modern religion feel very uncomfortable.

To those who uphold clear territorial distinctions between science and religion, YEC damages the credibility of both science and religion. To an outsider, this is both bad science and bad religion. But the YEC insider cannot accept the manner in which Christians who claim adherence to miraculous and metaphysical truths can accept a double-truth outlook on reality—one in which science and religion do not integrate coherently. This is particularly concerning to evangelical Protestants for whom a "plain meaning" doctrine of scriptural inerrancy is one of the most primary miraculous and metaphysical claims they adhere to.

Leaving to one side the inherent difficulties with a positivist scientific interpretation of the meaning of ancient Scripture, there really are serious cosmological difficulties that make modern science very hard to coherently integrate with Christian theology. These difficulties shed an interesting light on the problems entailed in the post-Victorian functional isolation of scientific truth from religious truth. This bears further thought.

There really is a **double-truth** problem.[19] Christian theology cannot ignore the problem of double truth when it tries to situate itself within a lifeworld

18. Latour, *We Have Never Been Modern.*
19. The manner in which Aquinas responded to the Latin Averroism of the likes of Boethius of Dacia and Siger of Brabant remains significant. Aquinas appealed to the unity of truth but

that carefully separates the facts of "science" from the meanings of "religion."
The Adamic fall is a particularly significant doctrinal issue in this regard. If sin,
death, and evil are not exogenous and aberrant to created nature, then how does
one account for a Creator of unmitigated goodness, and what need is there of
a divine redeemer? The Christian understanding of the passion, where God
himself is the sacrificial agent of redemption, overcoming the three primeval
enemies of humanity (sin, death, and devil),[20] is premised on something having gone profoundly wrong in the natural order of things, something that only
God can fix. If disease, death, violent struggle, and competition for survival are
simply natural features of the entirely good reality we have been gifted, then the
redemption narrative of the Christian religion is—on the face of it—profoundly
out of step with reality. Again, applying a "plain meaning" hermeneutic, the
obvious conclusion to reach is not that a reductively naturalistic view of natural
history is telling us a different aspect of the *same* truth as Christian theology
but, rather, that reductive naturalism is telling us an entirely *different* story
than Christian salvation history. Here the unity of truth really does clash with
a wishful desire for "peace" between incommensurate truth discourses.

Unless modern natural history is taken to be totally separate from religious
truth and religious truth is understood as totally mythic in nature, natural
history as we currently understand it is incommensurate with the salvation
narrative of the Christian faith. I am not here proposing any sort of attempted
answer to this problem, but the problem itself cannot simply be ignored by
means of artificial terrain demarcation accompanied by wishful thinking
in the name of peace, aspiring to mutual respect between incommensurate
truth discourses. Aquinas is right to insist that truth actually *is* a unity. The
separated territories of science and religion invite the problem of double
truth. The problem could be as much with how we presently understand the
territory of science (can it really be reductively naturalistic?) as with how
we presently understand the territory of religion (can it really be discretely

also to the priority of revealed theology over speculative natural reason, should they disagree.
In this manner Roman Catholic thinking has largely maintained that what we now call science
and Christian theology cannot contradict each other as regards truth, but if there is an apparent
incoherence, revelation is the first truth discourse that the Christian should hold to, and then
the passage toward a coherent integration of natural philosophy with divine revelation will arise
over time. Notably, thinkers like Thomas Huxley also appeal to the unity of truth but maintain
that science is the first truth discourse and religion should—over time—come to be coherent
with it (or disappear). In this manner, the "science and religion" discourse continuous with
Huxley's stance does not put "science" first for no reason. On Aquinas's response to double
truth, see McInerny, *Aquinas against the Averroists*.

20. This understanding of the meaning of the narrative arc of salvation history is the *Christus
Victor* outlook. See Aulén, *Christus Victor*.

supernatural?), but respect for the unity of truth means that incommensurate truth discourses require attempts at unification.

Whatever Young Earth Creationists may have gotten wrong about science and theology, their awareness of the problem of double truth is right—and they share this awareness with the evangelical atheists of recent times.[21] In some way, Christian theology and a credible knowledge of the natural world must be capable of integration, or else one (or both) of them must be false. The YEC response to this awareness, however, is deeply entrenched in modernity itself: they have not left the early modern age, where nominalist, voluntarist, pure-matter Christian theology produced positivist and instrumental modern science. They have not adapted to the great reversal in which science became the first truth discourse of public knowledge and theology was banished from the public domain. Now that science has entirely separated itself from Christian theology, the YEC failure to come into line with that separation makes their appropriation of science to their theology profoundly out of step with the times. But the picture is more complex, more nuanced than it seems.

The fact that there is still no credible scientific understanding of *any* natural process whereby prebiotic chemicals spontaneously (or highly contrivedly) produce life; the fact that ecological systems and species adaptations are typically cooperative and mutually enhancing, rather than reductively survivalistic and inherently competitive; and the fact that—as the agnostic analytical philosopher Thomas Nagel puts it—"the materialist neo-Darwinian conception of nature is almost certainly false"[22] throws some interesting wrenches into the works when it comes to thinking about Christian theology and evolutionary biology. Christian evolutionists who are very keen to avoid any association with what they see as the crackpot anti-scientific errors of the Young Earth Creationists can readily end up being more committed to a reductively materialist and survivalist, orthodox Darwinian outlook in their science than open-minded non-religious scientists exploring the big problems of contemporary biology.

Truth really *is* a unity, and the methodological materialism that goes along with the modern scientific method may not be able to help us get anywhere with such astonishing realities as mind, life, and the sort of cosmos in which life and minds can be found. If we are determined to keep the thought world of theology away from the thought world of nature, we may curtail very significant thinking, thinking from which the next (and much needed) big breakthrough might come. Science-engaged theology working on the philosophy

21. For this reason, Ken Ham and Richard Dawkins are strangely akin. What they both have in common—and this seems to me an intellectual virtue, not a fault—is their insistence on unifying the fields of fact and meaning.
22. Nagel, *Mind and Cosmos*.

and theology of matter—such as the fascinating work of Nathan Lyons[23]—is an emerging and promising area on the theological borderlands of contemporary biology, which people interested in such things should watch closely.

The "science and religion" strategies of functional demarcation, autonomous overlap, and integration, as pursued by post-1870s Christians, are all seriously problematic. I think the reason for this is that Christian thinkers have not dug deep enough into the first-order framing questions that give us artificially rigid (and finally unbelievable) assumptions about the very nature of modern science and religion. It could be that our real problem is that we are trying to work within frameworks that are themselves inherently problematic for both natural philosophy and Christian theology.

The remarkable reversal has put Christian theology into a religious box that leaves science free to define public truth in entirely non-metaphysical and non-miraculous terms. Over the past 150 years or so, this boxing in has pretty well killed Christian theology as the first truth discourse of Western modernity. Many celebrate this demise as progress and liberation—including many modern Christians. But it does not seem likely that Christian theology can accept this container and remain Christian theology, as regards its own truth claims. So let us take one final look at Christian theology's own role in its public demise before trying to think of a few possible pathways out of this "religious freedom" box, which looks more like a coffin than a sanctuary to me.

5.4 The Unremarkable Remarkable Reversal

The passage from Hermann Reimarus, to Friedrich Schleiermacher, to David Strauss, to Ludwig Feuerbach, and to Karl Marx is a complex yet bold line of conceptual influence. This is the passage from eighteenth-century rationalistic and deistic humanism, to romantic liberalism, to scientific theological reductionism, to a reductively anthropological understanding of religion, to an atheistic understanding of the social sciences wherein religion is the opiate of the ignorant and exploited masses. Once we arrive at 1848, progressive forces are ready to tear up the entire cultural fabric of Christian Europe.

The above paragraph is not intended as a shrill cry of fear about the revolutionary appearance of anti-Christian progressives. In the latter half of the nineteenth century, Christian social-reforming activists and atheist socialists often worked side by side, seeking to improve the circumstances of highly

---

23. Lyons, *Signs in the Dust.*

exploited and impoverished women, children, and workers. Progressive reform was by no means simply a revolution in ideas. The manner in which the long-settled customs, ways of life, and sacred traditions of Christian Europe were being violently torn up by the Industrial Revolution cannot be underestimated. The Industrial Revolution, too, is a function of the rise of modern science. Its instrumental power, its physical reductionism, its calculative rationalism as applied to technology and profit ushered in a new age of humanity's relations with nature and between those who must sell their labor and those who own the technological means of production. And the nineteenth century was also the high age of European colonialism. This was an age of global plunder economics, where the rich and technologically advanced did as they willed and the pre-industrial "savage" suffered what they must.[24]

Perhaps it is no mere coincidence that the concept of natural selection through the morally indifferent struggle for dominance became a scientific truth in the nineteenth century. Knowledge really is always integral with power, and power tends to find its own justification, and often in the terms of the knowledge that enables it. This also is an unavoidable aspect of nineteenth-century science.

It seems to me that the dominant intellectual currents of nineteenth-century European Protestant theology did not—in general—have the theological or philosophical resources to resist the infatuating pull of scientistic compromise with their most foundational truth commitments. Some great thinkers—such as Kierkegaard—did powerfully resist, even though they were largely marginalized in their own times. But when Christian theologians find it impossible to believe in orthodox Christology because such belief is incompatible with Enlightenment rationalism, Humean empiricism, and materialist reductionism, then why would any intelligent and well-read person have any interest in Christian theology at all? Western Christendom was theologically white-anted (eroded from within) and ready to fall over long before the 1870s, long before Darwin (inadvertently) and Huxley (intentionally) gave it that last little nudge in initiating a culture war between science and religion.

In broad cultural terms, we live in the afterglow of Western European Christianity[25]—and hence the afterglow of Christian theology as our first public truth discourse—and in the full radiance of modern, functionally

24. See Boyce, *1835*, for an account of the illegal establishment of the town of Melbourne. The destruction of Indigenous people and the plunder of the land was all too normative of that era.

25. For a few helpful texts in this area, focused on the United States (the last major Western culture to try to come to terms with this), see Dreher, *Benedict Option*; Hauerwas, *After Christendom*; Harvey, *Can These Bones Live?*

materialist science. Indeed, as I have tried to show, there are direct causal links between the way in which our lifeworld has embraced the truth radiance of modern science and the way in which we have abandoned the light of Christian theology. The Christian, and particularly the Christian theologian, cannot ignore this. Even so, if Christian theology is actually true, if Christ is actually the light of the world, then Western modernity has put that light under a bushel and the remarkable reversal has been a massive mistake.

There is nothing one can do about massive historical mistakes, but there is nothing to be gained by pretending that the mere fact that a mistake was historically successful makes it somehow not a mistake. And, indeed, it is simply *not* true that science is the light of truth for the world.[26] For one thing, when we practice modern science, we are always seeking truth, but our ideas remain revisable. For another thing, there is no one thing called "science," as different branches of science may not coherently integrate. But most fundamentally, there is no such thing as a clearly defined factual knowledge territory or unified final truth authority called "science." Science is not, as the historian Peter Harrison puts it, "a natural kind."[27] Science is not a natural object in the world that can be defined; rather, it is an ever-changing, historically situated, and culturally, philosophically, linguistically, and politically embedded human activity.

The Christian theologian thinking about modern science, then, cannot afford to treat science as a fixed knowledge system of absolute truth (as if a trans-historical, theoretically locked, and singular science exists) and Christian theology as adaptable around the current state of natural knowledge (wherein, for all practical purposes, God does not exist). Perhaps, even, the Christian theologian might try doing the opposite: treat "science" as if it does not exist[28] and God as if he does exist.[29] This would entail thinking about natural philosophy "after" science, without thinking "after" Christian theology. This is not as impossible as it sounds.

26. Berger, *Desecularization of the World*.

27. Harrison, *Territories of Science and Religion*, 4.

28. I don't, of course, mean to imply that scientists don't exist or that the production of scientific knowledge does not happen. But as a point of historical fact, there is no trans-historical reality, no once-and-for-all-time secure and definable "thing" called "science."

29. In complete agreement with Maximus the Confessor (*Quaestiones et dubia* 2.14.4–6), I do not hold that God is a "thing" among things that "exist" in the spatiotemporal world. See "Maximus' Apophaticism: God Does Not Exist," in Mitralexis, *Ever-Moving Repose*, 45–48. With Augustine, I take it that God *is* Being (the "I Am") and the ontological ground of all created beings. With Aquinas, I take our knowledge of God to be expressible only in analogical terms. God's "existence" is never univocally compatible with our understanding of what existence, for a creature, is. But the sentence here noted upholds a stance in which science is a contingent, adaptable, and malleable human practice that can't be decisively, trans-historically defined and the only God worthy of the title is more real and primary than any existing created being.

6

Thinking "After" Science but *Not* "After" Christian Theology

At the outset of this book, I set up two provisional definitions of science and Christian theology. I must now come clean with you and confess that I do not believe there are any such definable things as science and religion.[1] This is not much of a problem for Christian theology, for that at least *is* doctrinally definable. I take it that the Nicene Creed is the basic definition of what Christians believe to be true, and that this definition is fixed, being (for the believing Christian) a function of church-embedded divine revelation, doctrinally hammered out over centuries, that is tied to unalterable historical events in the life of Jesus the Christ, which actually happened.[2] Clearly,

1. On being unable to define science, see Dear, "What Is the History of Science the History Of?"; and Harrison, Numbers, and Shank, *Wrestling with Nature*. On the deep fluidity between "science" and "religion" (and "magic") in the early history of modern science, see Webster, *Paracelsus*; and Funkenstein, *Theology and the Scientific Imagination*. In religious studies there is a long-standing critique of the idea of religion, beginning with Wilfred Cantwell Smith's classic *The Meaning and End of Religion* (released in 1963). For more recent commentary, see Stroumsa, *New Science*; and Nongbri, *Before Religion*. On the interface of politics and religious studies, see Hurd, *Beyond Religious Freedom*. In theology, exploring the way in which the modern and Western category of religion is politically constructed, see Lash, *Beginning and End of "Religion"*; and Cavanaugh, *Myth of Religious Violence*.

2. I am aware that the sentence here noted does a lot of work. For one thing, the evaluation of Emperor Constantine's role in the anti-Arian formulation of catholic Christian doctrinal orthodoxy and the emperor's role in the transformation of the Christian faith into the official cult of the Roman Empire is increasingly, in modern times, the subject of strong controversy. See

Christian theology continues to unfold and develop in various ways, but the core remains clear and unchanging. Many times in the history of theology, there comes a point where some brilliant theological innovator is no longer developing but simply abandoning Christian theology, and at that point the innovator has ceased to be doing Christian theology. If one has the Nicene Creed as a canon—a rule—for orthodox Christian truth, then the points of departure are not that hard to find. But science is different.[3]

6.1 "After" Science

There is no *one* science, and there is no *one* true knowledge of nature.

For countless generations the Australian Aborigines have had the most intimate knowledge of the natural environment in which they have lived.[4] This is a real knowledge of nature, and a highly sophisticated knowledge at that. Indeed, the manner in which wisdom and knowledge are intimately integrated in Aboriginal customs makes modern technological society look, in this respect, backward and dangerous by comparison.[5] Traditional Aboriginal natural knowledge systems[6] are enmeshed in sophisticated and ancient metaphysics and theology, in a distinctive range of approaches to technology

---

Drake, *Constantine and the Bishops*; and Leithart, *Defending Constantine*. Undoubtedly, the first three hundred years of the church was a period of enormous development and transition, and there are many today in our anti-authoritarian times who lament the manner in which this settled down doctrinally, firstly with the Apostles' Creed and then with the Nicene Creed. On the other hand, the mainstream view within the catholic Christian tradition—upheld by most of the church's lay believers to this day—sees the Holy Spirit working *through* the astonishing twists and turns of ecclesial history. For a masterly scholarly account of the complex historical process of the formation of the creeds, see Pelikan, *Credo*. However one evaluates it, this distillation of doctrine into short formulations that act as a basis for discriminating between orthodoxy and heresy is characteristic of the central trajectories of historical Christianity, and the Nicene Creed has been the gold standard of Christian orthodoxy for the past 1,700 years. This remains true for the large majority of contemporary practicing Christians, whatever heterodox doctrinal innovations modern academic theologians may come up with.

3. Perhaps this is a problem for Western science. Perhaps because the Western lifeworld still *culturally* assumes an orthodox Christian idea of defined and functionally revealed truth, it tends to treat "science" as a body of true doctrines that can be decisively and for all times defined. Within the sociology of scientific knowledge, both the inescapable pluralism and the "dogmatic" impossibility of scientific truth are well understood. See Feyerabend, *Philosophical Papers*.

4. Note: there is no meaningful way of delineating the natural from the spiritual in an Aboriginal account of nature.

5. Yunkaporta, *Sand Talk*.

6. There were about five hundred Indigenous nations with their own dialects and languages, distinctive cultures, knowledge, and modes of living in the Southern Continent when the British colonized Australia in the late eighteenth century. See "Our People," Australian Government, https://www.australia.gov.au/about-australia/our-country/our-people.

and land management, and in uniquely fitted forms of social organization. The point is, there is more than one way of knowing nature, and every way we have of knowing nature is in fact embedded in human culture and our distinctive practices of living in the natural world.[7] So there is no reason why we should not do science differently. We can change our science.[8]

The idea that "true science" is definable only as modern Western empiricist, rationalist, and physically reductive natural knowledge is unjustifiable. That is, our extrinsic, mechanistic, and pure-matter approach to the knowledge of nature certainly works (in some respects), and it delivers instrumental power like no other system of natural knowledge we know of; but that does not make it the only approach to natural knowledge that we could have. It works because it really does have has some highly credible relation to reality, but that does not mean it is a full-truth system. In fact, its efficient power is bought at the cost of it decisively excluding features of reality from its epistemic framework, and these exclusions are not trivial: value, meaning, purpose, aesthetics, transcendence. By the boundaries of its own territorial terms, it *cannot* provide a complete-truth vision of reality without being hubristically reductive. "Science" presuming to define the entire nature of reality within its reductively physical epistemic categories—science, that is, as an all-encompassing ideology—is usually called "scientism."

Even so, it is not surprising that we largely assume that there is only one true way of doing real science. For, as far as technology goes, as far as mathematico-theoretical sophistication goes, and as far as perception-assisting observation tools go, there is nothing like modern science in the history of human knowledge. Modern science does indeed have a better grasp of physically measurable facts than any previous natural knowledge system, a more extensive international network of knowledge seekers who agree on methodology and criteria than any previous network, a more expensive and powerful set of knowledge tools, and a more open and unified set of intellectual institutions than any previous institutional arrangements could have made possible. And modern science, thanks to its reductive nature, has a far simpler set of operational metaphysical premises that it works with than more metaphysically sophisticated knowledge systems. This simplicity has facilitated

7. Regarding the distinctive historical and sociological embedding of modern Western knowledge, see Kuhn, *Structure of Scientific Revolutions*. Kuhn's text (originally released in 1962) is quite dated now but remains a significant milestone in the sociology of scientific knowledge. However, Polanyi's *Personal Knowledge*, from much the same time (1958), is bearing up very well as a significant contribution to our understanding of what a humanly contextual business modern Western scientific knowledge actually is.

8. See the fascinating book *Another Science Is Possible*, by the Belgian philosopher of science Isabelle Stengers.

the linear development of a very limited range of theory types that makes "science" far more global than the distinct schools of natural knowledge of the West's pre-modern past.[9] Modern science is a crowning achievement of the human intellect and human institutional organization. And yet, while it has wonderful life-enhancing gifts to offer, it is also profoundly dangerous.

In the age of continuous upheaval produced by the great acceleration,[10] surveillance capitalism,[11] global financial alchemy,[12] unprecedented refugee flows,[13] staggering military hardware,[14] and global environmental degradation and climate change,[15] are we still hoping that science will save us? Are we still thinking that scientific innovations and human progress are the same thing? As Jacques Ellul warned some time back, one of the most concerning features of living in our highly instrumental technological society is that we become the tools of our tools.[16] The age of modern science could end very badly.[17]

With great power comes great responsibility. Commercially lucrative applied science might be the means of the demise of our species.[18] Military technology might be the means of the demise of our species. And theologically, science has become a functional idolatry; it is the knowledge and power of our own making in which we place our first trust for the present and our first hope for the future. Our deep embeddedness in sophisticated communications technologies increasingly comes to shape and define the very purposes of our daily lives and the very pathways of our thinking and relating.[19] We are re-creating humanity in the image of our technologies, and we are not uninclined to worship the works of our hands. But, as the psalmist warns,

9. The situation is really more complex than this. It is the medieval university that provided Western Christendom with a unified (Christian Aristotelian) intellectual natural knowledge culture, and this is why we have modern science. See Rubenstein, *Aristotle's Children*. It is true that institutes like the Royal Society were set up outside the universities, but by the eighteenth century the new natural philosophy was firmly within the universities, and the late Victorian professionalization of "the scientist" has meant that the universities have become largely defined by a modern scientific conception of truth since the early twentieth century.

10. McNeill and Engelke, *Great Acceleration*.

11. Zuboff, *Surveillance Capitalism*; P. W. Singer and Brooking, *LikeWar*.

12. Das, *Extreme Money*; Shaxson, *Treasure Islands*; Soros, *Alchemy of Finance*.

13. Maley, *What Is a Refugee?*

14. P. W. Singer, *Wired for War*; P. W. Singer, *Corporate Warriors*; Feinstein, *Shadow World*.

15. Houghton, *Global Warming*; Klein, *On Fire*; Serreze, *Brave New Arctic*.

16. Ellul, *Technological Society*.

17. For a profoundly sobering understanding of the political and military consequences of the failure of world leaders to address climate change, see Cribb, *Food or War*. For a deeply thought-through understanding of the type of outlook and action needed to avert terrifying disaster, see Northcott, *Political Theology of Climate Change*.

18. Hamilton, *Requiem for a Species*.

19. Greenfield, *Mind Change*; Lanier, *Ten Arguments*; Gillespie, *Teen Brain*.

one becomes like the idol one worships—a lifeless object fashioned, used, and ultimately discarded by human hands (Ps. 115:8).

Here are two problems that the Christian theologian notices when thinking about modern science. First, it has been the primary intellectual means of the collapse of Christian theology as the truth foundation of the Western lifeworld. Second, technologically enhanced commercial, political, and military power is now the first cause of the destruction of the earth.[20] Our modern technological way of life is deeply implicated in the extinction of so many of our fellow creatures, and it is the means of unprecedented new forms of violence, surveillance, and oppression within the human race. For these two reasons, the Christian theologian will want to push past a romantic and reified faith in "science" and try to rethink, in the light of Christian theology, some of the basic features of how modern science works and what assumptions it makes. That is, the Christian theologian will want to think "after" science (no longer infatuated with science, no longer subservient to the truth criteria of science as applied to Christian theology) but *not* "after" Christian theology.

6.2 *Not* "After" Christian Theology

When post-1870s naturalistic scientific credibility becomes the acceptable truth criterion for Christian theology, all the defining features of creedal Christian theology, other than the crucifixion, must go. Jesus of Nazareth might still be a remarkable moral teacher of astonishing personal charisma, and to the early believers he clearly was the legendary embodiment of the mythos of the Cosmic Christ, but to us scientific modernists he can no longer be the Christ of the ancient creeds. He cannot have been born of a virgin, for that is just not how babies are born. Jesus cannot have performed miracles and driven out demons, though primitive and superstitious credulity was obviously widespread among his uneducated early followers. Jesus certainly could not have risen from the dead in anything like a literal sense; that is not the way sophisticated modern people interpret the *true* meaning of the resurrection narratives. The fantasy that Jesus ascended into heaven and will return on the last day is clearly a wish-fulfillment delusion. All these strange ideas about resurrection and heaven seem tangled up in a Greco-Roman, Platonist heaven and in pagan mythology, no doubt superimposed on the original Aramaic-speaking rabbi by his hysterically deluded followers who were psychologically unable to come to terms with the crucifixion of their Messiah.

20. Note this eschatological warning: "We give thanks to thee, Lord God Almighty, . . . for destroying the destroyers of the earth" (Rev. 11:17–18 RSV).

Starting from a sophisticated modern understanding of the higher meaning of Christian faith—with theologians such as Schleiermacher, Strauss, Harnack, Schillebeeckx, and Spong—we would see that there is obviously a delusional credulity in any belief commitment to the factual truth of creedal orthodoxy. From here, theologians and biblical scholars readily advance the idea that intelligent apostolic Christians—Saint Paul in particular—must have been Hellenist perverters of the true teachings of Jesus. And then, all that Greek metaphysical mumbo jumbo about the eternal Word in the prologue of John's Gospel, any allusion to some immaterial "place" called heaven, and any degrading suspicion of "the flesh" is clearly a Platonic perversion of the concrete and wholesome Hebraic original. Modern progressive biblical theology rather likes to think that original Christianity is a very flesh-affirming, materially grounded, non-transcendence-framed outlook on the world. Interestingly, this supposedly authentic and original "Jesus of history" seems to entirely affirm the post-nineteenth-century scientistic worldview of our sophisticated modern debunkers of crude creedal orthodoxy. What a remarkable coincidence!

To take up the post-1870s scientific credibility lens and view Christian theology through that lens is to seek to be a Christian "after" creedal Christian theology. But this is a denial of the faith as handed down to us through the historical church. As this sort of apostasy was alive and well among theologians long before the 1870s, it is not surprising that this has remained a firm feature of twentieth- and twenty-first-century academic theology and biblical scholarship. But whatever this new theology is, it is not Christian as measured by the ancient rule of the Nicene Creed. This is theology and biblical scholarship done "after" *Christian* theology, and its Christology is defined by a modern, functionally materialist anthropology. This sort of theology often has a very vague *theos* component that is entirely defined by culture-generated poetic mythos, if it has one at all.

As we have rehearsed, there is a clear line from the new historiography of the late eighteenth century,[21] to the early nineteenth-century German higher criticism, to the increasing prevalence of the denial of the very possibility of the factual truth of creedal Christian doctrine. We can see this line from Ferdinand Baur's Hegelian synthesis of Jewish (Petrine) and Hellenistic (Pauline) Christian constructions, to Adolf von Harnack's jettisoning of Platonic transcendent perversions of an authentic and earthy Hebrew Christianity, to

---

21. Herbert Butterfield writes with considerable insight about the connections between biblical and classical scholarship in the eighteenth century, particularly at the University of Göttingen, and the rise of distinctly modern historiography. See Butterfield, *Origins of History*, 185–97.

Žižek's happily atheistic and materialistic appropriation of certain features of Christianity in the present day.

Those wishing to retain creedal Christian theology after the 1870s have generally taken one of two pathways in response to the remarkable reversal of the late nineteenth century. Either they have withdrawn from public truth into the safe and discrete territory of "religion," or they have entered the public truth domain on "science's" terms while seeking to uphold their private orthodoxy as outside the purview of science. Both of these responses have sounded the death knell for a living and public Christian theology within Western knowledge and culture.

Christianity is not a religion of private salvation; it makes public truth claims about the historically situated revelation of God in the past and about the ongoing reality and activity of the Holy Spirit as expressed in the church today. Christian theology is incompatible with the truth criteria of modern empiricism and rationalism premised on non-miraculous, non-metaphysical physical reductionism. If one enters the science domain as a Christian on secular, reductively naturalistic science's terms, one must leave the substantive truth content of one's Christian faith at the door. Thus have Christians been encouraged to take up their faith "after" Christian theology in the public square or else to withdraw from the public square and reconstruct their faith as discretely religious, as a personal and subjective piety concerned only with private belief and the discretely supernatural.

Let us try something different. Let us try to rethink the parameters of *science* in such a way that science can be both truth revealing and compatible with Christian theology. Let us try to reason afresh from Christian theology as our first truth discourse. Such an enterprise entails the now-radical Thomistic idea that if, after careful consideration, it seems that Christian theology is incompatible with our prevailing natural philosophy's way of approaching and understanding public truth, then there is something wrong with our natural philosophy rather than something wrong with Christian theology.

In this investigation thus far, we have found no compelling reason to believe that a post-Victorian scientific outlook defined by Humean empiricism, secular rationalism, and reductive materialism should, or even could, be considered expansively truth revealing. Post-Victorian, secular EEF (egocentric epistemological foundationalist) outlooks on knowledge give us a highly stylized and abstracted vision of truth precisely because they exclude theology and metaphysics from the domain of nature. Such a knowledge of nature does give us extrinsic, instrumental power over nature, so it must have *some sort* of truth relationship to physical reality. But this science, as Western modernity's first truth discourse, is self-defeating—for when the *real* truth about reality

is that material objects and forces acting on material objects alone qualify
as real, that materialist vision of reality itself becomes an ephemeral epiphe-
nomenon of mere matter. Such a physically reductive outlook presupposes a
bizarre faith in a non-intellective, non-meaningful, non-transcendently situated cosmology, which makes a mockery of both the understanding mind and
the genuinely intelligible cosmos.

There is, then, no compelling reason why modern Christians should evaluate the truth of orthodox Christology by the standards of post-1870s science.
The "science and religion" project—where the public first truth discourse of
science sits as judge of the credibility and veracity of religion—should be
abandoned by Christians.

In this book we are attempting to revive a religion-to-science interpretive
outlook on natural knowledge. We are looking for a theology of science in
which Christian truth is not disciplined away from its primary interpretive
commitments by reductive naturalism. To do this, we have to recover an often-
overlooked feature of traditional Christian theology: theological epistemology.

Rediscovering Christian Theological Epistemology

Epistemology is the branch of modern philosophy concerned with the nature and meaning of knowledge. Modern knowledge theories are not theologically neutral. There is a basic difference between modern philosophical epistemology and traditional Christian Realist approaches to knowledge. For modern secular philosophy, the source of knowledge is the human mind and perceived material reality only; but for a Realist Christian theology, the source of knowledge is God first, and then the human mind and the perceived natural world. This is the difference between modern anthropocentric epistemology and Christian theocentric epistemology.

I do not think it is possible to overemphasize what a profound impact the above difference has on our approach to scientific knowledge and our understanding of the nature of reality. If you approach knowledge itself from a reductively anthropocentric and functionally materialist modernist stance, you are going to come to an entirely different outlook on the nature and meaning of scientific knowledge and natural reality than if you approach knowledge itself from an overtly theological and metaphysical stance.[1] It is a blindness to this starting-place issue that bedevils contemporary Christian "science and

1. I am not here conceding that you can approach knowledge without metaphysical and theological commitments, as the commitment to not have any metaphysical and theological commitments is itself a metaphysical and theological commitment. That is, I am very happy to accept materialism and atheism as entirely respectable metaphysical and theological commitments,

religion" discourse. Conceding the anthropocentric and materialist starting
point of secular scientific knowledge, we think we are entering into a reasonable and fair contract with supposedly objective and neutral scientific facts
and theories. We suppose that signing up to this contract enables us to be
taken seriously in the contemporary knowledge environment. And yet, in
such an arrangement we are selling our metaphysical birthright in order to
get our spoon into an epistemological mess of potage. We will get nowhere in
trying to restart a meaningful "science and religion" discourse that takes the
starting premises of a Christian theology of knowledge seriously if we don't
closely examine our approach to knowledge itself. We need to ask, then, what
a genuinely Christian theological epistemology looks like.

Strictly speaking, it is anachronistic to use the phrase *Christian theological
epistemology*. Christian understandings of knowledge well predate the recent
emergence of modern epistemology and are often metaphysically incompatible with what modern epistemology thinks of as knowledge. So, in this book,
the phrase **Christian theological epistemology** is shorthand for "Christian
philosophical theologies concerning the matrix of divine grace, human sin,
an intelligible and ordered world, sensory perception, mental illumination,
meaning, and scientific and other truth." Revelation (both general and special); the interpretive impact of sin; and the intellectively, morally, and spiritually transformative impact of divine grace are all intimately entailed in what
I am calling Christian theological epistemology. None of these theological,
moral, and metaphysical features are entailed in the rigorously formal and
supposedly non-metaphysical thin gruel of modern academic epistemology,
at least in its dominant analytic and pragmatist Anglo-American trajectories.[2]

A further complication in the term *Christian theological epistemology* is
that there is no single way in which different Christian outlooks understand
knowledge. For example, a fourteenth-century Franciscan approach to how
and what one knows of natural and divine truths is different from knowledge
embedded within a patristic Realist outlook, and both are different from early

but in no manner do I accept that they are simply realistic or merely useful post-metaphysical
and non-theological commitments.

2. For two classic twentieth-century texts reducing the truth value of knowledge to a pragmatic appreciation of functionally materialist science and the logical analysis of symbolic language, see Russell, *Problems of Philosophy*; and Ayer, *Language, Truth and Logic*. For a more
recent expression of the same tradition, see Blackburn, *Truth*. Of course, nothing sits still in
philosophy, and many highly brilliant contemporary thinkers and many shades of approaches
are present in contemporary epistemology. See Steup, Turri, and Sosa, *Contemporary Debates
in Epistemology*. Even so "epistemology" as a specialist branch of contemporary academic
philosophy still largely functions in the shadow of Kant as something that at least aspires to
being *not* metaphysical and *not* theological.

modern Puritan approaches to knowledge. So there is a sense in which *Christian theological epistemology* is a generic term covering an expansive range of options. But there is considerable unity in the basic categories of the discourse itself. The long Western traditions of Christian philosophical theology are often concerned with how we know and understand natural light and divine light (these categories will be unpacked below) and with the different ways in which sin and grace impact both knowledge and understanding (the difference between knowledge and understanding will also be unpacked below).

Significantly, over the past two hundred years the epistemic and higher-meaning categories of Christian thinking have gone out of vogue in the academic mainstream of Western modernity. From the perspective of Christian faith, this development has had a catastrophic effect on both academic theology and modern philosophy.[3] Theological epistemology really matters as regards both a Christian understanding of reality and the ability to maintain an intellectually credible commitment to the truth claims of creedal orthodoxy in the public square within Western intellectual culture. Further, not consciously thinking about knowledge in Christian theological categories has far-ranging sociological implications for modern Christians. Sociologically, conformity to the taken-for-granted knowledge categories of the lifeworld one is intellectually and practically formed by is more or less automatic. Unless the Christian makes concerted and discerning effort to "be not configured to this age"[4] (Rom. 12:2), epistemic configuration by the lifeworld one inhabits is basically guaranteed.

Why Christian theological epistemology went out of vogue in Western modernity is a very long story. Our earlier look at nominalism, voluntarism, and the rise of pure matter has a lot to do with the backstory to this decline in the eighteenth and nineteenth centuries. Suffice it to say that serious problems for our understanding of the truth-carrying capacity of sensory and rational knowledge and the truth-carrying capacity of divinely aided understanding have arisen in Western modernity since Christian theological epistemology declined. I also think that a broadly Realist[5] trajectory within pre-modern Christian theological epistemology remains viable today, and that at least

3. Of course, this evaluation depends on how you see things. This same discarding of the long heritage of Christian traditional understandings of knowledge is a major epistemic advance—nothing short of Enlightenment itself—if those old Christian epistemic categories can be effectively shown to be misguided and wrong. Notoriously, Immanuel Kant claimed to be saving faith by entirely separating faith from knowledge.

4. Hart, *New Testament*, 311.

5. The classical and medieval meaning of *Realist*, as used here, is quite neatly the opposite of the modern meaning of *realist*. To the pre-modern Realist, it is the invisible, eternal, essential, divine, and spiritual truths that carry the proper meaning of ultimate reality. To the

Christians would do well to both rediscover and reimagine this astonishing intellectual resource. This is not as nostalgic an enterprise as its critics might wish to maintain, for we are not as removed from traditional theological outlooks as modernists would like us to assume. Indeed, the final collapse of a Christian theology in underpinning Western intellectual culture did not occur until the late nineteenth century.[6]

Until quite recently, natural light and divine light—as truth-enabling intellectual illumination categories—were not seen as being discretely separated into "religious" and "natural" boxes. Divine illumination, even in early and high modernity, was often *naturally* accessed via Scripture reading and devotional practices, and natural light was often seen as a form of *divine* revelation. But after the territories of science and religion were delineated in the late nineteenth century, Christian theological epistemology became something of a lost art in modern Western circles. This is because, when theology became a discretely religious affair, theology was confined to the systematic exposition of strictly doctrinal and supernatural matters (not philosophical matters) and to biblical studies. By this process Christian academic thinking became increasingly reduced to naturalistic exegetical and hermeneutic forms of textual criticism, which, presupposing scientific neutrality, purported to have no philosophical or even theological commitments. So the very idea of theological epistemology seems rather strange to those of us formed by modern and Western academic culture after the nineteenth century. But it was not always thus, and actually, theological epistemology has never really gone away.

The relation of God to both human natural knowledge and the human reception of special revelation is a very important feature of the Western intellectual tradition. The Western understanding of the human experience of common graces, in which we all experience natural and divine goodness, as well as sin, which is the now "natural" human tendency to fall short of truth and goodness, is integral to the West's long Christian traditions of theological epistemology. Hence, notions of the originary and remaining goodness of creation, and of the deformed and non-essential nature (which is now, alas, "natural") of human sin and travailing creation, are basic to creedally orthodox Christian approaches to knowledge.

---

modern realist, it is visible, temporal, existential, natural, and material truths that carry the only meaning of reality.

6. And such a collapse has not occurred in some of the greatest Christian thinkers of the past two centuries, such as (at random) Søren Kierkegaard, John Henry Newman, C. S. Lewis, G. K. Chesterton, Henri de Lubac, Hans Urs von Balthasar, Hans Boersma, John Milbank, and William Desmond.

We will have to come back to this matter, but it is clear that the Edenic myth cannot be meaningfully extracted from traditional and creedally orthodox Christian understandings of knowledge, as the category of the **fall** is not only of basic soteriological significance but also of basic epistemic significance to Christian theology. This, since the early twentieth century, has been a serious point of tension in the "science and religion" context. But this tension did not start in 1859 with the publication of Darwin's *Origin of Species*. The eighteenth century's historicization of biblical studies and its de-biblicizing trajectories in deistic rationalism are what started this pulling away of natural knowledge from the West's creedally orthodox theological framework and its deep embedding in divinely revealed (hence true) myth. But at the start of the modern era—and for many of the pioneering figures of the new natural philosophy—what we now call science was deeply grounded in a range of theological epistemology stances derived directly from the Western doctrine of the fall. The Edenic myth and Christian theological epistemic categories are, as a matter of historical fact, profoundly important to the rise of modern science.

7.1 The Fall, the Foundations of Science, and Two Theological Anthropology Trajectories

In *The Fall of Man and the Foundations of Science*, Peter Harrison unpacks how two theological anthropology trajectories—broadly Augustinian and broadly Thomistic—are intimately connected to the generation of seventeenth-century empiricist and rationalist approaches to knowledge. Christian theology is the ground out of which the tree of knowledge itself grows at the dawn of the modern scientific age. That is, broadly skeptical and empiricist early modern approaches to knowledge are deeply embedded in the **Augustinian epistemic anthropology** trajectory, which takes the fall of Adam as profoundly affecting the human capacity to know truth. On the other hand, the more rationalist and positivist approaches to knowledge draw on the **Thomistic epistemic anthropology** trajectory, which sees natural knowledge as, in many regards, continuous with a faith-enabled appreciation of divine revelation.[7] These two trajectories combine in interesting ways in

7. Again, by pointing out differences in emphasis, I am not intending to imply a polarity here. It is only really in the eighteenth century that the rational and the empirical become recognizable as potentially opposed intellectual approaches. As regards Aquinas, he is deeply indebted to Augustine, whom he constantly references, and to the Christian Platonist apophaticism of Dionysus the Areopagite. In a firmly Socratic tone, Thomas notes, "This is what is ultimate in the human knowledge of God: to know that we do not know God" (*Quaestio Disputata de*

the seventeenth century and solidify into a fully synthesized rational-and-empirical approach to natural knowledge by the late eighteenth century. But these two broad epistemic trajectories have roots that go back further than Christian theology in the main streams of the Western intellectual tradition.

The difference in emphasis between Plato and Aristotle[8] in their approaches to both natural and high knowledge is integral with the Augustinian and Thomistic trajectories that set the modern approach to natural philosophy alight. Plato is less interested in what we would now call science than Aristotle is. Plato's metaphysical interest in the immortal soul somewhat links up with Augustine's skepticism about our fallen capacity to know truth. Equally, Aristotle's profound interest in natural philosophy links up with Aquinas's synthetic melding of natural knowledge and theology into a unified whole. We will come back to these matters below, but what is significant just here is that the final collapse of both **Platonist/Augustinian** and **Aristotelian/Thomistic epistemic anthropologies** (understandings of human knowledge) in the late nineteenth century produces an entirely unprecedented (and unworkable) context for relations between Christian theology and natural philosophy. I will argue that only by recovering aspects of that pre-nineteenth-century Christian epistemic heritage can a viable arrangement be renegotiated between creedal Christian theology and modern science. To start that recovery now, let us look a little more closely at how Platonist and Aristotelian philosophical trajectories about the knowability (or otherwise) of nature get linked into Augustinian and Thomistic theological trajectories concerning the relationships between sin and grace and human knowledge.

7.2 Is Nature Knowable?

Let us start with the philosophical question about the knowable (or otherwise) nature of the apparent world. Plato and Aristotle both affirm that some sort of knowledge about the tangible world is possible. This must be so because

---

Potentia Dei 7.5 ad 14, as quoted in Pieper, *Silence of St. Thomas*, 64.). This failure of epistemic mastery does not apply only to God. Thomas also says, "The essential grounds of things are unknown to us" (*Commentary on Aristotle's "De anima,"* 1.1.15, as quoted in Pieper, *Silence of St. Thomas*, 65). There is, in many regards, one complex and theologically grounded Western tradition of reasoning and experiencing that passes through Plato, Aristotle, Augustine, and Aquinas. This tradition only disintegrates, with the loss of its theological ground, in the nineteenth century.

8. It is important to recognize that polarities drawn between Plato and Aristotle should not be overemphasized. Aristotle is far more a modified Platonist than a stark alternative to Plato. Lloyd P. Gerson (*Aristotle and Other Platonists*) brings this out very clearly in his analysis of the way that late classical Neoplatonism was a happy synthesis of Plato and Aristotle.

the world that is apparent to our sensory experience is in some manner intelligible to our minds. But Plato and Aristotle approach the intelligibility of the perceived world in different ways.

To Plato—drawing on Heraclitus and Parmenides—the apparent world is hard to know because we are embedded in the flux and contingency of the perceived spatiotemporal manifold. To Plato, only that which is always itself—that which never changes from one thing into another thing—actually *is*, and only what *is* can be decisively known, and that the apparent world is intelligible at all must entail that all the changelings of spatiotemporal flux and contingency somehow partially participate in eternal and essential being. Plato posits an invisible realm of intellectual being that leaves traces of eternal, unchanging essences in the transient physical realm of becoming and unbecoming. The tangible world is thus a shadow of real being. Here, the high source of essential intelligibility is partially gifted to tangible nature, but the home of being is beyond the world of becoming and unbecoming and is in no manner dependent on the apparent world for its own being (though the apparent world is dependent on the high realm of being for the limited degree of intelligibility and reality it has). This is where we get our high transcendent metaphysics from in Western philosophy, and our anti-realist approach to science.[9] To Plato, what we now call "science" never amounts to more than opinion (it can never be real knowledge), for it is concerned with apparent nature, which is always undergoing change and cannot, finally, be really real in itself. To Plato, the seeker after truth should be firstly concerned with the transcendent *source* of essential meanings and rational order that is given to apparent nature—the realm accessible only to the contemplations of the spiritually and morally enlightened mind. That is, the realm of **transcendent being** is immaterial; it is eternal; it is intellective; it is the realm of **high ideas** (Beauty, Truth, Goodness) as well as of **low ideas** (mathematics); it is the home of the mind and the source and destiny of one's eternal and immaterial soul.

9. In modern philosophy, an anti-realist approach to science takes human knowledge to be a construction of human culture that is always inherently different from nature itself. In effect nature itself is unknowable, and all we know is our symbolic systems that seek to describe this unknowable thing that we call nature, which, being not a function of thought but a function of matter, is intrinsically unlike human thought and language. Here, we only "know" our own thinking and speaking about nature when we do science; human knowledge and material reality never really connect up in any directly caused manner. The difference between Platonism and modern anti-realism is that the modern anti-realist somehow assumes that the ultimately unknowable and yet perceived material world is real; the Platonist assumes that the world accessible to the mind is real. To the modern anti-realist, all we know is unreal knowledge, because our knowledge is mental and reality is material. To the Platonist, mental knowledge is the only knowledge that can be of reality, because reality is inherently intellective and only derivatively material.

God, as the Goodness Beyond Being, is the luminous source of mental reality (Ideas) and the focus of the highest devotion of the wise and good soul.[10] The realm of Mind is thus above the realm of bodies. Nature (*physis*, from which we get the word *physics*) is the material world of semi-real appearances (material bodies) that change, that come in and out of being, where embodied lives are always profoundly contingent on conditions that they have no final control over. Physical bodies, for the duration of their fleeting existence, are always changing and are never really stably themselves. Here physics is not the realm of the real; rather, metaphysics,[11] the immaterial and eternal realm beyond physics and upon which physics depends, is the realm of the real.

Aristotle modifies this outlook. To him, the material realm of temporal change is only comprehensible because essence (intellective form) is always materialized in reality. To Aristotle—apart from a totally self-absorbed, purely mental Deity—matter is always informed with ideas, and there is no realm of immaterial Ideas separated from material nature. Aristotle integrates the Platonic heaven of essential ideas very firmly into the particular and material reality of concrete beings. Nature is thus decisively knowable for Aristotle in a way that it is not for Plato. Sensory knowledge is most definitely of primary epistemic clarity to Aristotle, and those divine metaphysical truths that stand prior to and above our normal rational-sensory understanding are less clearly knowable, even though the attempt to understand the eternal first things remains exalted above all other types of contemplation.[12] The physical world is now very real, even though the divine metaphysical first principles of reality remain superlatively philosophically desirable, even as they escape all but the most tentative comprehension by our mortal minds. Thus a positivist confidence in the truth of observable nature and what we would now call naturalistic realism are very much the heritage of an Aristotelian epistemic attitude toward the human knowledge of nature.[13]

10. Plato, *Republic* 509b8–10.

11. "Metaphysics" is not a term that either Plato or Aristotle used. It is a viable term, however, for speaking of certainly Plato's understanding of the transcendent source of being itself as beyond (*meta*) physics.

12. In his introduction to the *Metaphysics*, Aristotle notes that "these things, the most universal, are on the whole the hardest for men to know; for they are furthest from the senses" (*Metaphysics* 1, 982a24–25), yet "the most divine science [first philosophy] is also the most honourable" (*Metaphysics* 1, 983a5). "All sciences, indeed, are more necessary than this, but none is better" (*Metaphysics* 1, 983a10–11).

13. A complex matrix is worth signaling here. Plato is skeptical when it comes to science and a rationalist when it comes to ideas; Augustine is skeptical about ideas as a part of natural knowledge. Aristotle is a positivist when it comes to sensory knowledge but skeptical about religion; Aquinas sees revelation and the traditions of the church as fully compatible with natural positivism and rational certainty. So while it is helpful to think of Plato, Augustine, and

The dominant Platonist and Neoplatonist[14] streams of ancient philosophy took physical reality to be between partially and highly knowable. In both cases "essence"—the intelligible characteristics of perceived things—is what our perceiving minds know, to varying degrees, via the embodied operations of sense perception and the mental operations of rational understanding. Here, it was taken as given that divine Reason in some manner governed the tangible cosmos such that it was an ordered unity and also knowable to our minds. Particularly in Aristotle, the ability of our perceptive apparatus to generate form-mapping phantasms in the mind, which then convey the essence of any perceived body to the reasoning mind of the knower, made a true knowledge of nature possible. That is, to Aristotle matter and form are always found together in the real and concrete world, but we only ever take the abstracted essential form of perceived bodies into our minds when we understand the sensory stimulus that makes us aware of any real body in the world.

Very briefly, patristic and medieval Christian theology tended to take and reject various aspects of both of these streams. With Aristotle, embodied reality is taken as firmly real and as inherently good. Creation is the work of God, and the incarnation elevates human flesh to unimaginable heights. On the other hand, the intimate dependence of temporal reality on an eternal and genuinely transcendent God—who is the source of all order, goodness, and essential meaning in the cosmos—has more in common with Plato than with Aristotle. In the early age of Christian theology, Plato was by far the easier of the two great Greek sages to integrate into a Christian theological vision of reality. When Aristotle's star rises in the West in the High Middle Ages, this new interest in particular concrete beings is overlaid on a high Platonist Realism, modifying that spiritual conception of reality considerably in the process but never removing features of high transcendence foreign to Aristotle, such as the genuine autonomy of eternal ontological reality from temporal flux and contingency.

In terms of the natural philosophy stances of the Platonist and Aristotelian central trajectories of Western intellectual culture, nature is knowable to some extent. But divine truths are the source of natural reality on both outlooks; physical nature itself is not self-standing. A theological philosophy is integral with both the Platonist and the Aristotelian understandings of reality and of how we know it. But neither stance is, of course, Christian.

---

skepticism toward natural knowledge as one broad trajectory in early modern approaches to knowledge, and Aristotle, positivism, rationalism, and Aquinas as the other broad trajectory, in reality this is more of a complex interactive matrix than a simple polarity of epistemic emphases.

14. Neoplatonism is the late classical synthesis of Aristotelian science, ethics, and logic with Platonist metaphysics.

7.3 Can Fallen Humanity Know Nature?

We turn now more specifically to Christian theology, where the question that arises in late antiquity—notably with Augustine—is whether fallen natural humanity can know the truth about anything.[15] This is no longer a question of whether nature itself is knowable, which exercised Plato and Aristotle, but this is a question of whether sin-stained humanity has the capacity to know truth at all, be it natural or divine. I'm going to introduce Aquinas at this point too, even though he enters the fray some seven centuries after Augustine. The two key concepts in Christian theology concerning the epistemic impact of sin that we shall now look at are **divine light** and **natural light**.

Broadly stated, the late classical Western doctrine of the fall, as derived initially from Saint Paul, and then as formulated by Augustine in the West, with the influence of Gregory of Nyssa's understanding of illumination in the East, led to long Christian traditions of thinking about Adam's pre-fallen knowledge as profoundly superior to what postlapsarian humanity is naturally able to attain. These traditions flourished in late classical and medieval Christian contexts and were alive and well in seventeenth-century Christian Europe. To these traditions, Adam in his state of created perfection had perfect knowledge as a function of his intimate and sinless mental fellowship with God. The divine and uncreated light of God's direct revelation illuminated his mind internally, such that his ordinary perceptual knowledge of created reality not only had our usual external inputs but also was integrated with essential insights as gifted to Adam directly from God himself. The way Adam understood what he perceived operated at an order of true intellective insight never achieved again since the fall—except, of course, by Christ.

In Christ, the second Adam, we see what "normal" human perception should have been like, and what the normal authority of humanity over nature should have looked like. The miracles of Christ, then, express what is natural to the true Son of Man and push back the fallen deformities and rebellious natural tendencies of redemption-awaiting creation. Christ is complete master of his own carnal nature and has authority over sickness, demonic bondage, sin, destructive elemental powers, and death itself. That is, the ordering high principalities under which creation exists are now in a "natural"—yet actually deformed, even unnatural (when viewed from the stance of Edenic primal origins)—state of rebellion, as introduced into creation by the fall.[16]

15. Augustine's pre-Christian tangle with academic skepticism informs his concerns on this point. See Augustine, *Against the Academicians*. See Brown, *Augustine of Hippo*, 69–78.
16. If you are now worried about how the Genesis cosmogenic origin myth and contemporary life sciences can both be understood with suitable respect for the differences in the truth

After the redemptive passion of Christ, it is possible for the minds of the saints to be so transfigured by grace as to receive essential knowledge directly from God. But even ordinary Christians are at an astonishing advantage to the great sages of the past, whom God favored with snippets of divine wisdom. For the Scriptures are inspired by God, and their reading gives every believer access to a form of spiritually transformative divine illumination.[17] Through the redemptive work of Christ, as mediated to the Christian by hearing and believing the Gospels and by participating in the divinely graced sacraments of the church, the Christian is able to "have the mind of Christ" (1 Cor. 2:16). The work of grace thus enables the Christian to know and participate in revealed heavenly realities that the fallen mind, unaided by this special epistemic grace, could no longer naturally grasp or experience. In the age of the Holy Spirit (the church age), Christ's redemptive work is underway such that through Scripture reading, theological contemplation, and mystical experience, the epistemic wound of the fall is starting to be healed. Saint Paul explains that "now I know in part," but when the eschaton comes, "then I shall know fully, even as I am fully known" (1 Cor. 13:12). Not incidentally, the Pauline category of full knowledge is love; this is not some extrinsic epistemic mastery—it is clear from the First Epistle to the Corinthians that the very categories of that sort of knowledge are fallen and unspiritual.

Significantly, there are various shades of understanding within Adamic theological epistemology, and those shades are often tied to whether the Christian approaches epistemological concerns more from the Platonist/Augustinian trajectory or more from the Aristotelian/Thomistic trajectory. In this context, divine and natural light take on different shades of meaning.

Roughly described, Aristotelian/Thomistic approaches to knowledge see divine illumination as a super-added high insight—with natural knowledge remaining truth revealing, though to a limited degree, even after the fall. Importantly, the super-added nature of divine illumination is integral with natural knowledge. Because of the unity of truth, there can be no incommensurability between **natural illumination** and **divine illumination**. Hence there is some continuity between natural and divine illumination, such that the high revelations of Christian doctrine and proper natural philosophy and sound reasoning always complement each other and cannot clash. In Romans

---

categories being drawn on, I would ask you to put that concern to one side for the present. We will return to that question, but for now the theological epistemology embedded in the Edenic myth needs to be clearly understood on its own terms, without it having to first bow down to the altar of the epistemic authority of modern science.

17. The disciplines and imaginative techniques of *lectio divina* (divine reading) were developed by the church to assist in the illumination of the mind through contemplative Scripture reading.

1:20, Saint Paul seems to imply such a continuity between natural revelation and divine truth.

Roughly described, Platonist/Augustinian approaches to knowledge see natural knowledge itself as corrupted by the fall, and thus natural knowledge and even valid reasoning will be servants of a corrupt and sinful intellect, a willfully futile mind, or simply a mind passively in bondage to original sin; and hence there is no obvious passage from natural light to the truths of divine light. Saint Paul warns that carnal people readily become "futile in their thinking," all the while "claiming to be wise" (Rom. 1:21–22 RSV). Thus, fallen appetites "naturally" corrupt the capacity for any pure and spiritual high knowledge, for the natural person, hardened by pride against God's grace, is without spiritual understanding (1 Cor. 2:14).

7.4 Complexity Issues regarding Natural Light and Divine Light

There are varying approaches to how natural and divine illumination integrate and delineate in the West's theological epistemology heritage. Centrally, it is a complexity of shared sources of illumination—both natural and divine—that differentiates that long theological heritage from the "purely" naturalistic trajectories of epistemology and skepticism that characterize modern and secular Western philosophy from the nineteenth century onward. This pre-nineteenth-century complexity—and how creedal orthodoxy requires it—needs to be unpacked a bit.

If Christians are to take the Nicene Creed as the catholic and orthodox[18] benchmark defining the central framework of Christian theology, then Christians are committed to the genuine transcendence of God, the genuine truth of the miraculous work of God in the historical birth, ministry, passion, resurrection, and ascension of Jesus of Nazareth, and the ongoing inbreaking of the Holy Spirit into the present age through the ministries and gospel message of the church. None of this is compatible with modern rational, empirical, or pragmatic epistemic sources as defined by reductively materialist naturalism. Reductively materialist naturalism (let us shorten this to "secular reason") rejects the very possibility of both genuine metaphysical reality and divine light. To the Christian, then, secular reason is not theologically or philosophically neutral but entails a genuine epistemic and metaphysical blindness to that which

---

18. By "catholic" I mean "universal," and by "orthodox" I mean "not heretical." Thus all Roman Catholics, Eastern Orthodox, and Protestant Christians can recognize one another as being broadly catholic and orthodox Christians in that to this day—in, for example, Roman Catholic, Lutheran, Anglican, and Eastern Orthodox liturgies every Sunday—the creed is still recited (plus or minus *filioque*) as a statement of what Christians believe.

is most important. So, for starters, the Christian cannot accept that secular reason is validly truth revealing as regards the central theological beliefs of the church. Christian doctrines entail a commitment to some form of genuinely truth-revealing illumination that is not visible to secular reason. Let us call this other form of understanding divinely illuminated wisdom. Given the Pauline understanding of the transcendent God being the ground of all created being (Acts 17:24–28), as reflected in the "I Am" proclamations of the divine name in the Hebrew Scriptures, as well as in Christ's "I Am" teachings, the Christian is also committed to some form of Platonist/Augustinian conception of immaterial transcendence as ontologically prior to and beyond material reality. God is, as the creed puts it, "the maker of all things visible and invisible" but is not himself made. The real nature of the ground of reality itself cannot be adequately grasped by the mindset of secular reason. If creation is thus dependent on God, then natural reality is not its own ground; its order and meaning is gifted to it from God, and traces of divine grace are evident within nature, detectable by those "who have eyes to see." And yet, because the goodness and reality of God and the truth of the Christian gospel are decisively *not* self-evident to all, a structural epistemic deformity must be seen as "natural" when it comes to our capacity to discern some reflected vision of God through nature. There remain profound, existentially relevant epistemic consequences of the fall as regards our comprehension of the true higher meanings that natural knowledge is seen to imply (or not).[19] Even so, it also seems self-evident that secular reason really *can* genuinely discern extrinsic and instrumentally effective valid knowledge of the physical world. Further, it seems evident that the data of sensory experience and the rational structure of human reason (the materials, if you like, of knowledge) are not the same thing as the interpretation and meaning of knowledge (the buildings, if you like, of theoretical knowledge).

We need a complex-enough model that can distinguish between natural and divine illumination sources and that can appreciate the difference between the empirical and rational dynamics of mental experience and the interpretation of experience, without excluding the higher categories that are metaphysically necessary for human experience to be genuinely meaningful. As it happens, such models have been around for a very long time. Plato is a good place to start, as the Augustinian and Thomistic trajectories of divine and natural light largely build on the basic framework for meaningful human knowledge laid down by Plato.

19. For a classic in nineteenth-century Lutheran theological epistemology, where sin and faith are epistemic categories with the most demanding existential as well as eternal implications, see Kierkegaard, *Concluding Unscientific Postscript*.

7.5 Distinguishing and Integrating Natural Light and Divine Light

In thinking about how natural and divine light are conceptually delineated and operationally integrated in human awareness, Plato's divided line analogy has the conceptual nuance and metaphysical categories that the positivist and reductively naturalistic post-Victorian epistemic framework of secular reason lacks.[20] Consider the diagram in figure 7.1.

Plato talks about four categories of awareness in this analogy. The top two categories concern eternal and essential knowledge regarding things that are visible to the mind (*nous*) but invisible to the physical eye. Plato uses the words *noēsis* and *dianoia* to describe these two intellective categories. The bottom two categories of awareness—*pistis* and *eikasia*—relate to the world as sensibly perceived. These lower categories concern imaginatively grasped temporal and existential opinions regarding those things that are apparent to the senses and practically useful.

Noēsis, then, translates as something like "high intellection," as it is concerned with the essential knowledge of the mind, a knowledge of eternal and qualitative truths. *Dianoia* translates as something like "low intellection"—as, like *noēsis*, it is a knowledge of the mind, but it concerns formal rational truths (logic, mathematics) rather than substantial essential knowledge. Geometry, for example, belongs to *dianoia* for Plato, as the universal truths of geometry are positioned above the merely visible world of sensory opinions but beneath the high intellection of essential, qualitative, and ultimate knowledge.

Moving into the realm of the senses, *pistis*, within the domain of opinion (*doxa*), translates as "faith/belief"; it is a historically contingent awareness of humanly constructed meanings. The opinions of belief are produced in us by our embeddedness in customs, conventions, and common understandings and practices. Plato calls the lowest awareness category within the domain of the tangible world *eikasia* (icon, image), which is the understanding of the images our senses reflect to our minds concerning the tangible world.

These categories can be related to the Christian notions of divine and natural illumination and their complex interactions. According to Plato's analogy, there are two awareness categories of natural belief (α and β) and two awareness categories of higher knowledge (γ and δ). Let us map natural illumination onto natural belief and divine illumination onto higher knowledge. But note: Plato's divided line is a ratio in which the two low categories of sense and intellection (α and γ) are in some manner connected and the two high categories of sense and intellection (β and δ) are in some manner connected. So immediate sensory knowledge (α) is the lowest yet also the most

20. Plato, *Republic* 509d1–511e3.

Figure 7.1

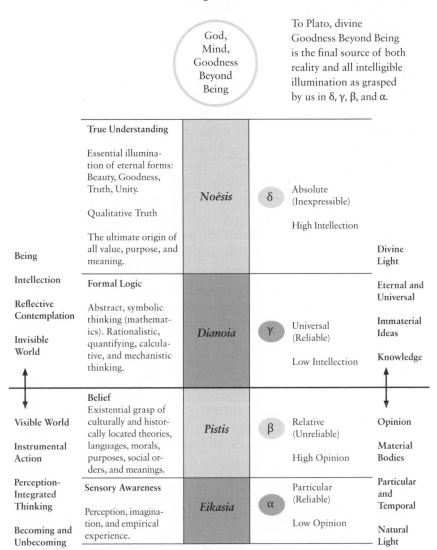

To Plato, divine Goodness Beyond Being is the final source of both reality and all intelligible illumination as grasped by us in δ, γ, β, and α.

immediate and practically reliable form of natural belief, and this has some intimate rational (i.e., "of ratio") relationship to the lowest form of higher knowledge, which is abstract mathematics (γ).

Perhaps both low natural belief (α) and low higher knowledge (γ) could be considered—from a Christian theological epistemology perspective—as largely unaffected by the fall. Which is to say that the basic empirical and rational ingredients of modern science are a combination of low natural illumination with low divine illumination, and these remain epistemically viable after the fall. This would make aspects of empirical and rational knowledge truth carrying within the limited terms of low natural belief and low higher knowledge.

The two low categories as combined (α and γ) we can call empiricocalculative awareness. Most animals and insects display powerful empiricocalculative awareness, combining sensory perception with exquisite calculative mental processing in simply moving around in the physical world. A jumping spider, with its truly tiny brain, performs astonishing calculations as it jumps from one moving blade of grass onto another moving blade of grass. Low intellection (logical and calculative reason) as a form of divine illumination is by no means a human-only category of knowledge.[21]

In passing, we should here note how this understanding of low intellection highlights the fact that pre-modern traditions did not think of divine aid as supernatural. People, animals, and insects using calculative reason appropriate divine illumination in an entirely natural manner. Nature is embedded in and upheld by divine reality here such that natural processes will always display some reflected divine glory that transcends any reductively physical view of the world. Thinking of the natural as entirely discrete from the supernatural is a very late-medieval and modern idea. It is also a theologically untenable idea for traditional Christian understandings of the ontological dependence of all created beings on the Creator. But we digress; let us return to Plato's divide line.

Plato also notices that there is a higher form of tangible and natural understanding (β) concerned with qualitative and purposive judgments regarding lived temporal life. This is rationally (of ratio) linked to the higher category in higher knowledge (δ). This high section of higher knowledge (δ) is an illumination granting some true appreciation of the transcendent source of moral and aesthetic qualities, essential meanings, and final purposes in eternal and spiritual reality. This divine illumination is distinct from the natural illumination of tangibly acquired belief, even though the source of all understanding in the mind (all four illumination categories) is the radiant Goodness of the divine Ground of Being. Beyond higher knowledge (though such high realms are too splendid for any mortal mind), the good and wise soul may even glimpse inexpressible intimations of the first object of the soul's devotion:

21. Plato seeks to demonstrate that Meno's uneducated slave has an innate and immediate (i.e., divinely gifted) understanding of mathematical truths. To Plato, mathematical knowledge is not actually learned; it is (hopefully) merely uncovered or recalled by the helpful promptings of formal education.

God. High natural understanding combined with high spiritual knowledge (β and δ) we could call qualitative awareness, linking the existential in some manner with the essential.

As we think about natural and divine illumination, Plato's belief category (β) is an inherently mixed bag. Qualitative awareness as expressed in cultural mediations is always relative and contextual, on the one hand, but also (hopefully) inspirationally related to the divine illumination of true wisdom, on the other hand. To take an example from the ancient world, Herodotus claimed that while it is the case that some societies cremate the bodies of their parents and would never dream of eating their dead bodies, other societies would never dream of cremating the bodies of their parents but show filial respect by eating their parents' dead bodies.[22] Thinking like Plato, we see that the cultural expression of respect is astonishingly relative, yet the transcendent wisdom that both contexts seek to express is deep and appropriate filial respect toward one's deceased parents. Here relative and contingent existential beliefs define social customs and moral norms, and yet customs and norms also (and must) reach beyond the existential horizon of specific and temporal conditions, toward transcendent and eternal truths. So qualitative belief (β) is an inherently composite illumination category, combining natural illumination with poetically expressed analogical traces of the ultimately inexpressible truths of divine illumination.

Plato's four illumination categories can also be paired with reference to the primary division in this analogy between the visible and the intellective. The two tangible belief categories (α and β) are concerned with existence, and the two intellective knowledge categories (γ and δ) are concerned with essence. The awareness categories of the visible domain concern our physical bodies as embedded in material, temporal, and particular existence. The awareness categories of the intelligible domain concern eternal and universal realities of importance to our immortal souls. But just as there are five senses and only one sensorium, these four awareness categories should function together such that illumination itself is a rich unity even though there are four types of illumination.

Let us now try and map these natural and divine illumination categories onto familiar aspects of modern ways of thinking about knowledge and understanding. A key difference between the two low categories of each domain (α and γ) and the two high categories of each domain (β and δ) is the difference between the perceptive (α) and rational (γ) reception of epistemic givens and the theoretical (β) and inspirational (δ) interpretation of the data and structure

22. Herodotus, *Histories* 3.38.

of ratio-calculative awareness. In modern categories, we can describe this as the difference between knowledge (α and γ) and understanding (β and δ).[23]

Let us now translate Plato's categories into a modern, English-language idiom, while also mapping them onto distinctively parsed knowledge and understanding registers. Consider the reframing of Plato's divided line analogy in figure 7.2.

Translating Plato's four awareness categories into more contemporary terms, I propose these English labels: **wisdom** for *noēsis*, **mathematics** for *dianoia*, **belief** for *pistis*, and **perception** for *eikasia*. I am aware that translating *pistis* as belief concerning cultural understandings and *eikasia* as sensory perception may not facilitate a clear understanding of what Plato means. The difficulty here is in how *we* understand belief and perception.

In translating *pistis* as "belief" (faith and belief have the same linguistic stem in Greek) and in tying belief to the cultural and common-sense world of our existential lives, I am seeking to convey Plato's understanding that all our conventions, and our sociological lifeworlds themselves, are defined by penultimate and never finally true "truth" categories. This does not mean that Plato is uninterested in conventional morality or the attempt to construct good social order. Far from it! But unlike us, Plato sees the cultural realm of belief as having subtle links to the intellectual and moral realm of wisdom. This upholding of belief as a constructivist and contingent cultural realm that yet does *not* entail constructivism toward moral and metaphysical truth itself is where Plato's understanding of belief and our modern understanding of belief tend to part ways. This is because we have set up a polarity in which mathematical and empirical criteria define true knowledge and any supposed truth categories outside ratio-empirical knowledge cannot be true. To us, ratio-empirical demonstration criteria define truth. But to Plato, such criteria cannot ultimately be true; they are always in the domain of opinion. We will look further at this below, but for now, let us think of *belief* as the domain of cultural understandings (which, to Plato, includes what we would now call scientific theories). I think this is a valid translation of the category of *pistis* as used in Plato's divided line analogy.

In translating *eikasia* as "perception" I am seeking to convey something very foreign to how we now typically naively approach empirical knowledge.

23. This is not Plato's way of speaking. To Plato, only what is intellective constitutes knowledge, and everything in the realm of sense and cultural construction—including what we would now call scientific theory—is opinion. To posit *eikasia* as describing "knowledge" and to posit *pistis* as describing "understanding" would not please the ancient sage. My sincere apology to Plato, but I am here attempting a useful reframing of his categories for the purpose of incorporating the complex notions of divine and natural light into our modern ways of talking about empirical and rational "knowledge."

Figure 7.2

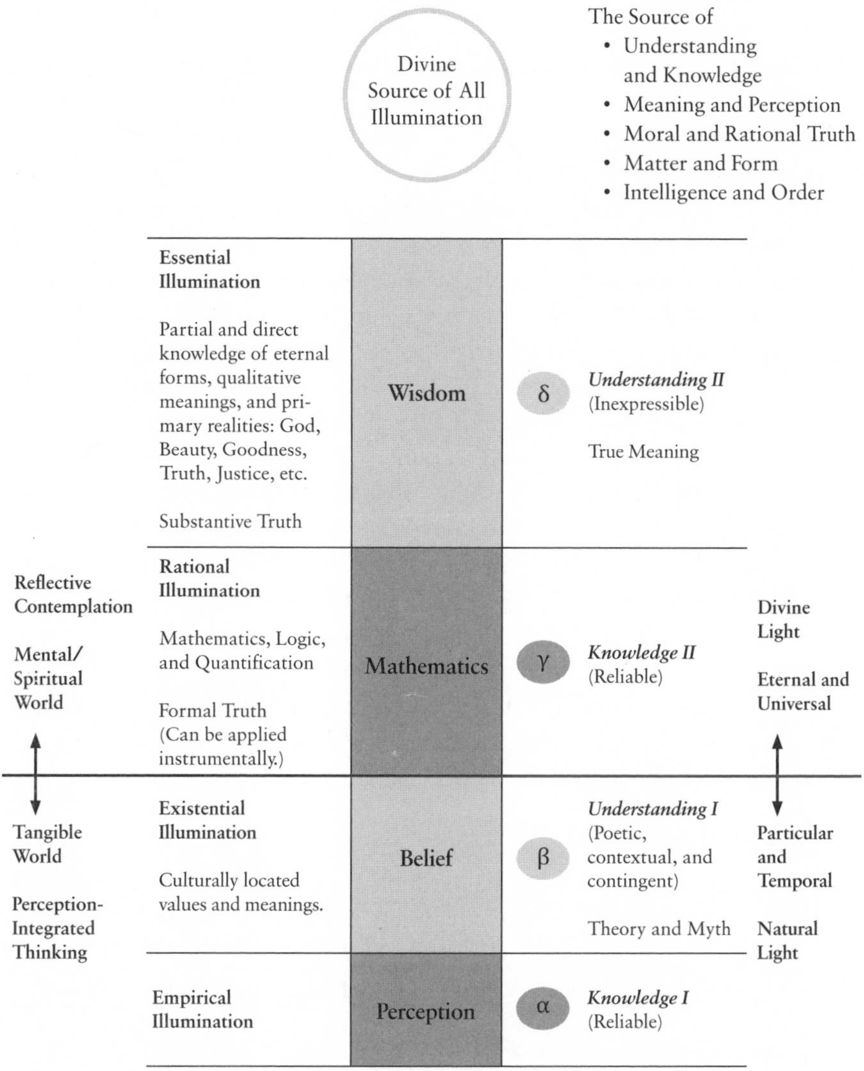

Divine
Source of All
Illumination

The Source of
- Understanding and Knowledge
- Meaning and Perception
- Moral and Rational Truth
- Matter and Form
- Intelligence and Order

	Essential Illumination Partial and direct knowledge of eternal forms, qualitative meanings, and primary realities: God, Beauty, Goodness, Truth, Justice, etc. Substantive Truth	**Wisdom**	δ	*Understanding II* (Inexpressible) True Meaning
Reflective Contemplation **Mental/ Spiritual World**	**Rational Illumination** Mathematics, Logic, and Quantification Formal Truth (Can be applied instrumentally.)	**Mathematics**	γ	*Knowledge II* (Reliable)	**Divine Light** Eternal and Universal
Tangible World **Perception-Integrated Thinking**	**Existential Illumination** Culturally located values and meanings.	**Belief**	β	*Understanding I* (Poetic, contextual, and contingent) Theory and Myth	**Particular and Temporal** **Natural Light**
	Empirical Illumination	**Perception**	α	*Knowledge I* (Reliable)	

To Plato, what we now call empirical knowledge is obviously practically useful, and by being careful in our observations we can be confident of the functional validity of sensory understanding, but this never amounts to knowledge. We have a high-truth view of sensory perception and a low-truth view of wisdom (which we tend to treat as belief). To Plato, it is the other way around, for he really does think that the world we perceive with our senses is a world of shadows, known through fragile sensory images, and that our imagination is always involved in whatever meaning constructions we build using our sensory experience.

The word *fact* has its roots in the Latin word *factum*, meaning "deed," from *facere*, meaning "to do, to make." As applied to a knowledge of the natural world, *factum* entails that we *make* or *enact* factual knowledge when the mind interacts with the sensorium of perception. To Aristotle, the mind views the phantasms produced in the imagination by the senses and must interpret the meaning of sensory appearance with reason. It is the mind that brings rational illumination to the senses; sensory data is not simply given to us as objective truth. For this reason, the interpretation of the sensorium can be done well or poorly. While Aristotle is one of the true greats of Western natural philosophy,[24] pioneering the entire discipline of biology, he does not think of facts in a modern way, as if the senses themselves provide us with an objective and self-evidently valid account of what we call factual truth. Even more so than Aristotle, Plato assumes what we might call a pre-modern view of facts—as imaginative human knowledge constructions that can be *done* well or poorly—which facilitate a partial understanding of the mysterious realm of tangible experience. So I think it is fair to identify Plato's category of *eikasia*—the understanding category apposite to interpreting the meaning of reflected images—with what we mean by perception.

So much for a working translation of Plato's Greek terms into a quite heavily qualified modern English idiom. But let us now think about perception and math as reliable knowledge categories, and belief and wisdom as categories of understanding.

We now almost reflexively think of science as concerned with a demonstrable factual knowledge of the natural world, and wisdom as situated in the cultural domain of entirely constructed values and beliefs.[25] Practically, this is because you can get demonstrable proof criteria that succeed or fail when it comes to empirical facts and rational coherence, but such proof cri-

24. See Rubenstein, *Aristotle's Children*.
25. Thinkers such as Alasdair MacIntyre (*After Virtue*), Charles Taylor (*Ethics of Authenticity*), and Jacques Derrida (*Of Grammatology*) deeply grasp the manner—for reductively naturalistic modern and postmodern philosophy—in which all value and meaning concepts have become relativized, constructed, and cut off from any transcendent ontological framework that could give them any truth and any knowable relation to reality. Wisdom must be a "cultural" construction that has no relation to a purely material understanding of reality. Theological epistemology is not possible in this context, but that does not mean that theological epistemology itself is impossible, only that the *context* of assumed reductive materialism makes true qualitative meaning (including any true meaning for materialism) impossible. Thus does the absence of high intellective knowledge categories destroy truth itself.

teria seem unavailable when it comes to belief, meaning, and interpretation. Because empirical and rational knowledge is at least functionally reliable and amenable to linear improvement, we tend to think of this as objective and solid knowledge in contrast to the fuzzy and endlessly contestable arenas of belief and interpretation.

Let us think this through a bit further. I am suggesting that we can think of two highly significant knowledge sources relevant to modern science—the empirical and the rational—as somewhat bare knowledge categories, without presupposing the modern meaning-making theories derived from those two knowledge categories that we now call empiricism and rationalism. That is, empiricism and rationalism actually belong to the domain of understanding (interpretation, meaning, and belief) rather than to the domain of knowledge. I am here dividing knowledge from understanding in conceptual categories, but this does not mean knowledge and understanding are actually separable in practice. Plato's four awareness categories all function together to produce a single awareness manifold—provided the lower, visible world does not occlude the higher, intellective world because of a false evaluation of the relationship between existence and essence.[26]

Significantly, in this model we locate interpretive theory, as regards the visible natural world, in the understanding category of belief rather than in either of the two knowledge categories (perception and mathematics). Belief, or *Understanding I*, is the domain of scientific theory; and whatever objectivist, scientistic ideologues may want to tell you, it is an inextricably cultural, meaning-laden, communal, linguistically framed, and imaginative domain of human belief.[27]

To help conceive a better relationship between Christian theological epistemology and modern science, I am using *Knowledge I* and *Knowledge II* and *Understanding I* and *Understanding II* in the following way. **Knowledge I** is a common-grace, natural-light awareness category, which happily links up

26. That is, to Plato, eternal essence is the proper domain of the real, and temporal existence is a derivate function of reality and not real in its own right. The reality priority of the intellective over the visible is upheld by Plato, even though he is very aware that the material, sensible world is more immediately present to our tangible experience and temporal existence than is the high world that only inspired thought can "see." It is possible that very tangibly focused and temporally defined people may never really grasp any genuine intellective truths, and thus their awareness manifold would be deprived of all high meaning categories and they would understand their own awareness only in the categories of sensory perception and culturally constructed beliefs. In his famous cave analogy, Plato describes such non-philosophers as the slaves of illusions and as easily manipulated by the unscrupulous. Such slavery entails a profound stunting of the human soul as far as Plato is concerned.

27. Michael Polanyi, as a brilliant theoretical chemist, understood this with profound insight. See Polanyi, *Personal Knowledge* and *The Tacit Dimension*.

with **Knowledge II**, which is a common-grace, divine-light category. In Kuyperian theology, everyone—be they Christian, atheist, Muslim, New Ager, or whatever—has the same access to **common graces**.[28] But, as mentioned, what we now call science also requires something that only high natural light (**Understanding I**) can give: interpretive **theory**. For all natural philosophies contain some overarching vision of the nature of nature itself. So it takes at least three awareness categories to produce modern science: two natural light categories and one divine light category. Yet the fourth awareness category cannot be absent either. We must hope that the incommunicable inspirations of **Understanding II** in some manner move our scientific theorists as they build our ever-evolving and poetic meaning constructions (scientific theories) within the communicable and culturally situated categories of **Understanding I**.

To clarify, the absence of linguistically framed and culturally situated theory (*theoria*, "vision") is why a jumping spider does not have science, even though it has natural-light perception and divine-light mathematics. Equally, the rich and complex presence of theory (**Understanding I**) is why, say, Australian Aboriginal natural understandings are genuine science, even though the profoundly spiritual theoretical presuppositions about the nature of nature in such understandings are strikingly incompatible with modern Western theoretical commitments.[29] There is a deep, intimate, and theoretically sophisticated integration of *scientia* and *sapientia*[30] characteristic of traditional Aboriginal knowledge systems as regards the physico-spiritual ways of the land, its creatures, its peoples, and its meanings.

So while—in our model—the two awareness categories of knowledge (perception and mathematics) look to be pretty reliably functional in fallen humanity, from a Christian epistemological theology perspective, understanding—from

28. Abraham Kuyper was a Reformed theologian and also the prime minister of the Netherlands at the turn of the twentieth century. His theology of common grace was controversial in some Calvinist circles in which a five-point Calvinist understanding of total depravity thought of divine grace as being given only to the elect. Without wishing to get embroiled in Calvinist theology, I think it reasonable to hold that a theology of common grace is a solidly biblical and catholic (universal) Christian stance. Jesus explains in Matthew 5:45 (RSV) that our Father in heaven "makes his sun rise on the evil and on the good, and sends rain on the just and on the unjust." See Kuyper, *Common Grace*.

29. For this reason there is no one thing called "science"; there are many sciences, and modern Western scientific theory is always undergoing change that is defined as much by culturally situated meanings as it is by new empirical knowledge and better mathematical models.

30. *Scientia* and *sapientia* are Latin words that we can loosely translate as "knowledge" and "wisdom," respectively. They do not map neatly onto the modern categories of "science" and "cultural tradition" precisely because they are integral, not separate, notions both in medieval Latin contexts and in Aboriginal contexts, and because *scientia*, unlike modern science, relates to any organized knowledge system (as in the German *Wissenschaft*), not just to "naturalistic" knowledge systems.

high essential insight down—has become unreliable after the fall. It may still be possible for a genuinely wise and virtuous non-Christian sage, aided by divine grace, to make approximately correct conjectures about high wisdom (patristic theologians like Augustine tended to think that Plato got quite a lot right), but there is no guarantee of truth in this speculative enterprise. In contrast, bivalent perceptual verification and rational validity is relatively unproblematic in both knowledge categories, if suitable observational accuracy and mathematical care are diligently employed. So knowledge can deliver on demonstrable truth, but it only provides truths of the low categories on both natural and mental knowledge. However, because of the fall, understanding now readily wanders from (or rebels against) the truth. Even so, there are limited natural checks preventing *Understanding I* (β) from totally departing from social and political truth, and these checks can be discovered by carefully examining the conditions for human flourishing.[31] However, there are no clear bivalent checks empirically available to *Understanding II* (δ)[32] such that wisdom itself seems characterized by fragmentation and distortion under the epistemic norms of fallen humanity. The aid of special graces that are not necessarily common graces is now necessary for the seeker of high metaphysical, moral, and theological truths.

And such special graces have been provided to us—so Christian patristic and medieval theologians maintained. For we now live after the incarnation of the very Word of God, the inspired writ of the Christian Scriptures has been given to the church, and the Holy Spirit has been given to the church to safeguard the truthful interpretation of divine revelation. This, as the church understands it, is the deposit of faith given to us by the Spirit of truth, which enables us to grasp the truths of moral and theological wisdom that are no longer certain to the understanding capacities of divinely unaided fallen humanity.

It needs to be reiterated that, in practice, a meaningful awareness of the world is unitary such that knowledge and understanding are integrated in our apprehension of the world and in the existential and social realities of

31. For example, any human society requires a (possibly very low) minimum level of trust and cooperation to function at all. The attempt to govern human society entirely by force will fail. One can "believe" that force alone is all one needs to take over and run a human society, but nature will refute such a belief, empirically. From the 1840s to the present, the British, the Russians, and the Americans were all unable to simply force the varying—often feuding—tribal peoples of Afghanistan to drop their own ways and submit to overwhelming displays of foreign force.

32. That is, wisdom and revelation discourses usually have at least some common elements and value commitments, and they can share significant substantive metaphysical claims (such as monotheism in the three Abrahamic faiths)—yet living wisdom traditions remain incommensurate as ultimate truth discourses.

our daily lives. It also needs to be said that both knowledge and (certainly low) understanding are always communally mediated and socially practiced human realities. Given these facts, it is no surprise that medieval Christendom made sure that while knowledge had its head in its own proper domain, understanding had a governing role in moral, religious, and legal judgment as well as in political power, and high truth claims were always held to be the prerogative of appropriately authorized religious understanding, not of academic knowledge (or "merely" academic theory).

The reality is that medieval thinking had a complex-enough grasp of the relationships between existential and essential knowledge and understanding categories—and between natural illumination and divine illumination—to be able to define zones of autonomy for "science" and "religion" (though neither of these modern categories existed in medieval times) while defining operational integrative zones in which science and technology were *subordinated* to wisdom and revelation.[33] We no longer have this level of complexity in our understanding of the sources of intelligibility, and—for Christian theology—this is a serious problem. But could we now build a new integrative zone?

7.6 An Integrative Zone for "Science and Religion" Today?

The arrangement between what we would now call science and religion from the Western explosion of Aristotelian natural philosophy in the thirteenth century to the late Victorian era looked something like the following.

Unlike the sharp territorial outlook that has (at least notionally) become assumed between science and religion over the past two centuries, a crucial zone of integrative overlap between methodologically and substantively discrete intellectual domains characterized medieval thinking about the relation of natural philosophy to Christian theology. Without such an integrative zone, our awareness of reality itself fragments, and a rupture opens up between natural facts/logic/power (the knowledge categories of awareness—including science and technology), on the one hand, and high cultural meaning/value/justice/purpose (the understanding categories of awareness—including moral truths, metaphysical *theoria*, and divine *theologia*), on the other. Such a rupture degrades the very possibility of integrative human awareness that is cohesive within a civilization. Where a common integrative human awareness becomes unviable—I contend—this is to the serious detriment of both science-technology and wisdom-theory-theology. For any vibrant human lifeworld

---

33. See, for example, Pasnau, *Cambridge History of Medieval Philosophy*; and Gaukroger, *Emergence of a Scientific Culture*.

strives to be oriented to the highest common good and requires at least some measure of integration in illumination itself. Our very humanity is degraded without some integrative apparatus mediating between quantitative/instrumental knowledge and qualitative/contemplative wisdom.

There are reasons to think that the medieval integrative-zone arrangement, far from being merely historically contingent, was in fact required theologically, politically, morally, and philosophically by the framework of human meaning and acting that was medieval Christendom. That distinctive integrative framework is now in the past—and yet, I shall argue, some sort of integrative zone remains necessary if there is to be any viable ongoing relationship between Christian theology and natural philosophy.

In the High Middle Ages, a naturalist methodology for natural philosophy—what Aquinas's teacher Albertus Magnus called *de naturalibus naturaliter*—was given a fairly high level of functional autonomy from Christian theology, but this was not a separation of reason from faith. In the thirteenth century, natural philosophy and logic were themselves understood as theologically significant and, indeed, as necessary prerequisites for higher theological knowledge. With theologians such as Albertus and Aquinas at the forefront of the learning revolution of the High Middle Ages, the very idea of our modern domain wars between science and religion was not conceivable. This is because nature itself was held to be graced with real sapiential truths that could be accessed by sensible natural belief (α and β), as bivalently and validly analyzed with formal reason (γ), without needing to have any recourse to divine revelation or high theology (δ), at least in the first instance. Even so, the unity of natural reason with divinely revealed wisdom was also assumed; there is only one cosmos—not two—even though the Creator is beyond creation.

What this points to is that there is more than one way of understanding what naturalism is. Correspondingly, there is more than one naturalistic epistemic methodology. The methodologically discrete yet theologically integrated medieval *naturalism* of Albertus Magnus and the reductively materialist modern scientific *naturalism* of Thomas Huxley have no substantive continuity with each other. They are incompatible conceptions of naturalism.

Back in the Middle Ages, the integrative zone for the methodologically and substantively discrete intellectual enterprises of natural philosophy and theology produced, at times, a bumpy ride. Integration was innately prone to being a bit edgy, as theological truth itself continually unfolds via its own intellectual pressures, and the cosmological, ethical, and technological implications of new developments in natural knowledge could challenge existing sociological forms of life. These dynamics entailed a steady re-jigging of intellectual norms and operational social, legal, political, and even ecclesial norms. But the bumpy ride was by and large workable. And, by and large, this integrative zone was not abandoned in early modernity. To repurpose Oliver O'Donovan's phrase, there were workable "bonds of imperfection" connecting theological and philosophical qualitative *understanding* with natural quantitative and observational *knowledge*. As universities were established by the church, a culturally accepted hierarchy of authority resting on ecclesially endorsed wisdom was largely acceptable to the medieval lifeworld in the governance of knowledge and power. But such an old-world arrangement came under increasing pressure as modernity matured, and it was the dropping (by design or by default) of the essentialist categories of divine illumination, as public knowledge categories, that ended any meaningful integrative zone. This has been highly problematic for Christian theology under the conditions of modern public knowledge. Integration was first replaced with demarcation, and then, increasingly, with the removal of *understanding* from the domain of truth itself.

7.7 Ockham's Pincer

Central institutional features of Western Christendom's integrated bonds of knowledge and understanding collapsed with the Reformation, and the old synthesis upheld by institutional linkages between the universities and the Roman Catholic Church was in serious trouble by the seventeenth century. The new learning happily rejected Aristotle's conception of natural purpose, natural value, and knowable natural essence, and this would lead to the idea of the complete autonomy of an entirely mechanical and reductively physical naturalism from theological and philosophical wisdom. Over time, nature itself—without Aristotle's hylomorphic categories—becomes seen as having no meaningful connection to any sort of higher essential understanding, and ethics and purpose are recast in entirely sensational, instinctive, and scientifically rational terms. Equally, the realm of the "supernatural" becomes radically removed from any mundane comportment with the realm of the "natural." Integrative categories linking natural light with divine light are increasingly abandoned after Kant (as is metaphysics itself), and this eventually produces the complete notional separation of the domain of science from the domain of religion as promoted by the secular scientific progressives of the late nineteenth century. By now, a sociologized and politico-economicized, methodologically atheistic understanding of the *true* (i.e., reductively physical) meaning of religion is firmly established in the progressive intelligentsia. In more culturally moderate intellectual circles, the perceived pre-scientific backwardness of orthodox belief leads to a sentimentalized, psychologized, mythologized, and internalized religious sensibility. Here, theology is isolated from public truth discourses and banished from presiding over the higher meaning implications and interpretations of natural knowledge.[34] Now the new naturalists' "cosmic feeling" has become the only scientifically respectable meaning of religion, and increasingly "religion" wants to find the blessing of science to be considered credible in the public domain of truth. This, for orthodox Christian theology, is an unmitigated disaster. The separation of science from religion, along with the dominance of science as secular, progressive modernity's first truth discourse, has resulted in the cultural death of the Christian religion within the public knowledge, meaning, and governance domains of Western modernity.

Losing the category of divine illumination is highly problematic for Christian theology, which has its source in the miraculous works of God in human history and in the divine illumination of the Christian revelation describing, expounding, and imbibing Christians into those works. I cannot see how Christian theology can meaningfully be Christian theology without divine illumination and a commitment to the primacy of transcendent reality (God). But this loss of the category of divine illumination in the public intellectual culture of post-nineteenth-century Western modernity also has a serious impact on how we now understand cultural knowledge—Plato's awareness category of belief (β).

When only perceptual/empirical (α) and mathematical/rational (γ) understanding categories are thought of as meaningful knowledge, and when reductive materialism is assumed (removing noetic wisdom [δ] from the domain of both knowledge and reality), then cultural knowledge has no transcendent meaning referent that it partially participates in. We then apply empirical, rational, and reductively naturalistic "knowledge"[35] categories to human meaning; this we call the social and human sciences. Which is to say, we use quantitative tools to try to understand qualitative categories. We use reductively quantitative and naturalistic science, as defined by a materialist theory of nature, to try to decode, epistemically master, and technologically harness qualitative, meaningful, and purposive understanding categories. To start with, this is a catastrophic category error. But redescribing meaning, purpose, and intelligibility in the categories of facts, quantities, and determinate naturalistic necessity has the effect of squeezing qualitative reality out of our

34. As Dorothy Sayers points out, this development and the subsequent decline of theology in basic and higher general education has severe consequences for the integrative intelligibility of Western culture. "Theology is the mistress-science, without which the whole educational structure will necessarily lack its final synthesis." Sayers, *Lost Tools of Learning*, 19.

35. But this "knowledge," in Plato's categories, is actually theoretically framed belief.

Figure 7.3

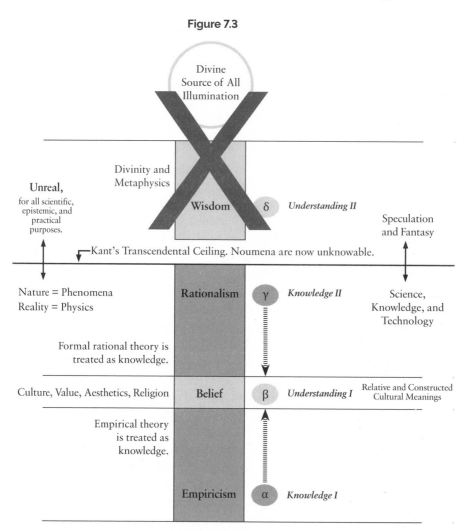

entire understanding of the world. This we can call Ockham's pincer, which can be pictorially presented as in figure 7.3.[36]

36. Ockham's razor is the principle of ontological economy—do not multiply entities more than is necessary. This was employed by the famous fourteenth-century Franciscan William of Ockham against medieval Realism, advancing a nominalist understanding of free-standing concrete beings that need no ontological participation in essential categories beyond their own concrete, matter-and-form-integrated substance. Over the centuries, this reductive particularism becomes part and parcel of how we now understand empirical knowledge. Ockham himself was an entirely medieval thinker, so modern science has no contact with how he saw the world, and yet this razor readily matures into Hume's fork by the eighteenth century, and Ockham becomes a darling of the reductively naturalistic, scientistic mythology of the twentieth century. So it

Empirical data, from below, and statistical and analytic modeling, from above, crush the domain of cultural belief between them and remove qualitative and transcendently referenced human meaning from existence. The humanities are increasingly trying to survive in the university context by adopting the methodologies of the natural sciences and the social and human sciences. But the more they adapt, the less case there is for keeping them at all, and the more they become subsumed into the social and human sciences and used by the technologies of human manipulation under the financialized pragmatism star of university administrations. Christian theology simply cannot adapt to these terms and remain Christian theology. Perhaps it is time for at least a serious minority of Christian philosophical theologians to depart from the academic cities and build monasteries in the desert again.

7.8 Christian Theological Epistemology and Post-Victorian Science

Now that we've reached the end of this chapter, I hope that a number of things have become clear.

First, the way in which we understand the nature and meaning of knowledge is of crucial importance if we wish to think about the first-order parameters in which the main games in the existing "science and religion" domain are played.

Second, divine and natural light and the epistemic impact of sin and grace are integral to the Augustinian and Thomistic trajectories of traditional Western theological epistemology. To the traditionally minded Christian, theology has a complex bearing on how empirical and rational knowledge categories, on the one hand, and belief and wisdom understanding categories, on the other, are understood and interact. But all theological and metaphysical understanding categories are now firmly placed outside the presumed objectivity and philosophical neutrality of scientific theory. Consequently, publicly valid knowledge is defined by a scientistic ideology, and theology is outside all public truth categories. Stated the other way around, the epistemic terms in which modern theology is allowed to enter the domain of scientific knowledge are profoundly problematic to the integrity of central features of the long and deep heritage of Western theological epistemology.

Third, the concepts of divine and natural illumination and of sin and grace are integral to a *Christian* theological perspective on both knowledge and understanding. This means that a Christian understanding of scientific theory

is this mythological Ockham of the twentieth century to whom I am attributing this reductive anti-sapiential pincer, rather than the fourteenth-century man himself.

is going to experience a primary outlook dissonance with the reductively materialist and anti-metaphysical theoretical commitments of the ideology of post-Victorian secular science. While the experience of such a dissonance does not entail the rejection of empirical and rational knowledge categories for Christians, it does have serious consequences. That is, Christians will experience serious incomprehension and misunderstanding if they seek to uphold a very different sort of partnership between knowledge and under-standing than is allowed by the assumed norms that currently structure the epistemic authority of our lifeworld. For this reason a theological engagement with science that retains the integrity of Christian epistemology is going to be characterized by first-order friction. This friction should not be feared and should not be construed as "anti-science"; it is a friction that is necessary to save the meaning and valid significance of science, if the high understanding categories of the Christian faith are to be treated as actually true. And if the high understanding categories of the Christian faith are not to be treated as true by Christians, then we might as well forget metaphysics and theology altogether and embrace a functionally reductive pragmatic materialism.

But perhaps the obvious question to try to address from here is, *Can* we still treat the high metaphysical and epistemological truth commitments of tradi-tional Christian theology as *primary* truth? Notably, the idea that there is such a thing as divine illumination, and that we are now somehow epistemically wounded by sin in apprehending that light, seems to imply that we believe an ancient cosmogenic fall myth to be true. Is this possible in our age of science? And if the Christian *believes* (in the categories of *Understanding I*) that we have been given divine graces that provide us with some sort of historically mediated access to the unsayable high truths of *Understanding II*, is it in any sense reasonable to maintain that divine revelation is really embedded in the very human texts, institutions, and practices of its historical transmissions? Even if we can *believe* this, could such belief claim higher truth authority than our current scientific truth discourse?

Now, perhaps, we can see exactly what the remarkable reversal has done to Christian theology in removing it from the place of Western culture's primary truth discourse. For after Ockham's pincer, modern scientific knowledge lays an assumed and largely unchallenged claim to a monopolistic control of truth itself. "Science"—as the authoritative canon of material facts and natural theories—now situates truth firmly within the demonstrable and public domain of ratio-empirical knowledge only. Truth does *not* reside in the now-private domain of belief anymore. *Understanding I* is now a territory apart from public truth, a territory in which non-factual and non-theoretical mythic understanding constructs ("religion") can be safely indulged in by those who have an infantile psychological need to believe such things.[37] In this manner, Christian theology has been firmly removed from its former status and function as the West's first public truth discourse. Beliefs that exist outside the domain of scientific knowledge—and outside the prevailing scientific theories that are derived from a reductively naturalistic interpretation of the knowledge categories of perception and mathematics—are, simply, *not true*. Myth has become equivalent to fiction. Indeed, all cultural meanings can no longer be true. The *true* meanings of culture are now reinterpreted by our dominant academic truth discourse as residing *within* the categories of perception and mathematics, as interpreted under the assumed theoretical banner of reductively materialist empirical rationalism. Culture herself might think she is all about the production and transmission of qualities, meanings, transcendent longings, and eternal and essential archetypes imaginatively expressed in myth, but we *know* that culture is actually an imaginative construct built over real material, instinctual, and rationally containable scientific facts.[38]

There is no getting around it. We can proceed no further without exploring a Christian theological understanding of the relationship between myth and history. This is the relationship between transcendence and immanence, eternity and time, essence and existence, knowledge and understanding. This is now very demanding, as these relationships have been radically reconfigured since the remarkable reversal. It is now taken for granted that myth is always subordinate to (and deemed objectively false by) history, transcendence is always subordinate to (and deemed objectively false by) immanence, eternity is always subordinate to (and deemed objectively false by) time, and essence is always subordinate to (and deemed objectively false by) existence. That is, myth and all these other metaphysical and theological categories are understood as—in reality—subjective projections of the imagination. To redraw Plato's divided line one last time, we now still put imagination (*eikasia*) at the bottom, but we connect it to archetypal categories of the unconscious, and we draw the line separating a true knowledge of reality from believed and culturally constructed impressions just above the category of myth, which we now see as the sub-empirical, the sub-rational, and the imagined world

37. A. J. Conyers (*The Long Truce*) points out that "religious liberty" has been carefully reconstructed after the remarkable reversal to protect the secular public domain *from* religion. If Conyers is right (and his case is persuasive), "religious liberty" has become something of a lobster trap that the theologically alert would be very unwise to enter into in order to defend the public integrity of expressions of their faith.

38. Perhaps Carolyn Merchant has a point about the tendency of a reductive and instrumental modern masculinist reason to stand over and control feminine nature and feminine insight. See Merchant, *Death of Nature*.

of the spiritual. The assumed outlook on knowledge and truth within the post-Victorian scientific lifeworld is now structured as shown in figure 7.4.

Figure 7.4

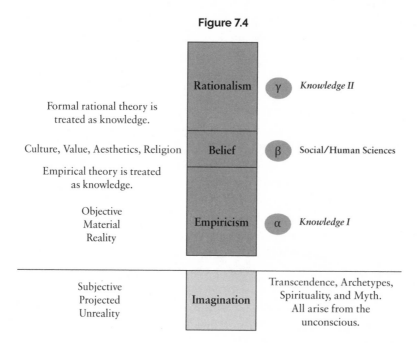

There is no place for traditional Christian theology at the table of truth under these epistemic conditions. If the price of entry to the table of knowledge is to accept these epistemic categories, the price is too high. But what if the modern truth outlook is itself mythically framed?

Myth and History—
the Fall and Science

The revolutionary and progressive attitude of secular academic modernity is stridently dismissive of its pre-modern origins in Christian theology and classical philosophy. More than dismissive—theocidal. Yet even killing our Father in heaven is not enough. According to the Freudian Oedipal myth, once we have killed and eaten our archaic and tyrannical father, we must then create a divine Father as the guarantor of the new social order (hence, to Freud, the relation of the superego to religion).[1] The historian Bernard Lightman argues that some of the most prominent English advocates of late nineteenth-century scientific naturalism—Thomas Huxley, Herbert Spencer, and John Tyndall—*replace* orthodox Christian theology with their own naturalistic theology, strangely created in the secularized image of Christian theology (which they have killed and eaten).[2] This, I think, is inevitable, for the low categories of natural knowledge are not self-standing in actual human

1. I have mentioned Freud here because he is thinking about religion, the soul, and morality in reductively naturalistic terms. Here, the psychological drivers of our deepest social motivations are intimately tangled in the dark cultural backstory of religion, but the real meaning of religion is not what the naive believer in any divine Father thinks it is. Now the faithless are calling the faithful delusional. That is, the dynamic of religious and moral motivation itself is not denied or suspended in Freud, but its meaning is inverted. Freudian psychology remains, in this sense, religious, albeit on its head.

2. See Lightman, "Theology of Victorian Scientific Naturalists."

experience.[3] For this reason there is a perennial human need to find *reasons*, *meanings*, and *purposes* in and beyond nature, and to attribute a continuity between the tangible and rationally understandable natural world and "who we are," "our place in the cosmos," "right and wrong," and "the meaning of life and death."

Science—having relegated religion to the private sphere of mere belief—now has to try to perform public religious functions for us that "bind us together" (*religo*) in a unified structure of high meaning, a center of common worth-ship.[4] If the individuals of modern secular society cannot be bound together in a high common truth, then the dogs of cultural fragmentation and unbridled private superstitions will be released on Western civilization with a vengeance. Yet "science" now does a fabulously bad job of supplying meaning, morality, and purpose, and it takes a particularly dry and abstract type of reductive materialist to find science, as a substitute for religion, in any way satisfying. The result of the meaning inadequacy of science as our first discourse of public truth can be a rather brutal kickback against scientific truth. If science had not been so effective in removing religion and wisdom from the categories of public knowledge and understanding, it may well have not set itself up for a powerful post-truth, anti-science blowback.

Alas, the entirely fabricated war between science and religion that was invented in the late nineteenth century, when secular reason was on the rise, may prove to be a picnic compared to what forces of anti-truth and superstition may be unleashed by the collapse of science as an ersatz public theology of first meaning for the secular age. For any unified lifeworld must have its guiding mythos. This leads us to ask very important questions about the adequacy of science as a first truth discourse for secular modernity and to consider how we can now understand the deep mythos frameworks of Christian theology—particularly in relation to knowledge—that are in serious dissonance with both modern epistemology and the materialistic mythos of modern consumer society.

As unpacked somewhat above, traditional Christian epistemic categories perform a complex set of operations: they synthesize a common-grace, low natural

3. Thomas Nagel's theologically agnostic and yet very decisive stance as to "why the materialist neo-Darwinian conception of nature is almost certainly false" (this is the subtitle of his *Mind and Cosmos*) is an expression of his inability to simply ignore our situation, where the very ideas of mind and cosmos are not compatible with reductively materialist naturalism and yet we can't possible make sense of our experience without them.

4. This is done in a thousand gentle and unobtrusive ways in the academy, but it is done quite overtly by the respectable advocates of scientism, such as Robyn Williams in the wonderfully expansive *Science Show* (Australian Broadcasting Corporation) and popular writers like Yuval Harari in, for example, his *Homo Deus*.

light with a common-grace, low divine light; they take account of the distorting epistemic influence of sin in the high natural light and high divine light categories; and they perform a complex set of philosophical and theological tasks that enable natural and divine light to operate both relatively autonomously and synergistically (though in some tension). This complexity is notably absent in post-Kantian epistemology, which renders the truth claims of traditional Christian theology not simply different from the truth claims of natural philosophy but incompatible with science and reason as our high culture's first truth discourses.

After Kant, the complex manner in which eternity (divine light) and temporality (natural light) were harmonized without being subsumed into each other is radically removed by a monist egocentric understanding of knowledge, located only in the framework of naturalistic perceived temporality and mathematic formal reason. Christian theology is simply removed from knowledge under these conditions. There is no getting around it—we have to look at the relationship between truth categories understood within the framework of eternity (myth) and truth categories understood within the framework of historical temporality. Our lifeworld-structured inability to interface these two categories is the huge and largely unaddressed crisis point for both Christian theology and scientific truth in the post-Kantian context of Western modernity's high intellectual culture.

As the epistemic impact of the fall is central to creedal conceptions of the relationship between common-grace forms of knowledge illumination (α and γ) and the faith-situated graces (β as temporally situated being; δ as eternally situated being), there can be no getting around the thorny problem of the relation of the Edenic myth of the fall to modern naturalistic interpretations of scientific truth. I appreciate we are now going where angels fear to tread, and I do so with appropriate fear and trembling!

8.1 Myth and History in Christian Theology

In a short and highly important paper written in 1942, the American medievalist Lynn White Jr. pointed out that a new and profound crisis had arisen in Western Christian theology by the late nineteenth century. This crisis is the dis-integration of time (**history**) from eternity (**myth**).[5] The intimate connection of time and eternity in the Christian doctrinal nexus of "historically **true myth**,"[6] and the development of this integrative stance in the liturgical

5. White, "Christian Myth and Christian History."
6. That is, a historical event sequence—such as the suffering, death, and resurrection of Christ—is seen as a "mythic event." It is an eruption of eternal reality into temporal reality. It is neither purely of eternity nor purely of time, but equally of both. This is different from the

performance of the relation of higher time to chronological time in the Christian calendar, had always been presupposed in the Christian faith until—as White identifies it—the late Victorian era. Ironically, it is the very serious interest in the historical nature of the Christian revelation that was the motivating force in the emergence of modern Western historiography, which—assuming various theological innovations that flowered in the early modern period— became determined to write *purely* natural histories of human affairs. This "purity" entails a new naturalism where nature becomes self-standing in relation to grace. Equally, this new stance entails a "pure" conception of the non-historical supernatural that emerges in the Enlightenment. The supernatural now becomes entirely unnatural, entirely separated from the natural realities of space and time, which prior to the eighteenth century had always been considered dependent on the divine for their very ground of being. Prior to the Enlightenment, the source and destiny of all natural cosmic order had been God, and qualitative and essential truths that must guide us as moral and intelligent beings were thought of as divine realities embedded in our normal experience of natural reality. The supernatural was, in effect, a very "natural" feature of human life. Put the other way around, naturalism was not pure; the natural was here embedded in the supernatural.

Modern historiography becomes the grounds of a sharp dualism between nature and supernature. As this trend matures, it gives rise to a new, purely natural naturalism that flowers in Thomas Huxley's firmly secular scientific naturalism. The theoretical vision of a purely natural naturalism and a purely supernatural supernaturalism is what guides Huxley and his reforming cohort of highly influential X Club friends. Steering by this theoretical star, Huxley and friends launch a highly successful coup to remove science from the hands of the clergy in the late nineteenth century.[7] This staggering revolution in Western culture—the metaphysical purification of both nature and supernature, and the firm political separation of the purely natural public truths of science from the purely supernatural private beliefs of religion—is still largely unaddressed by Christian theologians. Yet the impact of this metaphysical purification and epistemic revolution on our high intellectual culture has been at the core of the decline of Christian theology as Western civilization's first truth discourse since the mid-nineteenth century.

Ironically, as we have seen, this crisis was largely produced by Christian theologians in the arena of biblical studies. Enlightenment-framed German

---

classical Greek understanding of the mythic, whereby inspired imagination makes up a story that carries an eternal truth, and from a modern understanding of the historical, where only naturalistic events and explanations count as historically valid truths.

7. See Barton, "'Huxley, Lubbock, and Half a Dozen Others.'"

biblical scholarship leads to the isolation of historically probable facts from scientifically incredible myths. Under the influence of eighteenth-century deistic rationalism, the realm of the eternal becomes increasingly "high" (non-contingent and universal, pulling away from any historical embedding), and under the influence of eighteenth-century empiricism, history becomes increasingly non-miraculous (the temporal realm becomes defined by regularized mechanistic determinism). The idea that God acts in time, so that historically contingent contexts not only carry but transmit divine revelation, becomes intellectually unpalatable, as it was in high Greek theology before Christianity. By this process the mythological Jesus will become entirely disassociated from the historical Jesus. Starting in earnest with David Strauss's *Life of Jesus* (1835), the quest for the historical Jesus—a historical Jesus that is explicitly not the Jesus of myth—has set traditional Christian belief, where history and myth are inseparable, on notice as no longer credible. At this point all the miraculous aspects of orthodox Christology become *purely* mythic, rather than historically real.[8]

One can integrate a Jesus of history with Thomas Huxley's secular scientific naturalism. And one can integrate a mythic sensibility that has *no* connection with historical fact but is a "religious feeling" with Huxley's outlook. But one can no longer integrate orthodox Christian theology that presupposes historically true myth with modern, secular, naturalistic science. In some manner, all Huxley does is formalize the eye of the needle through which modern scientific reason requires religious consciousness to pass in order to be acceptable to the full separation of myth from history, the full separation of nature from grace, the complete isolation of immanence from transcendence. But once religion has passed through the eye of this needle and shed any integrative understanding of historically true myth, is it—in any sense at all—still Christian?[9] White is right; this is the central problem for the credibility and integrity of modern Western Christianity.

8. It bears noticing that the relation of the eternal and transcendent to the temporal and immanent in Platonist thinking is considered impossible after Kant, and moral Realism dies back drastically in the academy in the nineteenth century leading to "post-metaphysical" ethics, notably pragmatic, utilitarian, and rationalist moral philosophies that are no longer informed by genuinely transcendent moral realities.

9. Thomas Huxley claims to have no difficulty with religion as a personal appreciation of that expansive and wonder-struck feeling of awe and apophatic ecstasy. It is theology and powerful religious institutions that he simply can't stand. The idea that one could put into propositional and—as it were—factual categories those sublime mysteries that stand beyond us simply insults his scientific and rational intelligence, on the one hand, and his religious feelings, on the other. The idea that religious institutions would have the ability to define social norms and influence policy decisions by appeal to the superstitious conflation of myth with history is an insult to scientific and moral progress in social organization. It is traditional Christian theology and the

The Christian doctrine of Adam's fall is a profoundly significant site for considering the relation of mythic eternity to historical time in Christian theology.

8.2 Eternity and Time

Let us consider what has happened to any traditional theological conception of the true myth of Adam's fall under the conditions of scientific modernity. This exploration must circle around this matter, as simple polarities and definitional precision won at the cost of reality tempt one to error on all fronts. Let us proceed with caution.

A number of initial and general observations can be made. First, human origin myths are usually intimately concerned with the nature of evil and profoundly shape a culture's understanding of ethical norms. Dropping an Adamic conception of the fall cannot help but profoundly impact Western conceptions of moral normativity, particularly as it pertains to violent power and eschatological destiny (progress). Second, the separation of myth from history does not really work; we cannot help but integrate time and eternity, fact and meaning. Mythic archetypes are a fundamental social reality. What then, mythically, happens to Western modernity when Adam's fall no longer seems culturally believable as a true myth? Third, what if orthodox Christian theology cannot be true to itself without some conception of the historically true nature of its primary myths—including Adam's fall? If this is the case, then after White's observation about the late Victorian separation of myth from history, orthodox Christian theology is going to have an inherently problematic relationship with truth discourses framed by modern secular naturalism (in other words, with the totalizing knowledge discourse that now flies under the banner of "science"). This is not just a theoretical problem; the relation of Christian theology to modern naturalistic cosmology and anthropology, and any post-Christian naturalistic ethics of violence and competitive dominance, is going to be inherently problematic. Let us look briefly at these matters.

8.3 Myth Defines Norms

For some reason we seem to forget that the social Darwinism and the eugenics of the early twentieth century were very popular among educated elites all over

---

power of religious institutions in the public arena that Huxley opposes. Religion itself—by his definition—he fully supports.

Europe and North America. Germany, the very place where—thanks to liberal Protestants—myth and history in Christian theology were first separated, was strongly influenced by early twentieth-century social Darwinism and eugenics. But there is an important nuance here. Nineteenth-century Catholics in Germany were prohibited from using the historical-critical method of Protestant biblical scholarship, and the differences between Lutheran-dominated Prussia and Catholic-dominated Bavaria played themselves out dramatically in the time of Hitler. Hitler did not get anything like the same level of support from Catholics as he did from Protestants.[10] Looking at Bonhoeffer's frustrations with German Protestants, it can be reasonably argued that dogmatic theology as it concerned the eternal had become effectively privatized within religion, removed from history (time), and made "safe" within the discretely supernatural inner world of the church. At the same time, Protestants related to the public realm of power and authority by upholding a more Kantian and authoritarian duty of submissive loyalty to governing authority, drawing on a rather fatalistic rendition of Luther's "two kingdoms" theology of state power. Protestants were also, under the highly stressed inter-war years, easily moved to anti-Semitic, anti-Communist, and anti-homosexual scapegoating. In many regards Protestant theology either was actively supportive of Nazi power on the grounds of nationalist pride and authoritarian submission or held to the church's complete indifference to temporal power, which had the effect of a silent complicity with temporal power.[11] Bonhoeffer is the Protestant exception who, in virtue of being such a striking and isolated exception, proves the rule.

The point I am making here goes beyond noting the serious disconnection between the eternal and the temporal in the German Protestant churches. A powerful anti-Christian mythos was at work in Nazi Germany that the German church failed to address. A social-Darwinian mythos of a pure naturalism that embraces a violent and survivalist "state of nature" account of origins is not a-mythic; rather, it signals the return to a largely pagan mythos that has profound political and moral implications. Listen to Sigmund Freud in 1930:

> Civilization is opposed by man's natural aggressive drive, the hostility of each against all and all against each. This aggressive drive is the descendant and principal representative of the Death drive, which we have found beside Eros and which rules the world jointly with him. And now, I think, the meaning of the development of civilization is no longer obscure to us. This development

10. Hawes, *Shortest History of Germany*, 164–70.
11. Kelly and Nelson, *Cost of Moral Leadership*, 18–22; de Gruchy, *Cambridge Companion to Dietrich Bonhoeffer*, 190–205. See also Bethge, *Dietrich Bonhoeffer*.

must show us the struggle between Eros and Death, between the life drive and the drive for destruction, as it is played out in the human race. This struggle is the essential content of all life; hence, the development of civilization may be described simply as humanity's struggle for existence. And this battle of the giants is what our nurse-maids seek to mitigate with their lullaby about heaven.[12]

The mythos of our new naturalism sees any belief in a salvation and heaven as a mythic expression of a neurotic fantasy—illusions of infantile wish fulfillment[13]—invoked by our abhorrence of the amoral and implacably violent and agonistic gigantic truths of the human condition. To Freud, the eternal truth about civilization is unceasing struggle. Ironically, given that Freud was Jewish, Freud and Nazi Germany shared a mythic ideology of intrinsic struggle—myth always has and always will define cultural normativity.

8.4 The Myth of Secular Progress Falters

After World War II, our secularized progress myth starts to run out of steam. Nuclear bombs and the Cold War put something of a dent in the ideology of a coming rational scientific utopia. What are we progressing toward if the sole purpose of civilization is to be a functionally constrained theater for the instinctively driven struggle for mere existence? With no genuine eschaton and no vision of a fully redeemed humanity guiding the strivings of personal and social improvement, contest itself becomes the *telos*, and the return of more pagan conceptions of agonistic power start reappearing in our social, political, legal, and commercial norms. While the postwar boom is chugging along in the "free world," this is still moderated by growing levels of wealth and comfort. But with the crash of the Bretton Woods system, in 1971, we see the return to an ideology of competitive struggle, and dominating elites seem liberated from restraint and set out with new vigor to pursue self-aggrandizing conquest. Which is to say, we can dispense with an Edenic origins myth, but this also entails dispensing with a Christian anthropology and a Christian eschatology; and it does not stop there. The human reality is, we can have no common framework of cultural meaning without some cosmogenic account; hence, the mythic and the teleological cannot be dispensed with just because our culture's high knowledge categories have become reductively naturalistic and materialistic. Because we simply cannot have no cosmogenic mythos, throwing out Adam will give us a different cultural mythos as regards human

12. Freud, *Civilization and Its Discontents*, 74–75.
13. Freud, *Future of an Illusion*.

origins and destinies; we cannot be genuinely post-mythic when it comes to the origins and destiny of the human condition.

We have seen this mythos shift in Australia. As I write (2020), the Brereton Report has released its initial findings regarding thirty-nine alleged war crimes—the murder of unarmed civilians and prisoners—by Australian Special Air Service personnel in Afghanistan between 2005 and 2016. If, in Freud's terms, our soldiers are trained to administer the death drive on behalf of the Australian polity, and if the point of civilization is to control and channel this implacable human drive, and if people are not made in the image of God and do not have intrinsic sacred value, then a return to a naturalistic warrior culture valorizing death itself is no surprise, whatever the legal protocols about war crimes may be. If our humanity is not defined by being created in the image of God—a key component of the Adamic myth—then it will be defined by what Saint Paul calls "the elemental spiritual forces of the [fallen] world" (Gal. 4:3). But these forces cannot be a-mythic or spiritually neutral; they are profoundly charged with essential meaning (atemporal archetypal meanings), they entail practices of action and ritual (cultus), and they cannot avoid being collectively doxologically entangled, as the primary mysteries of life and death always confront us with matters of our highest moral and existential commitments. Freud and Paul, from astonishingly different stances, have notable areas of similar appreciation about the normal subjugation of "natural man" to powerful and dark cosmic forces that are only thinly pasted over by the mild facade of civilized peace.

8.5 Ricœur on the Four Basic Mythic Archetypes

Four French philosophical theologians—Paul Ricœur, René Girard, Simone Weil, and Jacques Ellul[14]—are particularly astute in this arena. Ricœur lists four basic cosmogenic myths that directly frame different basic attitudes to violence, evil, and justified social order.[15]

8.5.1 The Mythos of Original Violence

In the first cosmogenic mythic archetype, chaotic evil is coextensive with the origin of all things. There is no "problem of evil" here, for chaos is primal and creation is achieved as a cosmic act of original violence. The dominance of life and order over death and chaos, by violent power, establishes "goodness"

---

14. Ricœur, *Symbolism of Evil*; Girard, *Violence and the Sacred*; Weil, "The Illiad, Poem of Might"; Ellul, *Violence*.
   15. Ricœur, *Symbolism of Evil*, 172–74.

out of chaos. If we revert to this sort of cosmogenic outlook via a Hobbesian/ Darwinian/Freudian naturalism, there cannot really be any such thing as a war crime, for violence, destruction, dominance, and death are primal and natural features of life and the human condition. And indeed, it could be that the war crime is a very recent invention, only really becoming institutional- ized in the twentieth century in what we now call international law, largely in response to atrocities from World War II. Perhaps this notion, along with the notion of universal human rights, is something of a parting gesture of Western Christendom, for while broadly Christian conceptions of moral normativity were assumed to be valid in the mid-twentieth century, the social collapse of Christian moral normativity in Western culture started in earnest in the 1960s. Consequently, human rights and war crimes have increasingly been defined in legally reduced categories as they are outside modern naturalistic ethical categories—utilitarian, pragmatic, and rationalistically formal conceptions of ethical constructivism. Ethics itself is increasingly understood in terms of legal liability and procedural regulations, as the categories of moral realism[16] become incomprehensible to our reductively naturalistic knowledge discourse.

8.5.2 The Fall Mythos

The second cosmogenic mythic archetype Ricœur identifies is that of a fall. Here primordial creation is entirely good, and evil/death/violence is an "un- natural" aberration requiring gap-stopping remedies while nature is subject to this aberrant order, and while we wait for some final divinely enabled redemptive restoration of the original goodness (salvation). Here violence, death, and evil are problems to be contained and fought against, rather than natural realities to simply accept, or govern. There is a real "problem of evil" here; evil is not accepted as a "natural" feature of human life—as something that is simply given to the natural order of human reality—but it is a strange invader, an alien oc- cupying force, a problem to be recognized as a problem and suitably managed.

8.5.3 The Tragic Mythos

The third myth of origins Ricœur identifies he labels as tragic. Here reality is governed by evil cosmic power or, in more naturalistic terms, the powers we

16. "Moral realism," as assumed in Shakespeare and the Bible, is the idea that there is a moral grain to human affairs that is in important regards "objective"—that is, something expressed in all times and places, even though customary modes of expression are always distinctive. This can be thought of in naturalistic terms or in metaphysical terms. Traditionally (and certainly in Shakespeare and the Bible) moral truths are considered to be Real in the metaphysical transcendent categories of classical and medieval Realism. See Rist, *Real Ethics*, for a powerful contemporary exposition of Realist moral realism.

are subject to are callously indifferent to human goods. Whatever one does, one is guilty; whatever one does, evil will triumph, as the elemental powers under which mortals live and die are implacably inhumane.

8.5.4 The Mythos of Exile

The fourth myth is of the exiled soul. Here physical reality itself is a prison and punishment for the spiritual soul. We pass through this strange theater of suffering, but we are not, finally, concerned with or by it.

8.6 Ricœur on Myth, Time, and Power

After establishing these fourfold cosmogenic archetypes as carrying different symbolic meanings concerning the nature of evil, guilt, and violence, Ricœur goes on to look at each in closer detail. His treatment of chaotic evil as coextensive with creation—of creation resulting from an original act of violence—is particularly interesting in unpacking the relation between cosmogenic myth and political and moral orders. Ricœur cites the Sumero-Akkadian theogenic myths as most clearly depicting the violent victory of order over chaos.[17] The myth of redemptive violence, which theologian Walter Wink identifies as alive and well in our popular narratives and military ideologies, is native to this mythos.[18]

Intriguingly, Ricœur points out that the "creation as original violence" mythos makes power and war ahistorical, whereas the "fall" mythos makes history itself necessary. Which is to say that when violence is native to creation, the political form of a culture re-enacts the primal truth of creation in the exercise of violent power in such a manner that makes what we might call concrete history superfluous. Here the symbolic eternal reality is maintained through the exercise of violent political power; the mesh of myth and history is so integrated that history becomes an enactment of myth, time becomes an expression of eternity. Time cannot be linear and directional to this outlook. But when violence is a historically introduced problem—as in any fall mythos—human evil and eschatological redemption become strongly historical, and the original harmony of pre-fallen creation becomes the eternal reality that our political forms only ever partially enact, as a fragile just peace. The primal myth of original harmony, original high goodness, remains beyond fallen history and the "natural" fallen order, and the mythos of redemptive salvation *within* time becomes the primary site of concern

17. Ricœur, *Symbolism of Evil*, 175–98.
18. Wink, "Myth of the Domination System."

for humans. For this reason Christian theology is intrinsically historical, as it is the events *within* time and place that are the crucial carriers of both the degrading and the redeeming meta-drama of salvation history. That is, according to the Christian salvation narrative, it is in unique historical moments—concrete and unrepeatable singularities—that the mystery of **exogenous evil** enters the world and is then countered by divine redemptive eternity. The eternal God of Christian faith breaks into human space, matter, and time in order to save his creatures. Historically true myths are central to Christian dogma.

History as composed of unrepeatable concrete singularities—historical events—is intrinsically important in Christian theology; but it is not important, for example, in the sacred mythic sagas of the Indian subcontinent. In these sagas, time is more cyclical than directional, the mythic battles of the gods illustrate the eternal integration of creation and destruction, and release from the endless and immense cycles of time is the high spiritual aim of salvation. This needs to be said not to make any particular comment on the profound and ancient spiritual traditions of the Indian subcontinent but to highlight, by contrast, the distinctive role that linear history and the distinctive, historically embedded mythos of divine inbreaking play in Christian theology as shaped by the cosmogenic mythos of fall-and-redemption salvation history.

The Edenic myth of the fall can in no sense be seen as a mythos of eternal struggle. In Christian salvation history, the fall—however genuinely mythic—is a historical singularity, and this is why fallenness is not an eternal truth but, rather, a present aberration. This cannot be overemphasized: within Christian theology, the fall of humanity and nature is not an eternal or essential truth about reality; the fall has an accidental relationship to the eternal and original Goodness that is the source and destiny of creation. The drama of divinely initiated and historically located salvation—in response to this exogenous fall from original harmony—is a historical drama, requiring real people, real events, and real inbreakings of eternity into time in the cosmically redemptive war of the Lamb.

Once—as White has described it—Western history and Christian myth become dissociated, this is, in fact, a very complete destruction of Christian theology, even if the doctrines seem to remain orthodox (but in some timeless, entirely supernatural, and discretely "mythic" and "religious" register). And it is naturalism in *human history*—a view of the concrete and linear particularity of historical events that is *exclusively natural*—that is the central reason for the decline of Christianity in the West, rather than the reductive naturalism of secular scientific natural history. More precisely, it is eighteenth-century historiography that comes before and produces reductively materialist nineteenth-century scientific natural history.

It was not the Darwinian account of evolution that dealt a death blow to modern Western Christian theology; it was late eighteenth-century and early nineteenth-century historical-critical biblical scholarship that did that. But shifting a civilization's approach to the mythos that underpins its views of violence and evil has profound lifeworld implications. The West today still retains deep cultural reflexes from Christendom about the aberrant and yet "natural" character of human sin, but increasingly the knowledge culture of the West is post-Christian and readily reverts to more reductively "naturalistic" forms of cultural mythos in which original violence is assumed and in which there is really no "problem of evil." The pagan "state of nature" inherent in Nazism, the naturalism of the contest for mere survival in social Darwinism, and the voluntarist dominance ideology and animal spirits of neoliberal global corporate power (bulls and bears) are all of the same mythic family. We cannot go from "myth" to "fact"; in actuality, facts are always mythically framed.

8.7 What Stands and Falls with the Edenic Fall?

Christian theological epistemology presupposes the fall. Here the fall has a profound epistemic impact on all human knowledge and understanding. A Christian theology of that branch of human knowledge and theory we call science is thus embedded in the myth of the fall. Christian theology understands the fall—even though this is an impossible category to modern naturalistic history and to post-Victorian science—as a historically true myth.

The traditional Christian doctrine of the fall carries a sophisticated set of theoretical understandings concerning the epistemically and ontologically transformative impacts of divine graces (both natural and special) normative to the church age, which map onto the categories of natural and divine illumination. Such a stance is committed to an entire suite of truth claims that are now culturally incredible to the prevailing knowledge discourse of contemporary scientific naturalism. There is a lot riding on whether the fall can be understood as true or not, and in what manner the high truths of revelation are understood to relate (or not) to the knowledge categories of perception and mathematics, and *which* theoretical understanding of nature[19] one

19. The doctrine of the fall of nature (Rom. 8:18–25) is integral with the Christian doctrine of the fall of humanity and directly relevant to seeing sickness, suffering, violent struggle, and death (both natural and human evils) as structural deformities in nature that need redeeming. The eschatological aspect of the New Testament writings (e.g., Matt. 24–25; Col. 1:15–20;

employs in one's scientific theories. If evil—at cosmic (devil), natural (death), and human (sin) levels—cannot be understood as exogenous to reality and as entering into the world in history (and not as eternal truths), then the entire narrative of Christian salvation is profoundly incoherent.[20]

On the face of it, it does not seem likely that the truth of an Adamic fall is an optional component of a genuinely Christian understanding of cosmic meaning and the narrative arc of biblical salvation history.[21] Even so, I am aware that there are cunning ways of seeking to integrate a strongly mythic (atemporal yet in some manner historical) notion of the Adamic fall with orthodox theology; the "Christology is protology" approach taken by Conor Cunningham is impressive on that front.[22]

Speaking here as a creedally orthodox Christian theologian, I have no interest in weighing in on the details of how the truth claims of our present natural history knowledge constructs, within a reductively naturalistic set of interpretive commitments, may or may not be compatible with the truth claims

---

Rev. 21:1–4) is a hope for the redemption of creation; the overcoming of natural, human, and demonic evil; and the establishment of a new natural and heavenly order. Again, while such a hope is entirely delusional to the categories of thought native to modern, reductively physical scientific naturalism, if you extract this aspect of orthodox Christian doctrine from Christian belief, what you are left with is no longer recognizable as creedal orthodoxy.

20. In this text I am presupposing what Gustaf Aulén calls a *Christus Victor* account of soteriology.

21. See J. Smith, "What Stands on the Fall?" Smith writes, "The grammar of Christian theology encapsulates the biblical narrative in a plot that begins with the goodness of creation, a fall into sin, redemption of all things in Christ, and the eschatological consummation of all things. . . . The principal way a community discerns whether theological developments are 'faithful extensions' of the tradition is by determining whether such developments are consistent with this core 'plot'" (51).

22. See Cunningham, *Darwin's Pious Idea*, 377–421. Here Christ is, atemporally, not only Saint Paul's second Adam but the first Adam as well. And if Christ is the true archetype for Adam (which is the only orthodox Christological stance available), then, so Cunningham argues, there is no need for a historical Adam at the temporal start of the human race, such that Eden prophetically and poetically points *forward* to Christ rather than backward to some historical time and place. Hence, Darwin's pious idea of evolutionary biology—in which death, disease, agonistic struggle, and suffering are the archaic principles of life on earth from its primordial, temporal start until now—is happily compatible with orthodox Christology. On the other hand, Aaron Riches upholds the idea that historicity is inherently entailed in Christian theology and that Adam must be understood by orthodox theology as a real historical person. See Riches, "Mystery of Adam," where he writes, "The Christian claim is at its core incarnate, personal, and historically concrete, an inbreaking of God in the middle of time. It presumes that God in Christ receives his incarnate and historical being from a pre-existing and carnal history. The history of Christ has a carnal root. That carnal root is the first man, who is the *figura* of the *Figura* to come. . . . The inscrutable mystery of the origin of human history is betrayed by a theological imagination overly determined by contemporary science, whether this takes the form of a tortured conceptual synthesis, the reduction of Adam to a metaphor, or in the creationist rejection of scientific evidence" (128, 135).

of an orthodox Christian belief in the fall of both humanity and nature. That is a subtle and complex matter. But I will say at a general level that our post-nineteenth-century, reductively naturalistic conception of natural history is not theologically neutral, and—over a much longer time scale—the categories of sin and evil, as exogenous historical inbreakings that must be managed rather than as eternal truths that must be accepted, are profoundly important in shaping Western legal and political institutions to this day.[23]

But before going further, it is important to underscore that no view of the origins of humanity is ever a-mythic or a matter of simple objective facts.

8.8 On Finding What You Are Looking for—the "Myth" of Epistemic Neutrality

Without delving too deeply into the dynamics of hermeneutic formation, some quick comments on epistemic neutrality are in order. In any epistemic enterprise you will find (or fail to find) only what you are looking for. If the metaphysical and theological presuppositions of our knowledge framework exclude divine light, exclude scriptural revelation, exclude divinely inspired wisdom (*Understanding II*) as real modes of reality awareness; if we cannot see value or purpose in a purely material nature; if we believe in advance that miracles are inherently impossible—then trying to make the truth claims of creedally orthodox Christian faith compatible with such natural knowledge is going to have a profoundly distorting impact on Christian theology. I would go so far as to say that any child of a marriage between reductively natural-istic science and orthodox Christian theology is not going to be recognizably Christian as judged by the ancient rule of the Nicene Creed. The only way a creedally Christian understanding of truth can be compatible with modern science is if the presumption of reductively materialist naturalism is not taken as the lens for our vision of nature itself and is not used as a tool to redescribe, ignore, or debunk revealed and mythic high truth.

Not taking reductively physical naturalism as an interpretive *a priori* is something that the secularized scientific establishment (established by Huxley et al.) will not now readily countenance. If that is the case, then it is up to Christians to do their own science. In my estimation, Young Earth Creation-ism's attempt to do something like this is characterized, to date, by an aston-ishing array of theological and scientific train wrecks. But what that enterprise

---

23. It has been a long time since the Western Christian doctrine of original sin as a valuable and active concept for legal and political institutional formation in Western modernity has received serious scholarly attention. The most recent exposition of this nature that I know of is Butterfield, *Christianity and History*.

has gotten admirably right is an awareness that the broader metaphysical tilt of reductively physicalist modern science is in opposition to the most foundational truth commitments of creedal Christian theology. Perhaps, over time, something constructive might emerge out of the reactive and highly modernist theologico-scientific adventures of post-1920s, evangelical, fundamentalist Christianity.[24] On the other hand, tidy sympathetic harmonizations between reductively physical naturalism and orthodox Christian belief usually politely bypass the genuinely difficult nature of creedal orthodoxy's relationship with modern science, particularly as it concerns human nature and the meaning of moral and religious consciousness and actions. There needs to be tension in this relationship if Christian orthodoxy is to resist simply sliding off the plain of orthodox truth in order to make itself compatible with the metaphysical tilt of respectable reductively naturalistic scientific orthodoxy. Addressing this tilt when there is such an intrinsically complex relationship between the pre-modern meanings of Scripture and the cultural conditions of the present generation and reception of scientific meaning is no easy matter at all.

The Christian faith has been around for two thousand years and by now is expressed within almost every cultural context on earth. Accordingly, Christian faith exhibits an enormous range of contextualized interpretive variations. And as it is a historically and culturally situated faith that yet claims a transcendent source of truth above all human culture, this diversity of interpretive expression is basic to it. Yet there is a difference between variation and multiplicity. For the variations to remain Christian and for there to remain only one, holy, catholic, and apostolic church, the original framing of Christian orthodoxy—in the work and ministry of Christ, in the New Testament writings of the apostolic era, and in the primary doctrinal definitions of creedally orthodox faith—must retain a culturally embedded primacy over the variations that follow. Transcendence, revelation, miracles, and a created cosmos with meaning and purpose gifted to it from God, native to that early milieu, remain basic to Christian theology in whatever milieu it subsequently takes root. There are—and have always been—lines that delineate variation from multiplicity. Trying to make Christian orthodoxy compatible with, say, the reductive naturalism of a Democritean atomist in late classical times would have been just as heretical then as it would be now. However you try to spin it, the Christian faith is simply not compatible with naturalism defined by

---

24. There is nothing medieval or pre-modern about Young Earth Creationism. To the contrary, this modern and primarily Protestant form of natural theology is in clear continuity with James Ussher's seventeenth-century reductively positivist historiographical biblical chronology and William Paley's eighteenth-century extrinsic and mechanistic natural theology.

reductive materialism. Yet saying this still dodges the questions: Was there a historical Adam and Eve? Was there a historical fall in the mythic past?

I have danced around these questions to this point for a very serious reason: the shibboleth reason. I will go on to attempt some answers to these questions, but not without first noting the shibboleth dynamic involved in *any* answers given to these questions.

8.9 Eden and the Shibboleth Dynamic

Any answer to questions about the relation of natural history and human history to Adam and Eve is a shibboleth. The term *shibboleth* comes from the Hebrew Scriptures. Judges 12:5–7 recounts a terrible battle between two Semitic tribes, the Ephraimites and the Gileadites. The Gileadites had the upper hand and controlled the fords of the river Jordan. When the fleeing Ephraimites tried to cross the fords to go home, the Gileadites would ask them to say the word *shibboleth* to work out if they were Gileadites or Ephraimites. This is because the Ephraimites did not have the *sh* sound in their dialect. When the fleeing Ephraimites said *shibboleth* the wrong way ("sibboleth"), they were killed on the spot.

A shibboleth, then, is a spoken sign that identifies you to the questioner as belonging to "us" or to "them." We might like to think we are not as barbaric as Bronze Age vendetta warriors, but actually, when it comes to culturally assumed (yet strangely fragile) first truth commitments, we are usually every bit as herd orientated as everyone else in human history.

A significant feature of the shibboleth dynamic is that it assumes there are only two camps one could belong to, only two riverbanks one could come to rest on. Should one give an answer to a shibboleth question that neither opposing side finds comprehensible, being drowned by both sides is the only likely outcome.

I am going to give an answer to the question about the facts of natural history and human history and their relation to the Edenic myth that is not going to be acceptable to either identifiable side on this topic. This is because the discourse of facts assumed by both flag-waving, opposing camps on this issue does not allow for any third alternative. In one camp, Young Earth Creationists assume a modern historical positivism as regards the factual truth of the Edenic myth; in the other camp, Christian and non-Christian Old Earth Evolutionists also assume a modern historical positivism as regards the factual falsity of the Edenic myth.

I will try and proceed without being either for or against either of the normal camps, because I am seeking a different sort of understanding of historically true myth than either of these camps allow. But because, to both camps, there is so much riding on the answer to this question, being for or against one or the other camp is almost inevitably how I will be heard. That is, competing camps in this matter feel that the very category of truth itself, and the subsidiary categories of valid knowledge and cosmological meaning, are entailed in how one answers these questions.

The first truth commitment of the Young Earth Creationists (YECs) is to the divinely given authority of the Scriptures. They understand this gift as delivered in the literal truth of the biblical record, and this is something they cannot sacrifice and still make sense of the world. To interpret the Scriptures through the lens of evolutionary naturalism, such that ancient-world accounts of creation and cosmic catastrophes are read as non-historical mythic fantasies in order to harmonize the Scriptures with present scientific knowledge, is understood by YECs as placing present human knowledge above divine revelation. And yet YECs are Thomistic enough to hold that natural knowledge and special revelation cannot contradict each other, so natural philosophy should be carefully subordinated to divine revelation where there is dissonance between them. This they have endeavored to do. Further, the history of scientific theory *does* display continuous change and development, as there are always features of the natural world that our present theories find anomalous. There are then reasonable grounds not to be overwhelmed by the assumed incontrovertible truth of the present reductively naturalistic state of scientific theory in the life sciences (which also has lifeworld implications as regards ethics and metaphysics that seem incompatible with ethical and metaphysical biblical revelations).

The first truth commitment of scientific mainstream Christians (Old Earth Evolutionists, OEE) who are knowledgeable in contemporary evolutionary biology is to credible truth itself, holding that Christ is "the truth" and therefore all truth is derived from the *Logos* of God. To fearlessly respect truth, wherever and however one finds it, is to respect Christ. If the carefully established facts credibly show us that evolutionary biological scientific theory is highly persuasive, and true as far as we can presently understand, then to refuse to concede that truth for religious reasons is to bring the truth of the Christian revelation and the gospel itself into disrepute. Myth and science can be harmonized by recognizing that they do different sorts of things and that the Scriptures are not science textbooks (Genesis is ancient lore).

Intriguingly, it is not in the area of basic theological commitments that I have any problem with either YECs or OEEs. The YEC religion-to-science first truth interpretive commitment (grounded in a theology of scriptural revelation) and the OEE unity-of-truth commitment (grounded in a Christian

Logos theology of cosmic meaning) are stances I agree with. What I disagree with both YECs and OEEs about is their modern Western voluntarist, nominalist, and pure-matter philosophies of science. And ironically, it is the unity of both stances in their view of what constitutes scientific proof and credible public truth that enables both sides to unite against any voice raised to offer a third alternative to YEC and OEE on the historicity of biblical myth. Like probably all major issues in the US culture war, the submerged assumptions that both "sides" share is where the real problems lie, and the heavily fought-over flash-point issues are actually second-order consequences of the same underlying problems. In general, progressives and conservatives alike are modernists—defined by the secular revolution of the late nineteenth century and captives of modern epistemological outlooks that are theologically and metaphysically inadequate.

So, bracing myself for a double drowning by both YECs and OEEs, let us proceed to the questions: Was there a historical Adam and Eve? Was there a historical fall in the mythic past?

8.10 Myth and History—Adam and the Fall

To give any sort of answer to the above two questions, I am rather forced to move to the first person so as to limit the scope of any attempted answers to a horizon that does not exceed reasonable philosophical and theological ambitions. That is, I can only write about how I try to answer these questions, rather than presume to answer these question in any final or objective manner.

This is my position: I do not know how revealed myth relates to natural history and human historicity.[25] On that plane, I am prepared to be firmly committed to *not* knowing rather than to assume that Adam and Eve are historiographical and natural-history impossibilities because the present state of historical knowledge (framed as it is by the interpretive presuppositions of physically reductive naturalism) and the present state of evolutionary biology (again, framed by the theoretical presuppositions of physically reductive naturalism) tell me they must be non-historical mythic fantasies. This does not mean I have a disregard for the current theoretical understandings and

---

25. Socratic ignorance is an awareness of what you don't know. I'd like to think that in this mytho-epistemic domain my one superpower is that I am prepared to own up to Socratic ignorance. And as mentioned, Plato's dialogue on knowledge (the *Theaetetus*) ends by revealing just what an astonishing mystery any sort of knowledge is and how little our most penetrating attempts at understanding knowledge can actually be certain of. Piety and humility producing an openness to divine aid is the proper result of Socratic ignorance concerning knowledge, and this—Plato tells us—is what will enable us to travel further into truth than any proud and falsely mastered attempt to produce epistemic certainty by our own efforts.

careful observations of natural history and the biological sciences. Darwinian evolution is a very practical and helpful way of understanding how current ecosystems and organisms interact and how genetic variation, at least at an observable scale, works. Extrapolations back into the long distant past and into huge ranges of species variation on the basis of our current theories, knowledge, and dating techniques are highly sophisticated and—within the limitations of their theoretical assumptions—valid knowledge enterprises. (Origin-of-life extrapolations based on the present categories of our naturalistic theories of life, however, are remarkably hard to believe.)[26] Broadly, there seems to me to be no reason why a devoted and committed Christian could not be a very enthusiastic professor of zoology or biochemistry, and I happen to know such fine Christian professors myself. Yet, because natural philosophies are themselves constantly evolving, it would be a mistake to observe dissonance between the current state of scientific knowledge and doctrinal truths and immediately adapt doctrine to be compatible with the current state of natural philosophy. This sort of adaptation is particularly important to resist as regards a doctrinal category of such pivotal significance to our understanding of anthropology, cosmology, metaphysics, epistemology, morality, and soteriology as the doctrine of the fall.

I am also prepared to not know whether—as a matter of natural history— Adam and Eve fell, because the biblical grounds of my understanding of this matter are not written in the genre of either modern historiography or modern natural history. I cannot extrapolate from Scripture directly to our contemporary knowledge categories.

In historiographical and natural history terms, I am, then, *committed to not knowing* on the grounds of the philosophy of knowledge and biblical hermeneutics. I am a faith-based skeptic as regards contemporary historical and scientific knowledge concerning the fall. It strikes me as quite ironic that skepticism toward the transcendent is considered virtuous for the "enlightened scientist" but skepticism toward reductive naturalism is considered an escapist defect. For skepticism itself is neither a virtue nor a vice, but *why* one is skeptical about any particular proposition says a lot about where one's first truth commitments lie.

Theologically, however, the Christian understanding of the biblical fall is an essential aspect of the narrative arc of salvation history, crucially framing the very need for that salvation history, and also framing the **eschatological** hope of cosmic redemption that the Gospels promise. "Behold, the dwelling of God is with men. . . . He will wipe away every tear from their eyes, and death

---

26. See Tour, "Animadversions of a Synthetic Chemist."

shall be no more, . . . for the former things have passed away" (Rev. 21:3–4 RSV). The good news of the Christian gospel is that Christ has defeated death itself and that divine love is stronger than the grave. This hope is hardly something that modern Christians can outgrow and still have Christian faith. The doctrine of the fall of nature (see Rom. 8:18–25) is hardly peripheral to the Christian gospel and is explicitly linked by Paul to the doctrine of the resurrection of the dead at the last day. Nature itself is in need of redemption.

Bear in mind that *nature* is also a mythically embedded notion. Naturalisms always entail tacit cosmogenic and teleological interpretive commitments. This is because cosmogenic and teleological interpretive commitments are the culturally primary carriers of different conceptions of the origin, nature, and destiny of nature. Cosmogenic myths are primary here because—as Paul Ricœur points out—origins are always concerned with social order and with how knowledge, power, and morality are understood and practiced, particularly with regard to justice, guilt, and violence.[27]

Theologically, a real fall is inescapable to creedal orthodoxy. So while I do not *know* about the natural history of Adam and Eve one way or another, I *believe* in the Edenic fall, as a category of divinely revealed high understanding. The fall of humanity is a revealed high truth. As such, it always has greater epistemic authority than any passing theory of natural knowledge can generate for the Christian who treats the first truth commitments of their faith as genuinely true.

To a broadly Augustinian outlook in which understanding (β and δ) is (after the fall) "naturally" uncertain, this uncertainty does not give us reason to elevate the authority of more certain knowledge categories (α and γ) above understanding *if* we can gain some divinely graced access to revealed high truth (β situated partial articulations of δ). To the Christian, the church has been entrusted with the divine gospel and graced with the gift of revelation by the Spirit of Truth. The divine gifts of wisdom and belief have been breathed into the church through the work of God in history, as recorded in the inspired Scriptures, and as interpreted, in the light of that same Spirit, by spiritually enlightened believers. Christians can now access aspects of these first truths by exercising faith in the reception of these high-understanding gifts. That is, theologically it is *reasonable* to hold that faith, as the gift of God, carries a higher truth authority than the knowledge categories of modern science.

I am aware that this might look like a double-truth account—one in which the credible authorities of our present natural philosophy are considered functionally true, on their own terms, and yet may be contradicted by theologically

27. Ricœur, *Symbolism of Evil.*

orthodox revealed high truths, which also are true on *their* own terms. As I am, with Aquinas, committed to the unity of truth, this is not the case. Indeed, I hold that, as a truth of faith, the fall of humanity cannot be simply false as regards both natural history and human history. So while I remain genuinely agnostic about natural and evolutionary history as regards what is or could be reasonably knowable about the historical reality of the fall of Adam and Eve, my agnosticism is tilted toward belief in the Scriptures, rather than tilted toward the apparently myth-busting epistemic virtue of scientifically naturalistic doubt.

At this juncture we can see how religious faith and naturalistic skepticism are both alike and unalike. Faith and skepticism both maintain a certain commitment to agnosticism. On the other hand, faith entails a humble acceptance of a revelation that tilts one toward belief, whereas (if there really is a God) skepticism entails a proud epistemic autonomy that tilts one toward doubt. Determining whether one is inclined to receive the gift of faith because one trusts the transmission of divinely given doctrinal truth through the church, or whether one's faith is the result of a psychological credulity derived from infantile wish fulfillments, again, is beyond the domain of any supposedly theory-free knowledge. For my faith can only be seen as an infantile wish-fulfillment psychosis by the skeptic who is already theoretically *committed* (as a matter of practical faith) to reductive physicalism. Equally, my faith can only be seen as enabled by the light of God by the faithful believer who is already hermeneutically *committed* to a Christian understanding of the reality of high understanding and a transcendent God. Whichever way you go, there remain cracks in any ambition for full epistemic mastery. (Leonard Cohen has a point!) This, I think, is a genuinely open question that no one can close down. But as an interpretive juncture, it is open to much more than a starkly binary choice between a scientifically rigorous and skeptical reductive physicalism, on the one hand, and a pre-modern and intellectually sloppy fideistic illumination, on the other.

I am aware that how modern Western people like myself interpret ancient cosmogenic narratives as either mythic and non-factual or factual and non-mythic is highly problematic. What little I know of the ancient cosmologies, deep-time categories, and metaphysical and theological complexities of traditional Australian Aboriginal modes of knowing and understanding shows me that I am a genuine foreigner to the inner-meaning world of non-scientifically framed ancient cosmogenic narratives.[28] A certain respect for

28. See Minniecon and Marshall, "Indigenous Faith," for a special journal issue from a Christian perspective. See Yunkaporta, *Sand Talk*, for some riveting expositions of "Indigenous thinking" (what I would call Indigenous Australian metaphysics and epistemology).

that which we no longer adequately understand is equally important in these matters if we are to avoid the Whig hubris that we, happening to live in the present, are obviously more able to understand the truth than people were at any time in the past.[29]

Greek and Latin pre-modern traditions of high metaphysical and theological wisdom have Christian resources that can be brought to bear on the philosophy and theology of time that need to be recovered. Sotiris Mitralexis's very helpful exposition of Maximus the Confessor's theory of time is an excellent place to start if one wants to enter the truly demanding domain of trying to think as a Christian about revealed myth partially unveiling eternal realities in relation to what we might now call normal historical temporality.[30] As Lynn White Jr. points out, a profound breakdown in the modern understanding of the Christian relation of myth to historical time is the real rock on which modern Christian theology has been sunk. We can't just patch the hole up and refloat modern theology, as modern Christian theology has largely broken up and disintegrated as a result of that collision. Some very serious first-order rethinking needs to happen regarding how Christian theology understands the relation of the eternal to "ordinary" temporality.

I find that when I try and think about the relation of the eternal to the temporal, I—as a born-and-bred member of the modern lifeworld—am reflexively a reductive and linear historical temporalist. That is, I reflexively assume that *real* time is linear historical time, and that mythic narratives of super-temporal cosmic and essential "events" are imaginative human glosses pasted over the (scientific) reality of temporal events. I know this to be the wrong way around; theologically, essential and eternal reality is the ground of temporal and particular historical time. Yet I experience the world through a culturally formed temporalist lens that is as immanent and reductive about time as it is about matter. If it were possible for me to learn from an Aboriginal Christian brother about a Christian lifeworld understanding grounded in the priority of eternal mythic reality over linear and particular temporal events, I might make theological progress with the problem of Christian myth and modern Western history. That is a very demanding enterprise, and it requires a degree of humility from the dominant cultural frame of Western modernity toward those lifeworld perspectives we reflexively think of as backward, when, to the contrary, they are—in the real sense of the word—*primitive*. That is, pre-modern understandings of myth and time are the *primary* human

29. The basic point about an assumed overdetermined confidence in modern progress as put forward in Butterfield's classic little text remains, I think, relevant. See Butterfield, *Whig Interpretation of History*.

30. Mitralexis, *Ever-Moving Repose*.

understandings of myth and time, and modern reductively temporalist notions of historical facts are not at all progressive and "adult" advances that leave behind primitive and "childish" fairytales about eternity; they are delusional escapes from primitive truth (i.e., primary truth). I can make this claim confidently because just as reductive physicalism is astonishingly powerful instrumentally and yet self-destructive theoretically, so also modern temporal reductionism is astonishingly powerful instrumentally and self-destructive theoretically. But that is the topic of another book.

The long and short of the above is that it strikes me as still necessary, and viable, to uphold a traditional Christian theological epistemology—one formed by the distinctions and integrations of the common graces of reliable knowledge categories and the special graces of divinely gifted high theological understanding, as historically and culturally mediated to us via the complex mixture of grace and natural light within low understanding. Here faith (the *pistis* category in Plato's divided line analogy) is epistemologically necessary, yet (contra Plato) such "oh so human" faith as embedded in the church has a higher truth authority than non-church-derived fallen understanding. But if this much is granted, then it is also necessary for faith to have a higher epistemic authority than rational and empirical knowledge, as all knowledge is now inevitably theorized from the fallen epistemic understanding category of natural light. That is, creedally orthodox Christian theological epistemology makes it necessary to maintain a certain skeptical distance from the epistemic authority claims of modern (and, indeed, any) science as they unbelievingly impinge on doctrinal orthodoxy. So the fact that the fall must be historically and cosmologically impossible to materialistically reductive, naturalistically theorized science should be of no particular concern to a Christian. Conversely, disbelief in the historical reality of Adam and Eve, disbelief in a human fall, and disbelief in the fall of nature should not be embraced by the theologically orthodox Christian. The epistemic authority of faith as regards high wisdom should not be made subservient to the epistemic authority of fallen, reductively physicalist scientific theorizing.

8.11 Myth and Christian Theological Epistemology

The rich categories of the longest and deepest traditional insights of Western Christian theological epistemology presuppose the existence of both divine light and the fully transcendent source of that light—the ground of creation—God. This First Cause of intelligibility, goodness, actuality, energy, light, life, beauty, love, and meaning in the cosmos radiates the divine light that reveals a partial awareness to us of essential high truths. Christian theological epistemology also presupposes that there is a problem for human-ity in validly apprehending this high illumination, and that problem is not an essential reality but an exogenous-yet-cosmic interference that Christians call the fall. As a result of this interference, our theoretical understanding of our knowledge is impacted by sin. But our theoretical understanding can also be graced by the redemptive work of the Holy Spirit, either directly or as mediated through the church, nature, reason, and all human cultures. It is ill-advised—simply on philosophical and historical grounds—to take the "truths" of any humanly constructed natural philosophy too seriously; these "truths" continually change over time and are always theoretically couched in the best ideas we have currently available. They are also subject to struc-tural epistemic weakness. So it is theoretical knowledge that is a construct—something situated within culture, time, and the complexities of perception, language, imagination, and human reasoning. If we place human knowledge constructs as first truths and divinely given understandings as subsidiary to those truths, we will become apostate in very short order. The mythic, then, must be given higher truth authority than the scientific. This, of course, is heresy to the moral imperatives of objective and evidence-based scientific knowledge, as our culture's first truth discourse, as set up by Thomas Huxley and company. But, in the end, you have your choice of heresy; trying to be fully orthodox to incompatible first authority communities is not going to end well for anyone.

Adam and Eve and the fall in the garden of Eden are mythic truths for Christian theological epistemology. These are truths we cannot discard or render as primitive fantasies so as to make Christian faith compatible with a functionally materialist and inherently agonistic and amoral view of natural reality and human origins. And indeed, the reductively materialist outlook does not escape mythological meaning either. There are only a few basic mythic options when it comes to the essential nature of reality, and while they might all be wrong, they can't all be right. Whichever view we embrace has profound lifeworld-ordering consequences. Choices have to be made in this regard, and systems of knowledge that construct useful theories about "natural truth" are not the basis but the outcome of such choices. Nature speaks back to our theories, of course, and so some of our theories are proved better than others at certain levels of understanding, but none of our theories are ever as complete as we might hope. Those exploring the edges of what our theories explain tend to be more aware of the ocean of mystery that sits outside the narrow terms of our best attempts to under-stand reality than those of us who never feel the desire or interest to look beyond what we think we can explain or at least instrumentally master. To the true child at heart, the true scientist, the true artist, the excitement of wonder never goes away.[31]

This chapter has sought to unpack a point of serious friction between the overt mythic framing of traditional Christian theological epistemology and a supposedly post-mythic, reductively materialist naturalism out of which our prevailing respectable science of human origins is now theorized. I hope I have shown that this tension is not simply resolvable, but also that this lack of resolution should not be feared by the Christian. We do not have to pretend that there is no problem here, nor that the problem requires one to choose between faith that is entirely separated from natural philosophy or natural philosophy that is entirely separated from faith (as if such a separation were possible). Perhaps, even, tension is a good thing here. Without friction between the bow and the string, the violin does not sing.

Moving on from here: How might we imagine a new sort of interface between Christian theology and science? Perhaps as a relationship of constructive friction.

31. See Desmond on astonishment in *The Voiding of Being*, chap. 3, "The Dearth of Astonishment: On Curiosity, Scientism, and Thinking as Negativity."

Recovering an Integrative Zone

Thinking about the need for a more complex interactive zone for Christian theology and natural philosophy than current "science and religion" possibilities allow, let us start by circling around that most touchy of post-Victorian mythologies: the demand and right for the complete autonomy of science from theology.

The autonomy of science from theology sits within the mythic and essential truth categories of our post-Victorian lifeworld. By "essential" I here mean "an idea about essence" purporting to belong to an eternal truth category properly at home in the high *Understanding II* category of wisdom (see fig. 7.2, p. 117), which then filters down into the cultural-belief domain via imaginative mythic narratives. That is, we have acquired a commonly assumed cultural belief about the archetypal nature of science that is *essentially* autonomous from the archetypal nature of theology. Further, the assumed essential difference in the "natures" of science and theology is now a normative difference (theology is backward and bad as a primary truth discourse; science is progressive and good as a primary truth discourse). There is also something of a realized eschatological dynamic to the prevailing mythos of the triumph of science over theology, complete with its own historical narrative arc. Thus it is culturally understood that, after a long struggle, scientific truth has broken free from superstitious theological oppression so that we now live in the enlightened age of factual scientific truth.

As with all mythic archetypes, the essential natures of science and theology must be grasped by inspiration and then embodied in the great men and women

157

who then live these truths out before us, partially materializing the eternal in the concrete and the temporal.[1] The pope—however nice and intelligent he may personally be—is still something of an archon of theological darkness in the mythic landscape constructed by the agnostic and atheist late-Victorian architects of the age of science. To those architects, Galileo and Newton are archons of illumination and truth. These iconic figures personify the mythos of science, and even though they had their own personal religious convictions, they are famous for rejecting the claims of authorized theology to define truth.

Cultural myths are complex and powerful things. If theology wants to reclaim an interactive relationship with science (and in some regards, a governing relationship with science), I can see no way around a mythic clash of the first degree between the frames of meaning that put either science or theology as first truth discourses. We proceed into highly volatile terrain.

9.1 The "Myth" of the Autonomy of Science from Theology

This topic is particularly touchy for Christians working professionally in science. The natural right of science to complete autonomy from theology has enormous cultural power as a function of the highly successful origins myth of modern science, as imagined by Thomas Huxley's X Club and others in late Victorian times. According to their origins myth, modern enlightened scientists, upholding the cause of objective and humane reason, have long been engaged in a titanic struggle against the oppressive, truth-stifling remnants of Dark Age religious superstition. Here science, struggling for intellectual independence against moribund Aristotelian philosophy (and speculative metaphysical moonshine in general) and fighting for its life against a backward-facing and authoritarian church, finally shakes itself free from superstitious and ignorant religion. This origin myth is integral with what, since the mid-twentieth century, we have come to call the Scientific Revolution.[2]

1. Peter Harrison, in his very helpful *Territories of Science and Religion*, points out that neither science nor religion are natural kinds, and neither term is amenable to positive or trans-historical definition. So the cultural creation of the territories of science and religion is a historically contingent collective fiction that governs the post-Victorian secular technological lifeworld in which we now live. However, while there are no positive or trans-historical definitions for science and religion, there really are mythic and essential definitions within the prevailing cultural imaginary. But such definitions are outside the knowledge categories in which modern historiography functions. The relationship between modern historiography and the invisibility of the mythic in its own essentialist categories (ironically, *because* Christian myth is historically embedded) means that history itself can no longer help us much in grappling with *any* sort of essentialist cultural reality.

2. Steven Shapin famously opens his exploration of this twentieth-century nomenclature thus: "There was no such thing as the Scientific Revolution, and this is a book about it" (*Scientific*

Here, scientists are brave seekers of truth, unflinchingly and morally committed to nothing but evidentially demonstrated truth, and fundamentalists and papists are trying to cling to inexorably vanishing pre-modern religious authorities. These wrong-facing religionists are the truth-terrified upholders of intellectual darkness, regressive morality, and oppressive power. In keeping with this profoundly moralistic and archetypal conflict narrative, the autonomy of science from theology is the most sacred article of modern scientistic faith. This origin myth and its first doctrine have become deeply embedded in the academic culture of secular modernity and define its tacit orthodoxy and cultus. So science *must* be autonomous from theology because theology is essentially the evil enemy of science. Ironically, secular myth and a deeply habituated "religious" formation in secular orthodoxy now rule the academy unchallenged.

But the above is a historically false myth. As is well understood by historians of science, Huxley's origin myth has no correlation with the actual history of modern science. Christian theology is actually the mother of modern Western science. Christian theology has had—in the past—complex ways of delineating and integrating itself with natural philosophy, and there is nothing inherently bad for science about such a relationship. There is no need to see Huxley's myth narrative about the intrinsic autonomy of science from theology as anything other than politically motivated (and highly successful) propaganda. Huxley wanted to dislodge the clergy from their prominent positions of cultural influence in the universities and broader society of his time, and in this he was amazingly successful. Let us, then, think about Christian theology and science without assuming Huxley's mythic archetypes, and without maintaining a super touchy fear about preserving the autonomy of glorious liberationist scientific truth from the superstitious intrusions of religious villainy. For this myth is simply false.

9.2 Obstacles to Recovering the Integration of Knowledge and Understanding

Knowledge I and *II* epistemic categories (see fig. 7.2, p. 117), as practiced by modern scientists, will yield genuine epistemic light at the level of perception-dependent and mathematically reasoned truth. At this level, science is, and

---

Revolution, 1). Shapin begins this book with a quick exploration of the history of the term "Scientific Revolution," finding that it does not come into common use until 1939, in the writings of Alexandre Koyré. Shapin's point is not that enormous changes in natural philosophy don't happen. To the contrary, because change is continually happening in natural philosophy, the present state of understanding is always deeply continuous with the past out of which it arises.

should be, entirely autonomous from Christian theology. However, natural philosophy is never a matter of merely empirical facts and rational operations. This is because theory is never simply a matter of objective scientific observation or mathematical necessity. Theory is an inescapably imaginative and interpretive act of the meaning-discerning mind. A scientific theory is never within the domain of empirical purity or rational purity, but it sits unavoidably in the lower domain of understanding. At this point, there should be integrative possibilities that enable genuinely philosophical and theological understandings of meaning, purpose, and cosmic order (metaphysics and theology) to creatively interact with the factual and rational categories of *Knowledge I* and *II*.[3]

There are three obvious obstacles in even trying to recover the meaningful integration of knowledge and understanding in our academic culture. All these obstacles are a function of the territories construct: the late Victorian view of science and religion as fully discrete domains.

First, after the strict demarcation boundaries constructed by the remarkable reversal, scientific *theory* (as distinct from its empirical content and mathematical analysis) is largely operationally blind to its own theoretical premises. As a result, modern science typically thinks of belief and wisdom as either outside its domain or outside the domain of reality altogether. This readily results—particularly in the social sciences—in "science" recasting the meaning of human belief and wisdom traditions in the terms of functionally materialist and reductively naturalistic knowledge (Ockham's pincer). This also results, *per impossibile*, in the assumption that scientific theories have no interest in the meaningful interpretation of nature and give us only "pure" functional models that simply explain factual truths. That is, when it comes to thinking about understanding, practical and theoretical scientists are often entirely unaware that meaningful belief and wisdom are *always* theoretically integral with scientific knowledge and its use. Presuming (ironically) a mythic autonomy of science from understanding, scientists, academics, and policymakers now often have no educated expertise in the scholarly terrains native to understanding,[4] or they disbelieve that an understanding

3. Referring back to Thomas Nagel's *Mind and Cosmos* again, it seems that this analytical philosopher is disturbed by the reductively physicalist determination to exclude a genuinely intellective understanding of consciousness and a genuinely metaphysically ordered understanding of cosmos. The apparent justification of this outlook derives from applying the demonstration categories of modern science to all domains of meaning. Ironically, this has made "science" itself blind to the non-materially reductive natural realities of thought and natural meaning, those very realities that make science possible.
4. This is an understandable problem as modern and postmodern philosophy from the nineteenth century onward has also often been pre-defined by categories of empirical and rational

of truths actually exists. A physical cosmologist such as Stephen Hawking, for example, could not, on the one hand, see that contemporary cosmology had anything to say about the meaning of the cosmos. On the other hand, he would occasionally drop the odd anti-God-framed cosmological pronouncement, which was typically received as something akin to inspired utterance by adoring scientistic atheists.[5]

Second, the myth of science's interpretive neutrality, as well as science's tight domain demarcation from anything religious or philosophical, means that science is now dogmatically resistant to integrative possibilities with wisdom.[6] Within the academy, scientific orthodoxy is now methodologically pragmatic, probabilistic, secular, and objectivist, and this epistemic paradigm is now largely assumed to be equivalent with true knowledge itself. Here the theoretical norms of science as an epistemic master discourse are now governed by the presupposition of the complete domain autonomy of science from all meaning discourses—such as theology, philosophy, Indigenous epistemologies, or art. Scientific knowledge now *must* be theorized as structurally isolated from understanding, and human understanding itself now *must* be assumed to be inherently fragmented (and actually, this is very convenient for amoral instrumental pragmatists and cultural constructivists).

Third, all scientific meanings are now largely theoretically governed by an operationally materialist realism. Orthodox respectability within science is often dogmatically committed to the epistemic authority lens of reductive materialism alone (*sola reductions, sola atomica*). A certain reformist zeal seems apparent in denouncing any *real* epistemic salvation by means other than *sola reductions*, such that old-fashioned appeals to divine revelation or metaphysical wisdom are equivalent to witchcraft or, at the very least, an infantile bondage to superstitious anti-reason. This is reductive naturalism

---

knowledge, so academic philosophy itself does not seem to have any living appreciation of the West's high wisdom traditions, as functions of understanding.

5. I intend no slight against Hawking via this observation. Hawking was a wonderful communicator of theoretical physics, and I have enjoyed his books immensely, even though his theology is not something I think anyone should take seriously.

6. Interdisciplinary work between the sciences and the humanities does not often happen, though when it happens it is often deeply rewarding to both the scientists and the humanities scholars doing it, because, in fact, knowledge and understanding—in real life—simply *are* functionally integrative. Knowledge and understanding are only abstractly separated in the academy, and only fictitiously separated in our lifeworld, so as to structure a pragmatic and secular "realism" in the public domain and unrestrained personal freedom in the private domain as regards all value, belief, and meaning commitments. However, interdisciplinary scholarship now done by science and humanities academics lacks any unifying meta-narrative that theology used to provide to Western learning, so the exercise is inherently piecemeal as regards its overall significance.

as a first truth discourse that unifies the entire field of valid knowledge and rightly interpreted "objective" meaning. This is reductive naturalism as a functional metaphysics, as a functional wisdom discourse, as a functional doctrinal orthodoxy (a theology even), but using only the language and epistemic categories of "objective science."

Putting the above three obstacles together, we can see that science is often unconsciously theoretically loaded away from engagement with the West's long wisdom traditions, and particularly—since late Victorian times—loaded against having any truth commerce with the West's own Christian theological belief and wisdom traditions. This makes it incredibly challenging to open up genuinely robust spaces for the understanding categories of Christian theology to engage with the knowledge and uses categories of modern science and technology in the zones where such engagement is most needed—theory and ethics. But Christian theology must insist on the need for such zones of engagement and must insist on engagement in terms not defined by natural-philosophy assumptions incompatible with Christian theology, however much academic orthodoxy may find this insistence heretical.

9.3 Christian Theology's Need for an Integrative Zone for Knowledge and Understanding

Using the categories of Christian theological epistemology outlined in chapter 7, it is clear that perception and mathematics, minimally theorized, and applied to measurable and observable phenomena, should be happily autonomous from Christian theology. Indeed, historically, Christian theologians have usually had a strong respect for observable facts and a careful appreciation of logically necessary relations. However, there really can be no such thing as theoretical autonomy between the domains of understanding and natural knowledge. This point needs to be underscored.

Scientific theorizing premised on reductively materialist naturalism, particularly as it relates to human meaning and behavior, is not, in any sense, pure and theologically neutral knowledge. Consider, for example, social Darwinism, eugenics, rational economic behavior theories, political science premised on amoral realism, reductively physicalist conceptions of mind, human resource management, advertising psychology, and the powerful communication- and behavior-conditioning technologies of social media. The theoretical understandings of natural meanings that guide these applied sciences are profoundly theory laden and normatively inflected—particularly when their normativity framework is defined by profit-driven amoral instrumentalism—in ways that cannot be attributed to facts and logic alone. When it comes to religious studies, holding up an epistemic lens that is cut by an inherently spiritually antagonistic theoretical naturalism to religious phenomena will reveal precisely nothing about any engagement of the divine with the human. Presumably, the divine is reasonably important to "religious" people themselves in *their* understanding of what "religion" actually is. Such a science of religious behavior systemically treats religious people as delusional. But even more troubling, simply accepting a tacitly atheistic theoretical stance on the meaning of nature is profoundly at odds with a Christian understanding of a wisdom-integrated *theoria* of nature. The Christian believes that the divine undergirding of nature is real, that meaning and purpose within nature, while transcendently sourced, are real, and that humans really are embodied immortal souls. Reductive naturalism theorizes the most significant features of reality out of a Christian understanding of a meaningful factual knowledge of nature. In what sense, then, can a Christian maintain that science theorized by reductive naturalism gives us a real understanding of nature?

What now seems to be endemic to academic knowledge, as defined only by the criteria of modern science, is that academic knowledge elevates science itself firmly above the domain of natural factual knowledge and into the domain of metaphysics and theology. As all *theoria* is of the domain of understanding, scientific theory as a belief- and wisdom-governed activity is not itself problematic, but it is the imposition of reductively naturalistic empirical and rationalist epistemic categories onto the domain of understanding that is the problem here. To Christian theology, the proper order of human meaning is inverted when knowledge categories disingenuously presume to define understanding (*theoria*). It is the domain of understanding that should be seeking to discern the meaning of the empirical and logical awareness that knowledge provides us with. If scientific theory and the materialist interpretation of human meanings and human thought and action were recognized as explicitly belief- and wisdom-embedded activities, this would greatly assist in making it possible for Christian theology to enter the terrain of scientific theory on its own understanding terms.[7]

Science has, in point of fact, no autonomy from interpretive theories of nature, and so scientific theories have, in point of fact, no genuine autonomy from theology. Empirical data collection and the mathematical modeling and analysis of empirical data is reasonably functionally autonomous from theory *until* that data is meaningfully interpreted (until it enters the domain of

7. Of course, this cannot be coherently done. Reductive materialism cannot accept that there are genuinely transcendent wisdom categories, or genuinely qualitative and meaningful belief categories analogically related to wisdom, and remain reductive materialism.

scientific theory).[8] So data collection and the detection and organization of rational structures in data sets is functionally theory minimal, and therefore its autonomy from theology is entirely laudable. But this is not our problem. Our problem is that functionally anti-theological empiricist and rationalist theory takes on the role of our master understanding discourse.

9.4 Rejecting the Sublimation of Understanding into Knowledge

Reductively materialist *theoria*—as a metaphysical stance—can lay no legitimate claim to a monopolistic interpretive role in defining valid scientific knowledge.[9] Yet functionally materialist "science," as our culture's first knowledge discourse, does play this monopolistic theoretical role in our academies. A category-confusing sleight of hand is going on here such that a simple correspondence is falsely assumed between valid scientific theory and the interpretive assumptions of metaphysical materialism. The trick goes like this.

The low natural category of understanding (β) perceives value, purpose, and meaning in particularized and spatiotemporally located categories. Because this is a category in the tangible lower portion of Plato's divided line, such qualities and meanings are known extrinsically through perception as regards an "objective" understanding, and culturally as regards interpretations of "subjective" meaning as framed by historical, relational, and linguistic contexts. This gives low understanding a natural affinity with low natural light (α, perception). Our reasoning powers also notice order in the observable world and in our social worlds. Thus low divine light (γ, mathematics) teams up with low natural light and usually simply assumes the interpretive-reality framework of its cultural context. When that framework presupposes functional materialism, the high wisdom category (δ) becomes entirely lost to view, as do the first-order realities of intelligibility, quality, and transcendence native to high wisdom. A loss of such awareness makes it seem "natural" to judge the categories of human meaning (β) in terms of perception (α) and logic (γ) alone. But where the real *meaning* of human meaning is reductive materialism, this is an inherently misleading sublimation of high theoretical truth

8. In point of fact, empirical data collection cannot be theory-free either. What data you are looking for, what data you expect to find, how you collect and mathematically model data, what data you consider you are entitled to know, even how you understand who or what "gives" the data (from *datum*, meaning "given") to you—all of these are theory-laden enterprises.
9. This is not just true for Christian thinking, which presupposes a transcendent God and a created cosmos gifted with divine intelligibility; it is true across the board. For a powerfully argued metaphysical rejection of reductively physicalist anti-metaphysics from a British idealist, see Bradley, *Appearance and Reality*. For a strongly argued postmodern rejection of the monopolistic meta-claims of scientific truth, see Lyotard, *Postmodern Condition*.

categories into the domain of perception and logic. This produces a phony high wisdom, which is actually not operative within the categories of high understanding at all. This faux high insight pretends to be a simple factual knowledge that theorizes the *real* meaning of all knowledge and understanding in empirically perceived and rationally analyzed materialist categories. This is a reversal of traditional ways of understanding the relationship between wisdom and knowledge. Traditionally, the meaning of the low understanding category is intellectually theorized as analogically related to and derived from the high understanding category of universal and transcendent conceptions of cosmic order, intrinsic value, final purpose, and essential meaning.

This confusion of categories, and this confusion of directional relationships between categories, is possible because human understanding as we actually experience it is inherently integrated across all four of Plato's awareness categories in the divided line analogy. Given this integration, confusion in these matters is inherently likely if high human epistemic categories are in any way dulled or broken. And clearly—whether one is theological about this or not—connections between perception and mathematics in *Knowledge I* and *II*, and natural and high understandings of value, meaning, and purpose in *Understanding I* and *II*, are now epistemically contestable in their very nature (Christian theology sees this as a function of the fall). In this context, the true meaning of the world remains inherently open to interpretation. This is why reductively materialist metaphysics is theoretically possible and should be given a seat at the theoretical table. Yet a "closed" scientific theorizing that presumes a reductively material meta-narrative for the theoretical interpretation of nature is overstepping its proper domain. Equally, Christian theology that theorizes divine causes defining true value, cosmic meaning, and ultimate human purpose is an "open" epistemic category in the context of our fallen natural epistemic powers. Christian theology now enjoys no first-philosophy status in Western modernity, so the integrative zone between first philosophy and natural philosophy is going to be genuinely pluralistic in this cultural context. But here we have the problem that the more linear, methodologically agreed, and bivalent knowledge and analysis categories of modern science have come to culturally define knowledge itself such that a non-pluralistic theoretical space is assumed to be required of genuine knowledge. Hence, science tends to impose reductively materialist naturalism as if it is a neutral unifying framework for valid *theoria*.

The outcome of this for the way Christian theology's theoretical wisdom heritage should seek to integrate itself with the knowledge discourse of modern science is that the proof categories appropriate to *Knowledge I* and *II* should not be assumed to apply to *any* theoretical framework as regards the

interpretation of nature. Proof (or instrumental viability, or statistical probability) as truth is fine for *Knowledge I* and *II* categories, but the assumption
that proof, probability, and instrumental power equate to truth in the domains
of understanding is simply false. Such an assumption is a fundamental category error, defining the qualitative and the intellective in the terms of the
quantitative and the material. This is not a realistic interpretive outlook at
all, because it disappears all those qualities, meanings, intelligibilities, and
purposes that are necessary to produce a truth-seeking natural philosophy in
the first place. Understanding should not be sublimated into knowledge. To
do so is to deny the possibility of intelligible theory itself.

The corollary of the above observation is that when it comes to theory,
understanding must (and actually always does) take interpretive and theoretical priority over knowledge. Understanding must interpret knowledge in
the categories of understanding. Of course, there is continuous interactive
communion between understanding and knowledge in human awareness
such that each is meaningless without the other.[10] However, when it comes
to theory, the discourse of science needs to be in some manner framed by an
inherently meaningful view (*theoria*) of nature itself. Without being up front
about having such a framing, two things happen: (a) knowledge cannot be
integrated into a meaningful vision of nature, thus it becomes fragmented
and meaningless, and (b) a meaningless frame of nature ends up being used
to interpret the world, leading to the demise of intelligible understanding.

In the history of modern science, the discarding of a distinctive meaning-
of-nature framework—Christian Aristotelianism—is seen as greatly liberating
the new ratio-empirical experimental knowledge. This is true. But, historically,
the first two centuries of the new natural philosophy were not advanced in a
theoretical or theological vacuum. Christian cosmology, metaphysics, and,
most importantly, eschatology and anthropology remained in place as Aristotelian metaphysics was displaced. The early modern desire to denude nature
of any ontological underpinning, any magical power, and any metaphysical
overshadowing—and hence to separate speculation and faith from reason,
and perception from piety and morality—was theologically driven. Once this
self-standing bare nature is revealed and a purely instrumental knowledge is
unleashed, the colonial conquest of the entire globe abroad and the Industrial
Revolution at home can proceed at pace. For, theologically, nature in the early
modern world was already seen as an arena for epistemic and political domination. The fearless application of calculative experimental knowledge—as

10. Aquinas's fondness for Aristotle's dictum "there is nothing in the mind that was not first
in the senses" well illustrates the unity of human awareness itself.

power *over* nature—was driven by a theological conception of the Principality of Man.[11] Here, Man has a divine mandate to rule, fill, and subdue the
earth. In exercising his sovereign will over nature, Man achieves his *imago
Dei*. Francis Bacon's guiding vision of recovering Adamic mastery over nature,
and bringing on the end times through the advancement of knowledge, was
indeed the theoretical star guiding the new learning.

This theological and anthropological vision, with its theoretical role in
underpinning and unifying modern science and technology, has been secularized and fully naturalized, but it has not gone away. We do in fact have a
theoretical framework of meaning integral to the advancement and use of
modern science. The early modern conception of the *imago Dei* got modern science into outer orbit, but that booster has now fallen away. We are,
however, still in flight because of its powerful initial thrust and its ongoing
momentum.

I will not follow this very interesting trajectory any further here.[12] But what
is clear for the larger argument of the book at this point is that the natural relationship between understanding and knowledge requires the higher-meaning
discourse to be understanding. If science refuses to be theoretically shaped
by theology, this is not because theology is misbehaving; it is because science
is misunderstanding the proper relation of theory to knowledge. But how
then might we set up a viable space in which the understanding categories

11. I am here drawing on Walter Wink's Anabaptist analysis of "the powers." The idea here
is that what the New Testament calls "principalities and powers" are the super-institutional,
super-cultural structures of power in which we live. In modernity, the categories of power that
were integral with the new natural philosophy that we now call modern science were explicitly
embedded in a gendered notion of dominion *over* nature as shaped by a particular (and decisively non-Anabaptist) reading of the Genesis creation narrative. "Man" here, as a principality,
concerns the divine mandate given to humans to *rule and subdue* the earth. Even though we
are now more feminist and inclusive in our attitudes toward gender and human sexuality than
we were in the seventeenth century, we are arguably just as taken with an idea of human power
itself that remains remarkably masculinist and dominating. As Carolyn Merchant (*Death of
Nature*) points out, our scientific knowledge culture is a culture of dissecting, uncovering,
deconstructing, instrumental mastering, and calculative control. This is a culture that is profoundly shaped by the Baconian masculinist subjugation of Nature to the utility and will of
Man. The fact that Francis Bacon did not find women to be sexually attractive illustrates the
point that domination as a masculinist category, as integral with his understanding of natural
knowledge, is not a reductively sex-defined category. Here, rather than gender and sexuality
simply structuring power, more fundamentally, modern instrumental power structures gender
and sexuality. Baconian epistemic power over nature is foreign to the more sympathetic and
sacramental concepts of natural philosophy that modern science displaced. On the Anabaptist concept of "the powers," see any of Wink's four powers books. See, for example, Wink,
Engaging the Powers.

12. This is the Christian dominationist and eschatological trajectory that produced modern
science. I have followed this trajectory in Tyson, *Theology and Climate Change*.

of Christian theology can be constructively interfaced with the knowledge
categories of modern science?

9.5 Obstacles to Integrating Christian Theological Understanding with Scientific Knowledge

This is going to be easier and harder than we might expect. On the hard
side, there are three problems. First, there is mythic cultural inertia against
theology playing any sort of theoretical role in the interpretation of empirical data and mathematical relationships. This is not simply a function of the
myth of conflict but also has to do with specialist guild prestige. Any scientist
with suitable interest, it is thought, can read and understand theology, or
history, but you have to be a highly trained and—let's face it—an unusually
intelligent person to really know what you're doing with dense data sets and
sophisticated analytical mathematics. The scientist is the priest of the first
truth discourse of our times, so she is going to want to have the final say on
the real theoretical meaning of scientific data and its correct analysis. (Of
course, scientists *are* highly trained and often have advanced procedural and
mathematical intelligence, and the accurate interpretation of data in different fields of the sciences does require long familiarity and enculturation into
the specialist language and tacit acute awareness of the particular specialty
in question.) Second, within the deep enculturation world of the community
of scientists, the operational fiction of science being understanding-neutral
is largely assumed. Third, the integration of non-science-defined metaphysical and theological theories into the domain of natural knowledge is going
to blow up any neat sense of that very thing we like most about science—its
capacity to advance. For the strong introduction of transcendently framed
understanding back into knowledge will also reintroduce a theoretical complexity and theoretical pluralism back into natural philosophy that we have
not seen since the ancient Greco-Roman world.

We have looked at the "autonomy of science" myth. We have looked at how
reductively naturalistic scientific theory is anything but neutral in metaphysical
and theological categories. So let us now have a go at pluralism.

Scientific theory itself should be pluralistic and—overall—directionally
undefined, if the empirical and mathematical aspects of natural knowledge
are to be properly integrated into the inherently open-ended understanding
categories of human meaning. This is not really that hard a concept, or that
far removed from what we actually do. Think of psychology, for example. The
psychological exploration of despair in Kierkegaard's *Sickness unto Death* is
an explicitly Christian theorizing about the nature, meaning, and appropriate

therapy for the human soul.[13] Psychological research—using empirical evidence and mathematical analysis—framed by a theological theoretical outlook will have a distinctive set of characteristics that are significantly different from research consistent with the theoretical commitments of Jacques Lacan or B. F. Skinner. But this would not simply be a distinction between materialist psychological science and theistic psychological science, for Lacan and Skinner are not exactly compatible, just as Kierkegaard and Viktor Frankl are not exactly compatible. Interpretive structures and theoretical meanings are inherently overextended if extrapolated out in overtly totalizing terms.[14] But, alas, we are now deeply enculturated to (wrongly) assume that science is a single, unified, and linear first truth discourse of perpetually advancing knowledge.

This is a bit complex. The systematic and incremental advancement methodologies and the universal validity categories of modern science really are successful—and *very* successful—in providing ever better mathematical models about, and ever more instrumental power over, physical nature. This success, however, masks the pluralist and directionless features of modern science that are also intrinsically present. Paul Feyerabend's detailed studies show a genuine anarchy in scientific knowledge that "advances" down linear pathways and theoretical frameworks in multiple directions, while never finally arriving at truth. However practically wondrous new scientific discoveries, theories, and inventions are, science itself does *not* advance in a singular, unified, and linear fashion. Instead, it grows in multiple theoretical[15] directions all the time, until various lines fall over and new lines start, and its only guiding principle is taking hold of whatever works in solving theoretical problems and gaining more empirical evidence, more calculative power, and more mastery over nature. Feyerabend is in no sense an enemy of scientific progress when he explains that "the only principle that does not inhibit progress is: anything goes."[16]

Our faith commitment that *science advances* is tied back—in a religiously appropriate manner—to that conviction's origins in Francis Bacon's eschatological convictions. This faith, however, is not clearly borne out (empirically!) in the history of science. To quickly qualify that observation, within a

13. See Evans, *Søren Kierkegaard's Christian Psychology.*
14. As a qualification, no theoretical truth claim avoids presupposing universality. No Kierkegaardian psychological truth claim would be a genuine truth claim if it were simply Kierkegaardian. However, as all truth claims are theoretically located, and no theory can presuppose that it alone is completely adequate for fully mastering truth, clarifying that a Kierkegaardian truth claim is as much a Kierkegaardian theoretical claim as a truth claim is important.
15. Here I mean "theoretical" as a technical subset of one basic theory—reductively naturalistic naturalism.
16. Feyerabend, *Against Method*, 7.

reductively physical theoretical umbrella, where epistemic mastery is rewarded by greater human powers of control over defined aspects of the natural world, science does indeed advance. But that science is a simple matter of incremental advance is not borne out in science's actual history, and to say that science is advancing toward truth (or anywhere in particular) is not actually possible within a theoretical framework that denies intelligible transcendent essence, and that denies any theological teleology to human knowledge that only an eschatological outlook can support.

Thinking about science that embraces theoretical pluralism in a far stronger manner than it currently does seems like resigning the myth of progress (which it actually is), and this seems like a terrible attack on the modern eschatological promises of Enlightenment reason (which, again, it actually is). This is, therefore, decidedly not welcome to the prevailing Enlightenment-framed secular naturalism and its mythic secular utopianism that unifies the scientific ideology of our age. So this is a hard problem.

But on the easy front, all that is being asked for in an integrative zone for Christian theology and science is access to points of crossover where data and logic interact with theory. This is not that big or disruptive an ask at all. We shall explore this further.

9.6 What a Working Integrative Zone for Christian Theology and Modern Science Might Look Like

We have come to define the scope of natural knowledge and publicly accepted truth in ways that are historically unique to Western modernity. We tend to see this as a mark of modern science's advanced standing in relation to other knowledge systems. But actually—if we are to take higher meaning seriously, and if we are to take the genuine openness of all theoretical systems seriously—this approach to knowledge illustrates a serious weakness in understanding. The fact that we have combined our experimental and mathematical knowledge of how nature works with our engineering capabilities means that we can do jet travel, where the ancient Greeks could not. But it does not mean that we have advanced in wisdom beyond the Greeks. In the context of the instrumental and cultural success of a totalizing and universal modern science, wisdom itself becomes epistemically obsolete. At this point Christian theology has a serious problem with modern scientific *theoria*.

To accept that divine light is now obsolete for an adequately realistic understanding of nature, and obsolete for the theoretical interpretation of the knowledge of nature, and obsolete for ethics, is to withdraw not only the epistemic form but also the metaphysical and moral content of creedal Christian theology from the most important public categories of Western truth. This leaves behind nothing but the dead shell of a culturally declining Christian religion within the Western academy and civics. But Western knowledge—and Western culture—is destructively impoverished by being theoretically reductive as regards higher meaning. This impoverishment has serious implications for knowledge.

Scientific knowledge as theoretically framed by physical reductionism—even just as an epistemic methodology—is simply blind to the obvious qualitative and transcendent features of the *natural* world: life, conscious thought (minds), the intelligibility of the cosmos (Mind), quality (both moral and aesthetic), and meaning and purpose.[17] Such a metaphysically impoverished knowledge does not ultimately reveal nature but conceals it behind a reductively abstracted and instrumental interpretive veil. And it is not as if what science can't see is unimportant—it is of the highest importance. When science is our first truth discourse, it reframes the higher-meaning categories of our actual experience of the world in the subcategories of its own reductive vision of nature. That is, what is bad for Christian theology after the remarkable reversal is equally bad for science. We are still under the spell of Newton, and it is time to break that spell.

Modern physics offers us a paradigm of natural knowledge that is (after Newton and until Einstein) pretty well contained within the knowledge categories of observation and mathematics. Here the careful measurements of the behavior of physical bodies, viewed theoretically as purely physical entities and abstracted in fully idealized mathematical models, really work (within appropriate error margins, at appropriate orders of magnitude) when predictively applied back to the real world. This is wonderful, technologically useful knowledge. *Theoria* applied to these strictly physical categories has advanced in bivalent, empirically demonstrable, and mathematically universal truth. Mapping the forces and properties of material objects (*as* purely material objects) has indeed vindicated the early Royal Society's expectation about the relationship between mathematico-experimental natural knowledge and instrumental human power. Western modernity has been culturally seduced by this success into thinking that theory itself is closed and demonstrable. Under the influence of this seduction, the norms of modern Western academic knowledge have also largely come to assume that wisdom, as an open and divinity-dependent epistemic category, was never a real awareness category in the first place.

17. See Tyson, *Seven Brief Lessons on Magic.*

Let us process this a bit. Forms of knowledge that really can be defined almost entirely within the epistemic categories native to minimally theorized empirical and rational understanding are unproblematic to the truth claims of Christian theology. But such theorizing must be explicitly methodologically reductive and make no claim on the meaning of natural phenomena. That smooth and hard balls rolling down friction-minimal slopes have uniform accelerating properties tells us facts about observable things and illustrates observable mathematically modelable natural necessities. Theorizing universal laws of nature from this is a reasonable and meaning-minimal activity, provided one does not want to think about the nature of universal physical regularity itself or ask the question "What is gravity?"

Yet the difficulty of the "science and religion" relationship for Christian theology since the triumph of a physically reductive understanding of demonstrable truth is a difficulty that will not go away until theory itself is rethought. Something like this is happening, but it is usually greeted with horror by both modern scientists and conservative advocates of modern religious truth. I speak here of the work of hermeneutic philosophers and postmodern critics of epistemically framed modern meta-narratives.

Imagine a future like this: We recover something of the ancient idea of schools. Here, as Pierre Hadot points out, a **school** is a theoretically framed way of life.[18] Knowledge and meaning are integrated not only theoretically but also existentially, communally, morally, and spiritually.[19] The ancients recognized that theoretically defined schools would be a pluralistic affair. Plenty of sharing of learning happened between different schools, and schools had an influence on one another, either reactively or sympathetically. However, nature itself, as well as higher meanings, was often interpreted in highly distinctive ways in different schools. In this context human understanding itself is accepted as functionally pluriform, even if each school is aiming at truth and believes it has found the best available interpretive angle on reality. In ancient times, overarching political, moral, and civic unity was provided by various forms of politically integrated "religion" and not by academic knowledge discourses. The Roman cultus shifts in the ancient world from pagan to imperial to Christian categories of public worship. Such civic-religious cultural unification would not work in secular, liberal societies today. But it was actually then that modern science was invented. There was not, however, an extensive body of scientific research available for a global community of scientists back then. So let us imagine a pluriform understanding of wisdom in a different way.

18. Hadot, *What Is Ancient Philosophy?*, 97–108.
19. Hadot, "Spiritual Exercises."

Let us assume (as is the case) that in our day there will be no civic religion unifying a functional framework of wisdom with knowledge and social and political norms. Let us assume (as remains the case)[20] that the residual wisdom of Christian civic-religious traditions retains its influence on Western legal, political, and ethical norms, but in a gently adaptive manner now entirely disconnected from civically enforceable ecclesial authority.[21] Let us also assume (as is the case) that experts in factual and natural knowledge remain a global intellectual community, enabling an incremental expansion of the frontiers of natural knowledge at a "workhorse" level, as well as providing opportunity for "pure science" to be experimentally curious and theoretically adventurous. But let us *not* assume the reduction of *Understanding I* and *II* to naturalistic *Knowledge I* and *II* categories in the academy. Let us also assume that interpretation, meaning, value, and purpose are always communally located, are essential for human flourishing, but cannot simply be read off from nature via "objective science." Here it is understood that a broadly "postmodern" stance is correct in its rejection of science as having a monopoly on truth, as well as in its rejection of the universal determinism of a totalizing and physically reductive "science" as a meta-narrative defining all genuine knowledge. In this context the relationship between mathematico-experimental knowledge categories, scientific theory, and explicitly religious and metaphysical schools of interpretation and practice could be far more pluralistic than our present academic norms allow. In this context, the relationship of the humanities to the sciences need not be one of the relentless invasion of scientistic categories into the wisdom and belief arenas of scholarship in human understanding; to the contrary, belief and wisdom would be expected to inform knowledge, but in a pluralistic manner.

From the stance of Christian theology, the return of genuinely Christian colleges of higher learning—as theoretically embedded schools of formation—could arise in this context. Ecclesially embedded intellectual communities could do science as integrated with the theoretical higher-wisdom insights of their religious traditions. A key thing to be carefully avoided here is importing the modern reduction of all categories of knowledge and understanding to the demonstration categories of ratio-empirical "proof" as if higher wisdom is a subset of reductively naturalistic modern knowledge. It is not. Practically, however, the way higher institutions are funded and regulated by the state,

---

20. For a popular yet scholarly recent work outlining the basic thesis that the liberal secular West remains profoundly shaped by well over a millennium of Christian cultural formation, see Holland, *Dominion*.

21. This would entail balancing tradition with change, rather than being radical progressive destroyers of traditional norms or stridently conservative reactionaries against change.

at least in places like Australia, means that any institution that tried to do theologically integrated natural philosophy theory, as well as experimental scientific research informed by such theologically integrated theory, would get defunded and de-authorized in no time flat.[22] The standards of higher learning in the religiously secular state are now rigorously naturalistic. And you can see why. There are many pseudo-science and pseudo-miracle cures on the market in—for example—the enormous alternative health industry, and, at least in terms of health products, rigorous objectivist testing standards about whether a health product can be clinically shown to actually work are important public safety issues. For this reason, Christian schools should not be dependent on secular government funding if they are going to undertake this sort of academic enterprise integrating knowledge and understanding.

This way forward is difficult on a number of practical and lifeworld fronts, but its advantages are significant. What it offers is the reintegration of knowledge with understanding, and on terms that a Christian school can pursue without sacrificing the foundational theological and metaphysical first principles of the Christian faith.

9.7 A Confident and Uncomfortable Stance

Because methodological physical reductionism is now largely taken for granted in our knowledge culture, this stance has functionally morphed into a tacitly materialist metaphysics that is now assumed to be epistemologically normative in the academy. This has been accompanied by the rise of physically reductive ethics and value systems within our publicly accepted knowledge culture and by an increasingly pragmatic and instrumental technological and commercial culture.

A Christian theology of nature cannot avoid the uncomfortable fact that it is incommensurate with a dominant knowledge culture now increasingly defined by reductive naturalism. The discomfort of this situation needs to be made explicit. Though the nineteenth-century "conflict myth" is indeed false propaganda, we need to stop pretending that there are no serious problems with the prevailing reductively naturalistic theoretical framework of modern

---

22. In the context of modern educational institutions, you can study whatever understanding discourse you like, provided your formal standards of academic rigor are adequate, provided you can attract students, and provided you are formally studying only the discourse itself but make no substantive claims to its qualitative or hermeneutic truth. That is, academic objectivity allows you to study only theologians and metaphysicians, but you cannot be a theologian and study God, or a metaphysician and study transcendent truth. Only knowledge-framed naturalistic categories *can* be true or false, or about anything real, to the modern academy.

science and orthodox Christian theology. For if it is to maintain a coherent commitment to its own truth claims, Christian theology must claim that the metaphysical materialism and the instrumental pragmatism that have crept into our knowledge culture are philosophically, morally, and theologically *wrong*. Christian theology must never concede that physical reductionism is anything other than an instrumentally useful methodological fiction. This is usually acceptable in theory, but in practice, the minute you appeal to "religious" truth warrants, you are usually off the screen of acceptable public knowledge in the academy. Despite strong pressure to look intellectually serious to the scientific establishment, Christian theology should be very cautious about making peace with methodological physical reductionism, which functionally is not metaphysically and theologically neutral. Christian theologians should be particularly aware that secular methodological reductionism comes with a set of serious moral and theological problems and that these problems are now profoundly embedded in our academic knowledge culture. But only Christian theologians are going to make an issue about the moral and theological problems embedded in our academic culture—the secularized Western academy itself, focused exclusively on the immanent, really isn't interested.

I think it is time for Christian theology to get discerning and busy about integrating an intellectually powerful Christian natural theology with modern science and technology. Increasingly, this is happening—but it is no easy task. To start with, a Christian theological account of perception and reason is not equivalent to a physically reductive account of both reason and perception, and of the world that is perceived, and of what it means to be a perceiver of the world. Equally, a Christian understanding of ethics is incompatible with a materialist and pragmatic account of ethics, for the Christian believes in the transcendent metaphysical origins of goodness. And there is the problem that in the secular academy materialist accounts of ethics are deemed valid public knowledge, but Christian accounts of ethics are deemed discretely religious, and hence a private or sectarian matter.

Also, as briefly touched on before, the categories of knowledge that science deals with are extrinsic, instrumental, calculative, and artificially reductive. These are—at least according to ancient Christian theological conceptions of prelapsarian Adamic knowledge and a biblical understanding of post-eschaton redemptive knowledge—knowledge categories that may not be much damaged in their truth-carrying value by the fall, but they are still inherently impacted by sin in their integration with theory and power. Manipulative power is accessed through these knowledge categories; and the use of power not guided by love, not ennobled by grace, not oriented by the Great Commandment, will result in both good and evil. That is, viewed theologically, the "natural light" of the postlapsarian human knower is an inherently inferior theoretical framework for natural knowledge compared with knowledge that is theoretically integral with intrinsic, love-defined, grace-enabled, empathetic, and spiritually discerning understanding. Knowledge is always theologically, relationally, metaphysically, and morally framed for the Christian. The idea that scientific knowledge is theologically and ethically neutral knowledge is terribly theologically naive.

If modern Western Christian theology does not remain true to its essential metaphysical and miraculous creedal commitments, if it adapts its core truth commitments to fit in with the now-dominant, reductively naturalistic knowledge culture, then it will die at the hands of modern science, even though it brought this science into the world. And perhaps—to paraphrase Stanley Hauerwas—such a death would be no bad thing.[23] But, speaking as a Western Christian living in the modern technological world, I have to say that I would find it sad. A better approach would be for Christian theology to stop trying to adapt itself to a functionally materialist and pragmatic conception of valid natural knowledge and rather to go on the front foot and reconfigure the interpretive lens of natural philosophy so that it is compatible with the first truths of Christian theology. A theologically creedal Christian outlook on natural knowledge must anticipate that this will make science *more* compatible with the real truth about creation.

23. Hauerwas says, "God is killing the church, and we goddamn well deserve it" (Hibbs, "Stanley Hauerwas's Pacifism"). Hauerwas, with a keen eye to the problems this text has sought to outline, is very interested in "science" and "natural theology" in the academy. See the book version of Hauerwas's 2000/2001 Gifford Lectures, *With the Grain of the Universe.*

Epilogue

The Future?

The need for a new theological interest in knowledge and a fully reconfigured way of approaching Christian theology and modern science has now been put forward. Even so, it remains true that modern science is a wonder. The knowledge we now have brings more and more of the natural world under our powerfully disclosive epistemic gaze. This knowledge in turn enables our technological creativity, ever enhancing our powers. Science is also simply an amazing human practice. The international cooperation, the brilliant creative thinking, and the designing and building of beautiful artifices of human ingenuity that scientists do are rightly to be praised. Take the example of GRACE.

The Gravity Recovery and Climate Experiment (GRACE) is astounding. This twin satellite system, conceived and implemented by NASA and the German Aerospace Center, circles the earth fifteen times a day, mapping the dynamic gravitational topography of the earth. It works by very accurately measuring the distance between its two satellites traveling over the earth in parallel paths. Tiny differences in the distance separating these two satellites are produced by the gravitational fluctuations over various parts of the earth, which shows us—among other things—the changing patterns of fresh-water distribution around the globe, both on and in the ground. We can now get a global picture of the water cycle in its entirety. Modern science partnered with modern technology is a dazzling wonder and a triumph of human ingenuity.

GRACE has been going since 2002.[1] Nearly twenty years on at the time of writing, what does GRACE tell us? It shows us that as the global climate heats up, the soil gets drier and absorbs more rain, so that rivers in their normal flooding seasons are running drier. Equally, under torrential rain produced by extreme weather events, drier and harder soil means more runoff and greater flood damage. We now know that the cumulative global effect of this trend is that fresh water in our catchment systems is becoming scarcer. The overwhelming consensus of the international community of climate scientists is that recent human activity is responsible for this global temperature rise,[2] which is now noticeably drying the planet's soil. The way modern, technologically advanced, power- and resource-hungry humanity now lives is producing a rising global scarcity in usable surface water.

We have wielded the power that science has given us over the earth in ways that are making a basic human need—fresh water—harder to meet at the same time that we have by far the largest population of people the planet has ever seen. Again, the global population explosion of the twentieth century was intimately tied to the Green Revolution—the fossil-fuel-enabled industrialization of farming. In the tradition of Francis Bacon, NASA's vision statement aims to put science to work for "the benefit of humanity," and yet it looks like many of the most obviously desirable gifts of modern science and technology have had serious planetary-destabilizing consequences that we did not see coming. Our powers are now so expansive that we are a significant nature-altering force along with other natural forces. But where these other natural forces are in an intricate relative stasis, our powers are new, and they disrupt the intimately interdependent stasis of nature on which we depend. Whether human technological power, as now a high natural power, will become a balanced natural force, or whether its disruption will seriously damage the natural regenerative balances on which life as we know it depends and largely extract us from the natural system, is yet to be seen.

Modern science is a marvel of factual-information production, theoretical creativity, and technological power provision. But while increasingly accurate predictions are within science's power, as we have already rehearsed, wisdom is not part of its brief. Indeed, the modern world has produced its knowledge

1. The original GRACE program wound up in 2017, but the Follow On version of this project (GRACE-FO) is still going. See https://gracefo.jpl.nasa.gov/mission/overview/.
2. "In its Fifth Assessment Report, the Intergovernmental Panel on Climate Change, a group of 1,300 independent scientific experts from countries all over the world under the auspices of the United Nations, concluded there's a more than 95 percent probability that human activities over the past 50 years have warmed our planet." NASA, "Causes of Climate Change." See also Houghton, *Global Warming*; and Ellis, *Anthropocene*.

by explicitly separating knowledge from wisdom, facts from meanings, science from religion. The modern world has valued use and power above metaphysics and theology—even though, ironically, it was the tacit metaphysics and theology of seventeenth-century Christian innovators in the new philosophy of nature that gave us modern science.

Modern technological power, the science that produces it, and the uses to which it is put urgently need to be firmly limited and wisely directed if we are not going to ruin the natural balances of the world in which we and our fellow creatures live. Yet the origin myth of post-Victorian modern science is one of a heroic escape from the superstitious constraints of Christian theology and the useless speculations of Aristotelian metaphysics. So modern science is reflexively ideologically committed to its autonomy from metaphysics and theology. This, in practice, means that only metaphysics and theology that accept a reductively physical outlook on reality can make an easy partnership with modern science. But science actually *needs* what scientifically reductive "metaphysics" and rationalized and empiricized "theology" cannot give it. For wisdom to genuinely limit and direct modernity's amoral knowledge and instrumental power, science needs a metaphysics capable of grasping the intrinsic value embedded in and beyond nature and a theology capable of genuine reverence and submission to that which stands over and beyond humanity. Christian theology should be showing us why modern Western science needs the distinctive theological and metaphysical wisdom commitments of creedal Christian faith, and it should be demonstrating how a fruitful integration of Christian theology and science might be achieved.[3]

The above is a very different sort of enterprise from the kind of ventures that have largely governed a Christian interest in "science and religion" since late Victorian times. Adaptation Christians of different stripes have tried to answer the following sorts of questions: How can modern scientists be persuaded to take Christian faith seriously? What can Christian faith add to modern science? How can Christian theology better understand modern science? How can Christian theology be better understood through the truth lens of modern science? And what can Christian theology learn from modern science? Modern fundamentalist Christians have tried to show that modern science can be integrated with the miraculous truth claims of their distinctive

3. I am here implying that non-Western high wisdom traditions should govern science and technology in non-Western contexts. I appreciate that this is now all very difficult to imagine, much less to implement. On the one hand, we have for the first time a globally unified knowledge culture that crosses (by ignoring) all wisdom traditions. On the other hand, there are so many wisdom traditions present in the West (and everywhere) that the "location" of different syntheses of wisdom, knowledge, and power cannot be one of physical, geographical territory.

understanding of the Christian Scriptures. This outlook has usually left the instrumental autonomy and eschatological progress myth of science native to modernity as found. Conservative systematic theology has largely retreated into "religion" and abandoned public factual and instrumental concerns, has vacated the public territory of science (both theoretical and applied), and has concerned itself only with theology for theology's sake. None of these approaches are seeking to show modern knowledge and technological power that they need to be governed by Christian understanding. None of these approaches are seeking to show that Christian theological understanding, incorporating a Christian metaphysics of nature, is worthy of governing modern knowledge, or that such an idea is even remotely possible.

Knowledge and understanding are not identical, and each has its own area of competence in which it should be functionally autonomous. However, if understanding and wisdom do not in some manner govern knowledge and power, knowledge and power can be astonishingly destructive. How, then, can we aspire to a cooperative relationship between Christian theology and modern science in which the governance of knowledge and power by wisdom is upheld within something like a unified knowledge and understanding field? This is the seriously hard challenge of Christian theology as regards the "science and religion" domain. But it does not seem to be getting much attention.

There has been a serious lack of first-order reflection in the post-nineteenth-century Christian "science and religion" field as regards what a Christian metaphysics of nature and a Christian epistemology really look like. Theologians have given very little attention to the question of what a Christian philosophy of perception and a Christian philosophy of reason could look like in our times. Equally, there has been a lack of first-order reflection on what modern science's tacit philosophy of nature, philosophy of perception, philosophy of reason, and assumed metaphysical implications really are—and on how these relate to Christian theology. That is, a great deal of the storm and stress of the "science and religion" domain has been over second-order matters. Numerous approaches to peaceful mutuality between Christian theology and modern science have refused to even acknowledge the existence of serious first-order difficulties in our post-Victorian epistemic norms. Straining out second-order gnats, we swallow first-order camels without ever noticing them.

It is high time for Christian theology to get serious about these first-order questions and to take a close look at its own role in setting up the first-order assumptions of the prevailing dysfunctional territories of science and religion. Yet we now live within a lifeworld governed by the strict secular demarcation between public and religious domains, and in this lifeworld we are increasingly using physically defined knowledge and amoral instrumental power as cultural unifiers, to the displacement of religious meaning in the public sphere. In this context, any attempt to implement a first-order, reworked Christian metaphysic of nature and a Christian epistemology of natural knowledge will get no oxygen in the public, secular sphere. No matter. There are still large-enough Christian communities and Christian knowledge institutions for Christians to start things rolling in their own spaces. I think Stanley Hauerwas is right to think that in our post-Christendom times we must think of the church—though in and for the world—as a polity apart.[4] Here an Augustinian City of God must operate on its own terms rather than on the terms acceptable to the City of Man. This attempt to think in decisively Christian ways, rather than simply trying to fit Christianity in with the norms of the contemporary academy[5] and secular consumer society,[6] *is* happening all over the Christian world. And yet, there is still a widespread failure to recognize that the remarkable reversal completely changes Christian theology's relationship to public truth and that Christian theology itself set this reversal up. This failure must be recognized. If the demanding first-order rethinking can be done, then the church can find its own way toward integrating its own vision of natural meaning and divine reality with the knowledge of nature and the use of instrumental power. This, I think, would be the most meaningful redemptive witness the church could offer in our cataclysmically troubled times. For it is the fragmentation of secular knowledge, a cold instrumentalism toward nature, and an inhumane and pragmatic "realism" toward people and power that are driving us toward civilizational implosion on an unprecedented scale. The qualitative and spiritual blindness of our scientific understanding of truth is the very engine of this glacial inertia toward destruction.

A renewed interest in the Christian theology of science is needed. Recovering Christian theology as the first truth discourse for Christians is integral with the development of a fruitful Christian theology of science. Any attempt at such a recovery will make for a deeply uncomfortable relationship with the secular, functionally materialist academy. Christian theology, then, needs to be confident enough of its own truths to refuse the tacit first truth discourse of science that is now deeply ingrained in the post-Victorian "science and religion" dialogue. As challenging and uncomfortable as these endeavors would be, there is much to gain from such an approach.

A great deal of the tension between modern science and Christian faith felt by young people has much more to do with theological questions of first

4. See Hauerwas, *Resident Aliens*, for his thoughts on the use of *politeuma* to describe the church in Phil. 3:20.
5. Hauerwas, *State of the University*.
6. Ross, *Gifts Glittering and Poisoned*.

truth than with questions of how one simply integrates current scientific knowledge and Christian doctrine *within* the prevailing academic knowledge culture. We can talk about faith and reason, creationism and evolution, genetic engineering, euthanasia, global warming and Christianity, and evidence and credulity till the cows come home, but the remarkable reversal is so taken for granted that the first-order tensions between the historical and the mythic, generated by our science-to-religion truth culture, never come up in the conversation. We automatically demarcate faith from knowledge, put theology in the private domain of belief, and then subordinate truth to science in the public domain of knowledge. Thus do we synthesize a "respectable" solution on the assumption that preserving the integrity of the notional and supposedly neutral silos of science and religion is the way to resolve all problems. This allows one to be an intelligent Christian in a secular scientific age, for sure, but it takes as a given that science is a viable first truth discourse for the domain of public knowledge. Christian theology, however, does not remain Christian if it is not a first truth discourse. Trying to think like a Christian about theories of nature and about how to live in the natural world (i.e., about morality) while presupposing the tacit reductive naturalism of the academy will end badly for intelligent faith.

There is much work to be done. Amazing pre-Victorian resources are available for those interested in reimagining a Christian theology of science for our times. But history does not repeat itself. Theorizing the Christian meaning of nature in our context will require a new conceptual language and a new integrative outlook as we create categories of meaning that partially reflect the essential truths of the Christian revelation in our times.

Glossary

In this book, I have explained my terms where they get their first serious treatment. The page location in parentheses listed with each glossary term below corresponds to an explanation of that term in the text.

adaptation (5): The response to the ascendancy of science that seeks to *adapt* Christian theology to the credibility parameters, knowledge methodologies, and functional materialism of modern science.

a posteriori (20): "After." An empirical knowledge of the world that comes to us *after* sensory perception.

a priori (22): "Before." A rational knowledge of mathematical principles and logic that is contributed by our minds to our understanding of the world *before* we receive sensory data.

appropriation (5): The response to the ascendancy of science that seeks to *appropriate* a modern scientific account of literal and positivist truth and to apply this account of truth to the Bible in order to defend modern, and usually fundamentalist, accounts of Christian doctrine.

Aristotelian/Thomistic epistemic anthropology (104): A confidence, shared by Aristotle and Aquinas, in natural knowledge and logic as viable pathways upon which the human knower can travel toward metaphysical and theological truth.

Augustinian epistemic anthropology (103): The view according to which inherited original sin makes true knowledge of any type—without special divine grace—inherently unachievable.

being (35): Being itself is "is-ness," that property that all created things participate in simply in virtue of the fact that they inhabit the one field of reality. Distinct "beings" are not Being itself, and in traditional Christian metaphysics, Being itself—also understood to be the Ground of Being upon which all beings stand, the ontological source of all things that are—is God. "I Am" is how God self-identifies to Moses. Each created being is given an essential nature (its form) by God, as beings are always beings of a particular type. The essential nature of every being is only ever partially existentially expressed in space and time, as essence is eternal but all temporal beings are continually changing.

belief/*pistis* (116): Trust and confidence in the obvious meanings that are assumed by our community and supported by our senses. Belief is shaped by the contingencies and particularities of existence and mediated to us via human language, culture, education, and formation. It includes customary values and meanings and is overshadowed in some manner by the wisdom of high intellection.

Christian theological epistemology (100): A Christian theological understanding of knowledge. This covers a lot more than recent secular, philosophical conceptions of epistemology allow—incorporating doctrine, hermeneutics, community transmission, and metaphysics into a Christian account of knowledge. Revelation (both general and special); the interpretive impact of sin; the intellectively, morally, and spiritually transformative impact of divine grace; the metaphysics of an intelligible and ordered creation; the relation of sensory perception and meaningful thought to the soul and its Creator—all this and more is entailed.

Christian theology (11): Christian reasoning about God.

common graces (120): Gifts of God given to all humanity, be they saints, sinners, pagans, atheists, or even Australians.

conservative (74): Of or relating to the idea that traditional Western (at least culturally Christian) values and beliefs need to be "conserved." The conservative usually expects that things naturally "go off course" over time unless efforts are made to protect and transmit the high values of the past for the present and the future.

contingency (23): A state of being more or less randomly dependent on other things. For example, I speak the language I happen to speak because of the parents, time, and location I happened to be born into. There is nothing necessary about which language I speak, as this fact about me is contingent on a set of historical variables that could have been otherwise.

deism (23): A rationalistic theology that removes all logical paradoxes and all historical contingencies from our knowledge of God.

Democritean atomic matter (65): A reductively physical account of matter. Only atoms in motion in void exist; nothing else.

dianoia/**mathematics** (112): Low intellection, concerned with universal rational truths. The divinely enabled illuminations of formal reason.

divine illumination (109): See **divine light**.

divine light (108): The intellectual radiance of God that facilitates mental illumination in us, concerning intelligible reality. The human mind grasps truths that are invisible to the physical eye—the truths of formal reason and qualitative reality—as the mind's eye is illuminated by the divine realities of the high forms (to Plato) and ultimately by the radiance of the goodness and glory of God. Intelligible luminosity rules over the mental realm just as the radiance of the sun rules over the visible realm. To a divine-light perspective, contemplative thought is a divinely enabled activity.

double truth (85): The embracing of incommensurate truth discourses such that a "truth" of natural philosophy (say, that there was no nature-deforming fall of humanity) can be incompatible with a "truth" of doctrine (say, that the theology of the fall is integral with the Christian salvation narrative) and yet, somehow, both can be considered "true." Double truth denies the unity of truth itself and obliterates the meaning of truth as a unity.

doxological (31): Concerning worship.

egocentric epistemological foundationalism (EEF) (32): The view according to which the locus of knowledge is the human knower. The knowledge of the human knower is the only valid foundation for truth.

egocentrism (33): The ego is the center.

eikasia/**perception** (112): The natural illumination of physical perception. Concerned with existence.

empiricism (13): A theory about what we can know, empiricism holds that only what we can experience by sensation (aided by sensibility-enhancing devices where necessary) and quantify counts as real. Empiricists take sense perception to be the *only* grounds of our knowledge of the world.

epistemology (33): The branch of philosophy that seeks to understand the nature of human knowledge. In the dominant streams of Western classical and medieval thinking, being and divinity were usually thought of as the grounds of human knowledge, so epistemology was not treated as separable from ontology and theology, or as a philosophical subdiscipline in its own right. However, in the nineteenth century, epistemology came to be seen not only as philosophically self-standing but as the secular grounds of truth,

often to the exclusion of metaphysics and theology. This "modern epistemology" is now very different from classical and medieval "epistemology,"
and the word itself was invented in the nineteenth century.

eschatological (150): A Christian theological term for that which concerns the
last days. Eschatological hope is hope for a divinely instigated radical conclusion and redemption of human history—a conclusion and redemption that
is, nevertheless, often thought to be something human agency can hurry
along. Secularized, eschatological hope becomes the ideology of progress.

essence (30): The intelligibly ordered nature of a tangible being that makes it
(to at least some degree) identifiable and knowable to our minds.

exegesis (21): Linguistic analysis and explanation of the precise content and
meaning of scriptural words and texts, taking account of their historical,
cultural, and linguistic contexts.

existence (30): The particular and concrete reality of a tangible being, as
expressed in matter, space, time, vitality (if living), and energy.

exogenous evil (142): Evil that is not intrinsic to reality. Evil as an unnatural
and inexplicable irruption into an inherently good creation. Evil that has
no eternal mythic reality.

extrinsic (31): Concerning what can be seen, understood, and influenced
externally.

fall (103): The entry of sin, death, and evil into the natural world, dulling
and damaging the human capacity to receive and correctly understand
divine illumination.

first truth discourse (1): A unifying framework of first-order metaphysical,
moral, and epistemic meanings. A set of interpretive commitments that
one brings to all knowledge and understanding.

foundationalism (33): A truth and meaning system built on a set of first
principles that are foundational. In classical contexts, foundational truth
and meaning premises were ontological and theological rather than epistemological (that is, the foundation of knowledge was divine *Being* rather
than human *knowing*). But modern epistemological foundationalism seeks
(unsuccessfully) to make human knowledge capacities the foundation of a
true knowledge of reality and of valid human meanings.

four causes (Aristotle) (63): Material cause (what something is made of); efficient cause (how something is mechanically and externally acted on); formal
cause (something's essential, inner nature); final cause (something's purpose).

hermeneutics (21): The methods and principles of interpretation, or the study
of the methods and principles of interpretation.

high ideas (105): That which high intellection partially grasps; essential and eternal qualities, such as Goodness, Beauty, Truth, Unity, Justice, and the like.

historical-critical method (21): A method of biblical analysis, influential from the eighteenth century on, that applies to the Bible the kind of source and credibility tests now used more broadly in modern historiography, as well as the linguistic and textual analysis tools developed by humanist literary scholars.

history (Christian) (133): Temporally and culturally situated accounts of existential events. The medium—in Christian theology—of God's dealings with humanity.

hylomorphism (14): Aristotle's understanding of informed matter. On this view, every physical being is a matter-and-form composite. Matter is never found without intellective form structuring and purposing it; form is never found (by us) without it being expressed in matter. Here meanings, qualities, and purposes belong to a natural being's form, and hence belong to material nature. Significantly, meanings, qualities, and purposes are not found in nature according to the modern theory of matter, for this atomist philosophy of matter does not entail any unity of matter with form and thinks of nature as defined only by matter. Meanings, qualities, and purposes are treated as artifacts of culture by the modern atomist theory of matter.

immanent frame (29): The idea that only tangible and non-transcendent reality is real. The worldview of naturalistic materialism.

informed matter (65): See **hylomorphism**.

intellectualism (Thomistic/Augustinian) (61): The idea that God's will is defined and limited by the reasons of love and goodness and that, consequently, love and goodness (rather than sovereign will) define human nature as well. God's goodness and self-giving love form the template for the image of God that defines our humanity.

intrinsic (30): Concerning the essential and inner nature of a being.

Knowledge I (119): Sensory knowledge, minimally theorized (that is, not empiricism).

Knowledge II (120): Mathematical knowledge, minimally theorized (that is, not rationalism).

lifeworld (27): Sociological way of life. A distinctive common matrix of practice, belief, and culture in which people live.

low ideas (105): Low intellection. Mathematics and logic. Formal reason.

mathematics/*dianoia* (116): Low intellection. Concerned with essence. The divinely enabled illuminations of formal reason.

metaphysics (12): The branch of philosophy that investigates the transcendent realities that are the grounds of observable, physical nature. Platonisms usually reason from metaphysics to physics when thinking about the final nature of things, not the other way around (because the eternal and the invisible are the grounds of the temporal and the visible, not the other way around). Modern philosophy seeks to reason from the physical to the metaphysical, which tends to make what modern philosophers call metaphysics (if they use the term at all) a branch of theoretical physics.

miracle (12): A singular act of God within nature that cannot be explained by our understanding of the regular operations of nature.

modern science (13): From the seventeenth century: physico-mathematical, experimental natural knowledge, usually presupposing the first truth discourse of some form of Christian theology. From the late nineteenth century onward: a first truth discourse in its own right, typically characterized by Humean empiricism, secular rationalism, and a reductively materialist understanding of reality.

myth (**Christian**) (133): A narrative conveying essential and eternal meaning, often in richly analogical and archetypal categories. In Christian myth, such narratives are integrated into historical time, as God is seen as breaking into time and events in revelations and actions that are later transmitted in Scripture by inspired writers.

naive empiricism (43): The belief that the world as I perceive it with my faculties of perception is how the world really is.

natural illumination (109): See **natural light**.

natural light (108): Mental illumination, gifted to the knower by God via natural sensory and natural cognitive processes.

noēsis/**wisdom** (37): High intellection. Concerned with essence. The high source of all qualities and meanings. A divinely enabled insight of revelation.

nominalism (57): The view that universal categories do not exist in reality. Here, only particular physical things in tangible nature exist. For the nominalist, words like *Beauty* and *Good* are "names only" and have no metaphysical existence independent of physical reality. Individual things (like Peter) do not participate in trans-individual realities (like humanity).

normative (16): Concerning and making value judgements. Judging something to be good or bad in relation to a qualitative truth standard. In moral Realist terms (where Good is a primary metaphysical reality), normative truth is usually defined as a function of right worship (attributing worth or value correctly to the source of reality, God). In modern moral non-Realist terms, normativity is defined by the social norm (what most people are doing becomes, by definition, the right thing to do).

noumena (42): Reality as it is in itself (as distinct from reality as it is known by a human subject).

ontological participation (58): The Greek word *ontos* means "being." Ontological participation, then, is reasoning about how beings participate in Being, and in the different qualitative and essential powers of Being. In contrast to nominalism, this outlook does not think of individual beings as belonging only to themselves. That is, all beings participate in Being, and then participate in essential meanings (forms, ideas, qualities) in order to be whatever particular being they are. Here, intangible, trans-individual, qualitative realities—such as Beauty and Goodness—are transcendent powers of Being that individual beings can participate in. Theologically, the Christian ontologically participates in the church, which is composed of individual Christians but is not reducible to the sum of its parts; the church has an essential nature in which, by divine gift, individual Christians take part.

ontology (35): The branch of philosophy concerned with understanding the nature of being.

perception/*eikasia* (116): The natural illumination of physical perception. Concerned with existence.

phenomena (42) Reality as it appears to the human subject's experience and knowledge (as distinct from reality as it is in itself).

PHIL100 (33): An immanent-frame outlook in which valid modern philosophy is thought to be epistemologically foundational and in which modern knowledge is seen as rationalistically or empirically indubitable, or as pragmatically justified.

physical reductionism (15): As a metaphysical outlook, physical reductionism is the "pure matter" perspective that takes physical reality to be the only reality that defines nature, and it assumes that such physical nature is all that there is. As a methodology, physical reductionism treats reality *as if* only the physical is real, but without asserting that the non-material either is or is not real. Methodologically, physical reductionism is a functional materialism that is agnostic as regards spiritual and intellective reality.

***pistis*/belief** (116): Trust and confidence in the obvious meanings that are assumed by our community and supported by our senses. *Pistis* is shaped by the contingencies and particularities of existence and mediated to us via human language, culture, education, and formation. It includes customary values and meanings and is overshadowed in some manner by the wisdom of high intellection.

Platonist/Augustinian epistemic anthropology (104): The view that for human knowledge to be true knowledge, it must be divinely enabled. This view is reflective of Plato's conviction that true knowledge is invisible to the natural eye and of Augustine's suspicion of human knowledge on account of its corruption by the fall.

pragmatism (42): The replacement of truth with use.

prime matter (65): The medieval Aristotelian notion of the unformed matter out of which every matter-and-form substantial being is made.

progressive (74): Of or relating to a secularized eschatology (often explicitly scientistic and anti-Christian from the mid-nineteenth century on) that believes we are evolving or improving or getting closer to a human-made and religion-free paradise in which all the obstacles to equality and the good life will be overcome. Having to do with the view that things are always naturally getting better.

pure matter (14): Matter viewed as entirely self-standing in relation to divine grace and supernatural spirit. Modern materialism is premised on this view of matter. In modern materialism, pure matter—not form, not essence, not purpose, not value—is all that really exists in nature, and material nature is coextensive with reality.

rationalism (13): A theory of reality according to which only that which makes universal logical sense can be true. This view takes mathematical reason to be the language that describes necessary and causal relationships in all spheres of reality: the natural, the human, and—if it is thought to exist—the supernatural.

Realist (medieval/ontological) (58): Of or relating to the belief that the things we can't see (God, Goodness, Beauty, Truth, etc.) are realer than the things we can see. On this view, the essential, eternal, transcendent, and immaterial are the grounds of the existential, temporal, immanent, and material—tangible, spatiotemporal reality is dependent for its being, qualities, and purposes on eternal, spiritual reality.

religion-to-science interpretive dynamic (26): Thinking from theology to science. Treating theology as a first truth discourse that interprets the meaning and theoretical credibility of scientific knowledge and theory.

remarkable reversal (31): The late nineteenth-century reversal from Christian theology interpreting the true meaning and validity of natural philosophy to science interpreting the true meaning and validity of Christian theology.

school (172): A community of belief and practice incorporating disciplines and spiritual development with moral and intellectual formation. A community united in basic interpretive and way-of-life commitments.

science-to-religion interpretive dynamic (27): Thinking from science to theology. Treating science as a first truth discourse that interprets the realistic meaning and judges the credibility of theological and doctrinal beliefs.

secularization (26): As a sociological thesis, the idea that the modern lifeworld naturally and inevitably moves us all away from the ecclesial and the religious. As a political and cultural ideal, the belief that the religious should be separate from the public domain. As a process, the de-religionizing of a culture. As an epistemological idea, the interpretation of all religious phenomena as merely human constructs and the separation of faith from knowledge.

skeptical empiricism (43): The belief that I cannot know how the world is, but my perceptions are reasonably useful even so.

skepticism (42): An epistemic philosophy of doubt. The belief that no belief can be epistemically indubitable.

supernatural (15): To Aquinas, the ground and goal of the natural. To the post-Victorian era, a completely discrete realm (if it exists at all) from the natural.

teleological (66): Having to do with teleology—that branch of Aristotelian natural philosophy concerned with understanding natural purposes. *Telos* is Greek for "end" (as in "purpose").

theocentric ontological foundationalism (TOF) (32): Instead of placing human knowledge as the locus of valid truth, TOF places the Being of God as the locus of the intelligible cosmos and the ground of valid human knowledge. Faith in God is hence the foundation of valid philosophical, scientific, moral, and theological insight and truth.

theocentrism (33): The view in which God is the center and source of reality and meaning. Theocentrism is contrasted with anthropocentrism, in which humanity is the center and source of all human meaning, and egocentrism, in which the "I" is the center and source of all personal values and meanings.

theory (*theoria*) (120): A vision of meaning. An inescapably imaginative and interpretive act of the meaning-discerning mind.

Thomistic epistemic anthropology (103): The view according to which the natural knowledge of sense and reason remains truth carrying after the fall. Special revelation goes beyond what natural knowledge can ascertain, but not in a manner that contradicts natural knowledge. Truths of natural sense and reason are, on this view, always compatible with truths of special revelation.

transcendent being (105): Non-physical, qualitative, intellective, and eternal spiritual realities.

true myth (133): A narrative account of the coincidence of eternal essence and temporal existence in historical events. The advent narrative regarding the incarnation of the eternal *Logos* of God, as the historical man Jesus of Nazareth, is an illustration of a historically true myth. Such events—and the passion of Christ in particular—are sacramentally re-enacted (such as in the eucharist) and participated in in a manner that is no longer tied to simply one place and time, as is the case for ordinary historical events.

truth (1): The unified field of knowledge and meaning. Due to the limits of our minds and our knowledge, the unity of the field of knowledge and meaning is ever beyond us. Such full unity is known only to God. Our understanding of truth is only ever partial. Fellowship with God provides the best pathway to those parts of truth that are relevant to us.

Understanding I (120): Existentially situated meaning, valuing, and purposive understanding. The domain of theories that pertain to understanding the perceived world (including scientific and philosophical theories). Always poetically expressed in human language.

Understanding II (120): Essentially situated meaning, valuing, and purposive understanding. Inexpressible in human language other than analogically and in the suggestive imagery of myth.

utilitarian (62): The idea that *use* (utility) defines value. That is, something is valuable if it is useful. Modern utilitarianism is also characterized by a hedonistic theory of value where pleasure is good and pain is bad. This typically results in constructing some sort of hedonistic calculus to determine what is useful, based on calculating what outcome is likely to produce more pleasure and less pain than any other outcome. As a collective idea (as distinct from pursuing what is pleasurable just for oneself), "the greatest good for the greatest number" defines utilitarian ethics.

voluntarism (61): The idea that sovereign freedom of the will is the most basic truth both of the divine nature and of human nature. According to this view, free will is the most important attribute of human nature because God's sovereign and entirely unconstrained will is the template for the image of God that defines our humanity.

wisdom/*noēsis* (116): High intellection. Concerned with essence. The high source of all qualities and meanings. A divinely enabled insight of revelation.

withdrawal (5): The response to the ascendancy of science that seeks to withdraw theology from the public domain of science and situate it exclusively within the discretely religious domain of the systematic analysis of supernatural doctrines.

Bibliography

Alfsvåg, Knut. *What No Mind Has Conceived: On the Significance of Christological Apophaticism.* Leuven: Peeters: 2010.

Aquinas, Thomas. *Quaestiones disputatae de veritate.* "S. Thomae De Aquino Opera Omnia." Corpus Thomisticum. https://www.corpusthomisticum.org/iopera.html.

Aristotle. *Metaphysics.* In *The Complete Works of Aristotle: The Revised Oxford Translation*, vol. 2, edited by Jonathan Barnes, 1552–1728. Princeton: Princeton University Press, 1984.

———. *Physics.* In *The Complete Works of Aristotle: The Revised Oxford Translation*, vol. 1, edited by Jonathan Barnes, 315–446. Princeton: Princeton University Press, 1984.

Augustine. *Against the Academicians and The Teacher.* Translated by Peter King. Indianapolis: Hackett, 1995.

———. *City of God.* Translated by Henry Bettenson. London: Penguin, 1984.

———. *On Genesis.* Translated by Matthew J. O'Connell. Hyde Park, NY: New City Press, 2002.

Aulén, Gustaf. *Christus Victor.* Eugene, OR: Wipf & Stock, 2003.

Ayer, A. J. *Language, Truth and Logic.* London: Penguin, 1971.

Barton, Ruth. "'Huxley, Lubbock, and Half a Dozen Others': Professionals and Gentlemen in the Formation of the X Club, 1851–1864." *Isis* 89, no. 3 (1998): 410–44.

Berger, Peter L., ed. *The Desecularization of the World: Resurgent Religion and World Politics.* Grand Rapids: Eerdmans, 1999.

Bethge, Eberhard. *Dietrich Bonhoeffer: A Biography.* Minneapolis: Fortress, 2000.

Blackburn, Simon. *Truth.* Oxford: Oxford University Press, 2005.

Boyce, James. *1835.* Melbourne: Black, 2013.

Bradley, F. H. *Appearance and Reality.* London: Oxford University Press, 1930.

Brown, Peter. *Augustine of Hippo*. Berkeley: University of California Press, 2000.

Brueggemann, Walter. *The Prophetic Imagination*. Minneapolis: Fortress, 2001.

Buber, Martin. *I and Thou*. Edinburgh: T&T Clark, 1937.

Buckley, Michael J. *At the Origins of Modern Atheism*. New Haven: Yale University Press, 1987.

Burkert, Walter. "Philosophical Religion." In *Greek Religion*, 305–38. Oxford: Blackwell, 1987.

Butterfield, Herbert. *Christianity and History*. London: Fontana Books, 1957.

———. *The Origins of History*. New York: Basic Books, 1981.

———. *The Whig Interpretation of History*. New York: Norton, 1965.

Cavanaugh, William T. *The Myth of Religious Violence*. Oxford: Oxford University Press, 2009.

Chadwick, Owen. *The Secularization of the European Mind in the Nineteenth Century*. Cambridge: Cambridge University Press, 1975.

Chalmers, Alan. *What Is This Thing Called Science?* 4th ed. New York: Open University Press, 2013.

Chesterton, G. K. *Orthodoxy*. Rockville, MD: Serenity, 2009.

Conyers, A. J. *The Long Truce: How Toleration Made the World Safe for Power and Profit*. Waco, TX: Baylor University Press, 2009.

Cribb, Julian. *Food or War*. Cambridge: Cambridge University Press, 2019.

Cunningham, Conor. *Darwin's Pious Idea*. Grand Rapids: Eerdmans, 2010.

Das, Satyajit. *Extreme Money: Masters of the Universe and the Cult of Risk*. New York: FT Press, 2011.

Davies, Paul. *The Mind of God*. London: Penguin, 1993.

Dawkins, Richard. *The God Delusion*. Boston: Mariner, 2006.

Dear, Peter. "What Is the History of Science the History Of?" *Isis* 96 (2005): 390–406.

de Gruchy, John W., ed. *The Cambridge Companion to Dietrich Bonhoeffer*. Cambridge: Cambridge University Press, 1999.

de Lubac, Henri. *The Mystery of the Supernatural*. New York: Herder & Herder, 2018.

Derrida, Jacques. *Of Grammatology*. Baltimore: Johns Hopkins University Press, 2016.

Desmond, William. *Being and the Between*. New York: State University of New York, 1995.

———. *Ethics and the Between*. New York: State University of New York, 2001.

———. *God and the Between*. Oxford: Blackwell, 2008.

———. *The Voiding of Being*. Washington, DC: Catholic University of America Press, 2020.

Dionysius the Areopagite. *The Divine Names and Mystical Theology*. London: SPCK, 1940.

Drake, H. A. *Constantine and the Bishops: The Politics of Intolerance*. Baltimore: Johns Hopkins University Press, 2000.

Draper, John William. *History of the Conflict between Religion and Science*. New York: Appleton, 1874.

Dreher, Rod. *The Benedict Option: A Strategy for Christians in a Post-Christian Nation*. Hoboken, NJ: Prentice Hall, 2018.

Dupré, Louis. *Passage to Modernity*. New Haven: Yale University Press, 1993.

Ebeling, Gerhard. *Word and Faith*. London: SCM, 2012.

Ellis, Erle C. *Anthropocene: A Very Short Introduction*. Oxford: Oxford University Press, 2018.

Ellul, Jacques. *The Technological Society*. New York: Vintage, 1964.

———. *Violence*. New York: The Seabury Press, 1969.

Empiricus, Sextus. *Outlines of Pyrrhonism*. New York: Prometheus Books, 1990.

Evans, C. Stephen. *Søren Kierkegaard's Christian Psychology*. Vancouver, BC: Regent College Publishing, 1990.

Feinstein, Andrew. *The Shadow World: Inside the Global Arms Trade*. London: Penguin, 2012.

Feyerabend, Paul. *Against Method*. 4th ed. London: Verso, 2010.

———. *Philosophical Papers*. 4 vols. Cambridge: Cambridge University Press, 2003–15.

Finnis, John. *Natural Law and Natural Rights*. 2nd ed. Oxford: Oxford University Press, 2011.

Foucault, Michel. *The Order of Things*. London: Routledge, 2002.

Franklin, James. *A History of Philosophy in Australia: Corrupting the Youth*. Sydney: Macleay, 2003.

Freud, Sigmund. *Civilization and Its Discontents*. London: Penguin, 2004.

———. *The Future of an Illusion: Religion Is the Universal Neurosis*. London: Penguin, 2004.

Funkenstein, Amos. *Theology and the Scientific Imagination*. Princeton: Princeton University Press, 1986.

Gaukroger, Stephen. *The Emergence of a Scientific Culture: Science and the Shaping of Modernity, 1210–1685*. Oxford: Oxford University Press, 2006.

———. *Francis Bacon*. Cambridge: Cambridge University Press, 2001.

———. *Objectivity: A Very Short Introduction*. Oxford: Oxford University Press, 2012.

Gavrilyuk, Paul L. *The Suffering of the Impassible God: The Dialectics of Patristic Thought*. Oxford: Oxford University Press, 2006.

Gay, Craig. *Cash Values*. Grand Rapids: Eerdmans, 2004.

Gerson, Lloyd P. *Ancient Epistemology*. Cambridge: Cambridge University Press, 2009.

———. *Aristotle and Other Platonists*. Ithaca, NY: Cornell University Press, 2005.

Gillespie, David. *Teen Brain: Why Screens Are Making Your Teenager Depressed, Anxious and Prone to Lifelong Addictive Illnesses—and How to Stop It Now.* Sydney: Macmillan, 2019.

Girard, René. *Violence and the Sacred.* Baltimore: Johns Hopkins University Press, 1977.

Greenfield, Susan. *Mind Change: How Digital Technologies Are Leaving Their Mark on Our Brains.* London: Penguin, 2014.

Gregory, Brad. *The Unintended Reformation.* Cambridge, MA: Harvard University Press, 2015.

Hadot, Pierre. "Spiritual Exercises." In *Philosophy as a Way of Life,* 79–144. Oxford: Blackwell, 1995.

———. *What Is Ancient Philosophy?* Cambridge, MA: Harvard University Press, 2002.

Hamilton, Clive. *Requiem for a Species.* New York: Earthscan, 2010.

Harari, Yuval Noah. *Homo Deus: A Brief History of Tomorrow.* London: Vintage, 2017.

Harrison, Peter. *The Bible, Protestantism, and the Rise of Natural Science.* Cambridge: Cambridge University Press, 1998.

———. *The Fall of Man and the Foundations of Science.* Cambridge: Cambridge University Press, 2007.

———. "'Science' and 'Religion.'" *Journal of Religion* 86, no. 1 (2006): 81–106.

———. *The Territories of Science and Religion.* Chicago: University of Chicago Press, 2015.

Harrison, Peter, and Paul Tyson, eds. *New Directions in Theology and Science.* London: Routledge, 2022.

Harrison, Peter, Ronald L. Numbers, and Michael H. Shank. *Wrestling with Nature: From Omens to Science.* Chicago: University of Chicago Press, 2011.

Hart, David Bentley. *Atheist Delusions.* New Haven: Yale University Press, 2009.

———. *The Experience of God.* New Haven: Yale University Press, 2013.

———. *The New Testament: A Translation.* New Haven: Yale University Press, 2017.

Harvey, Barry. *Can These Bones Live?* Grand Rapids: Brazos, 2008.

Hauerwas, Stanley. *After Christendom.* Nashville: Abingdon, 1999.

———. *Resident Aliens.* Nashville: Abingdon, 2014.

———. *The State of the University: Academic Knowledges and the Knowledge of God.* Oxford: Blackwell, 2007.

———. *With the Grain of the Universe: The Church's Witness and Natural Theology.* London: SCM, 2002.

Hawes, James. *The Shortest History of Germany.* Devon: Old Street, 2018.

Henry, John. *Knowledge Is Power: How Magic, the Government and an Apocalyptic Vision Helped Francis Bacon to Create Modern Science*. London: Icon Books, 2017.

Herodotus. *The Histories*. Translated by Tom Holland. London: Penguin, 2013.

Hibbs, Thomas. "Stanley Hauerwas's Pacifism." *Washington Examiner*, May 13, 2002. https://www.washingtonexaminer.com/weekly-standard/stanley-hauerwass-pacifism.

Holland, Tom. *Dominion*. London: Little, Brown, 2019.

Hooykaas, Reijer. *Religion and the Rise of Modern Science*. Vancouver, BC: Regent College Publishing, 2000.

Houghton, John. *Global Warming*. 5th ed. Cambridge: Cambridge University Press, 2015.

Hume, David. *An Enquiry Concerning Human Understanding*. New York: Dover, 2004.

———. *Treatise of Human Nature*. New York: Prometheus Books, 1992.

Hunter, Michael. "Founder Members of the Royal Society." *Oxford Dictionary of National Biography*, May 25, 2006. https://www.oxforddnb.com/view/10.1093/ref:odnb/9780198614128.001.0001/odnb-9780198614128-e-59221.

Hurd, Elizabeth Shakman. *Beyond Religious Freedom*. Princeton: Princeton University Press, 2015.

Huxley, Thomas H. "The Evidence of the Miracle of the Resurrection." *Metaphysical Society*, January 11, 1876. https://mathcs.clarku.edu/huxley/Mss/RESURR.html.

Jenkins, Philip. *God's Continent*. Oxford: Oxford University Press, 2007.

Josephson-Storm, Jason. *The Myth of Disenchantment*. Chicago: University of Chicago Press, 2017.

Joy, Lynn Sumida. *Gassendi the Atomist*. Cambridge: Cambridge University Press, 1987.

Keele, Rondo. *Ockham Explained*. Chicago: Open Court, 2010.

Kelly, Geffrey B., and F. Burton Nelson. *The Cost of Moral Leadership: The Spirituality of Dietrich Bonhoeffer*. Grand Rapids: Eerdmans, 2003.

Kierkegaard, Søren. *Concluding Unscientific Postscript to the Philosophical Fragments*. Edited and translated by Howard V. Hong and Edna H. Hong. Princeton: Princeton University Press, 1992.

———. *Philosophical Fragments, Johannes Climacus*. Edited and translated by Howard V. Hong and Edna H. Hong. Princeton: Princeton University Press, 1985.

———. *Practice in Christianity*. Edited and translated by Howard V. Hong and Edna H. Hong. Princeton: Princeton University Press, 1991.

———. *The Sickness unto Death*. Edited and translated by Howard V. Hong and Edna H. Hong. Princeton: Princeton University Press, 1980.

———. *Two Ages*. Edited and translated by Howard V. Hong and Edna H. Hong. Princeton: Princeton University Press, 1978.

Kimmel, Michael S. *Classical Sociological Theory*. New York: Oxford University Press, 2006.

Klein, Naomi. *On Fire: The Burning Case for a Green New Deal*. London: Penguin, 2019.

Kuhn, Thomas. *The Structure of Scientific Revolutions*. Chicago: University of Chicago Press, 2012.

Kuyper, Abraham. *Common Grace: God's Gifts for a Fallen World*. 3 vols. Bellingham, WA: Lexham, 2015–20.

Lanier, Jaron. *Ten Arguments for Deleting Your Social Media Accounts Right Now*. London: The Bodley Head, 2018.

Lash, Nicholas. *The Beginning and End of "Religion."* Cambridge: Cambridge University Press, 1996.

Latour, Bruno. *We Have Never Been Modern*. Cambridge, MA: Harvard University Press, 1993.

Leithart, Peter J. *Defending Constantine: The Twilight of Empire and the Dawn of Christendom*. Downers Grove, IL: IVP Academic, 2010.

Lessing, Gotthold. "On the Proof of the Spirit and of Power (1777)." In *Lessing: Philosophical and Theological Writings*, translated and edited by H. B. Nisbet, 83–88. Cambridge: Cambridge University Press, 2005.

Lewis, C. S. *The Four Loves*. London: HarperCollins, 2012.

Lightman, Bernard. "The Theology of Victorian Scientific Naturalists." In *Science without God?*, edited by Peter Harrison and Jon H. Roberts, 235–53. Oxford: Oxford University Press, 2019.

Locke, John. *An Essay Concerning Human Understanding*. London: Penguin, 1998.

Lyons, Nathan. *Signs in the Dust*. New York: Oxford University Press, 2019.

Lyotard, Jean-François. *The Postmodern Condition: A Report on Knowledge*. Manchester: Manchester University Press, 1986.

MacDonald, George. *The Princess and the Goblin*. London: Puffin Classics, 1996.

MacIntyre, Alasdair. *After Virtue*. London: Bloomsbury, 2011.

Maley, William. *What Is a Refugee?* London: Hurst, 2016.

McInerny, Ralph. *Aquinas against the Averroists*. West Lafayette, IN: Purdue University Press, 1993.

McNeill, J. R., and Peter Engelke. *The Great Acceleration: An Environmental History of the Anthropocene since 1945*. Cambridge, MA: Harvard University Press, 2014.

Merchant, Carolyn. *The Death of Nature: Women, Ecology, and the Scientific Revolution*. New York: HarperOne, 1990.

Merleau-Ponty, Maurice. *The World of Perception*. London: Routledge, 2008.

Milbank, John. *Theology and Social Theory*. Oxford: Blackwell, 2006.

Milbank, John, and Peter Harrison, eds. *After Science and Religion*. Cambridge: Cambridge University Press, 2022.

Minniecon, Ray, and Chris Marshall, eds. "Indigenous Faith." *Zadok Perspectives* 144 (Spring 2019).

Mitralexis, Sotiris. *Ever-Moving Repose: A Contemporary Reading of Maximus the Confessor's Theory of Time*. Eugene, OR: Cascade Books, 2017.

Nagel, Thomas. *Mind and Cosmos: Why the Materialist Neo-Darwinian Conception of Nature Is Almost Certainly False*. New York: Oxford University Press, 2012.

NASA. "The Causes of Climate Change." Accessed February 13, 2020. https://climate .nasa.gov/causes/.

Nicholas of Cusa. *Of Learned Ignorance*. Eugene, OR: Wipf & Stock, 2007.

Nongbri, Brent. *Before Religion: The History of a Modern Concept*. New Haven: Yale University Press, 2013.

Northcott, Michael S. *A Political Theology of Climate Change*. London: SPCK, 2014.

Numbers, Ronald L., ed. *Galileo Goes to Jail and Other Myths about Science and Religion*. Cambridge, MA: Harvard University Press, 2010.

Oliver, Simon. *Creation: A Guide for the Perplexed*. London: Bloomsbury, 2017.

Pasnau, Robert. *After Certainty: A History of Our Epistemic Ideals and Illusions*. Oxford: Oxford University Press, 2017.

———, ed. *The Cambridge History of Medieval Philosophy*. Cambridge: Cambridge University Press, 2014.

———. *Metaphysical Themes 1274–1671*. Oxford: Oxford University Press, 2011.

Pelikan, Jaroslav. *Credo*. New Haven: Yale University Press, 2005.

Pieper, Josef. *Scholasticism: Personalities and Problems of Medieval Philosophy*. South Bend, IN: St. Augustine's Press, 2001.

———. *The Silence of St. Thomas*. South Bend, IN: St. Augustine Press, 1999.

Plato. *Complete Works*. Edited by John M. Cooper. Indianapolis: Hackett, 1997.

Polanyi, Michael. *Personal Knowledge*. Chicago: University of Chicago Press, 1974.

———. *The Tacit Dimension*. Chicago: University of Chicago Press, 2009.

Polkinghorne, John. *Exploring Reality: The Intertwining of Science and Religion*. New Haven: Yale University Press, 2007.

Reeves, Josh. *Against Methodology in Science and Religion*. London: Routledge, 2019.

Riches, Aaron. "The Mystery of Adam." In *Evolution and the Fall*, edited by William T. Cavanaugh and James K. A. Smith, 117–35. Grand Rapids: Eerdmans, 2017.

Ricœur, Paul. *The Symbolism of Evil*. Boston: Beacon, 1969.

Rist, John M. *Real Ethics: Reconsidering the Foundations of Morality*. Cambridge: Cambridge University Press, 2002.

Ross, Chanon. *Gifts Glittering and Poisoned: Spectacle, Empire, and Metaphysics*. Eugene, OR: Cascade Books, 2014.

Rubenstein, Richard. *Aristotle's Children*. New York: Harcourt, 2003.

Russell, Bertrand. *The Problems of Philosophy*. Oxford: Oxford University Press, 2001.

Sayers, Dorothy. *The Lost Tools of Learning*. Louisville: GLH, 2017.

Schmitt, Charles B. *Aristotle and the Renaissance*. Cambridge, MA: Harvard University Press, 1983.

Schumacher, Lydia. *Divine Illumination: The History and Future of Augustine's Theory of Knowledge*. Chichester: Wiley-Blackwell, 2011

Serreze, Mark C. *Brave New Arctic: The Untold Story of the Melting of the North*. Princeton: Princeton University Press, 2018.

Shapin, Steven. *The Scientific Life*. Chicago: University of Chicago Press, 2008.

———. *The Scientific Revolution*. 2nd ed. Chicago: University of Chicago Press, 2018.

Shaxson, Nicholas. *Treasure Islands: Tax Havens and the Men Who Stole the World*. London: Vintage, 2012.

Simpson, Christopher B. *The Truth Is the Way: Kierkegaard's Theologia Viatorum*. Eugene, OR: Cascade Books, 2011.

Singer, P. W. *Corporate Warriors: The Rise of the Privatized Military Industry*. Ithaca, NY: Cornell University Press, 2008.

———. *Wired for War: The Robotics Revolution and Conflict in the 21st Century*. New York: Penguin, 2009.

Singer, P. W., and Emerson T. Brooking. *LikeWar: The Weaponization of Social Media*. Boston: Dolan, 2018.

Singer, Peter. *Karl Marx: A Very Short Introduction*. 2nd ed. Oxford: Oxford University Press, 2018.

Smith, James K. A. "What Stands on the Fall?" In *Evolution and the Fall*, edited by William T. Cavanaugh and James K. A. Smith, 48–64. Grand Rapids: Eerdmans, 2017.

Smith, Wilfred Cantwell. *The Meaning and End of Religion*. London: SPCK, 1978.

Soros, George. *The Alchemy of Finance*. Hoboken, NJ: Wiley, 2003.

Spencer, Nick. *Atheists: The Origin of the Species*. London: Bloomsbury, 2014.

Stengers, Isabelle. *Another Science Is Possible*. Cambridge: Polity, 2018.

Steup, Matthias, John Turri, and Ernest Sosa, eds. *Contemporary Debates in Epistemology*. 2nd ed. Chichester: Wiley-Blackwell, 2013.

Stroumsa, Guy. *A New Science: The Discovery of Religion in the Age of Reason*. Cambridge, MA: Harvard University Press, 2010.

Taibbi, Matt. *Griftopia: Bubble Machines, Vampire Squids, and the Long Con That Is Breaking America*. New York: Spiegel & Grau, 2010.

Taylor, Charles. *The Ethics of Authenticity*. Cambridge, MA: Harvard University Press, 2010.

———. *A Secular Age*. Cambridge, MA: Harvard University Press, 2007.

Theissen, Gerd, and Dagmar Winter. *The Quest for the Plausible Jesus*. Louisville: Westminster John Knox, 2002.

Thomas, Keith. *Religion and the Decline of Magic*. London: Penguin, 1973.

Tour, James. "Animadversions of a Synthetic Chemist." *Inference* 2, no. 2 (May 2016). https://inference-review.com/article/animadversions-of-a-synthetic-chemist.

Tyson, Paul. *De-fragmenting Modernity*. Eugene, OR: Cascade Books, 2017.

———. *Kierkegaard's Theological Sociology*. Eugene, OR: Cascade Books, 2019.

———. *Returning to Reality: Christian Platonism for Our Times*. Eugene, OR: Cascade Books, 2014.

———. *Seven Brief Lessons on Magic*. Eugene, OR: Cascade Books, 2019.

———. *Theology and Climate Change*. London: Routledge, 2021.

Varoufakis, Yanis. *And the Weak Suffer What They Must?* New York: Nation Books, 2016.

Webster, Charles. *Paracelsus: Medicine, Magic and Mission at the End of Time*. New Haven: Yale University Press, 2008.

Weil, Simone. "The Illiad, Poem of Might." In *Intimations of Christianity among the Greeks*, 24–55. London: Routledge, 1998.

Weil, Simone, and Rachel Bespaloff. *War and the Iliad*. New York: New York Review Books, 2005.

White, Andrew Dickson. *A History of the Warfare of Science with Theology in Christendom*. 1896. Reprint, Cambridge: Cambridge University Press, 2009.

White, Lynn, Jr. "Christian Myth and Christian History." *Journal of the History of Ideas* 3, no. 2 (April 1942): 145–58.

Wink, Walter. *Engaging the Powers*. Minneapolis: Fortress, 1992.

———. "The Myth of the Domination System." In *Engaging the Powers*, 13–31. Minneapolis: Fortress, 1992.

Yunkaporta, Tyson. *Sand Talk: How Indigenous Thinking Can Save the World*. Melbourne: Text, 2019.

Zimmermann, Jens. *Hermeneutics: A Very Short Introduction*. Oxford: Oxford University Press, 2015.

Zuboff, Shoshana. *Surveillance Capitalism: The Fight for a Human Future at the New Frontier of Power*. London: Profile, 2019.

Index

Note: Bold indicates principal areas of definition or discussion.